❖ To all those doctors who died un-mourned in the Kashmir conflict.

❖ To all those doctors who stood upright in the Kashmir conflict.

❖ To all those boys and girls who aspired to be doctors but were killed in the Kashmir conflict before their dream was realised.

❖ To Daddy, Mummy, Nayil, my lovely little angels—Maryam, Madeeha, and Fatima

WHITE MAN in Dark

Dr. Rumana Makhdoomi

PARTRIDGE

A Penguin Random House Company

To order additional copies of this book, contact
Partridge India
000 800 10062 62
www.partridgepublishing.com/india
orders.india@partridgepublishing.com

CONTENTS

Each moment some new trouble terrifies,
And parrots there are panic stricken flies.
(Farid Attar)

Preface

I am human enough to feel pain. Human enough to cry when my brethren cry. I was trained to have a scientific mind-but what could be done, if it turned out to be sensitive too; sensitive enough—to feel sad at how we were trapped in whirlpools of pain and death. Our history remained our dreadful companion. It haunted each one of us. Each bullet ricocheted with the song of a forgotten ballad. We witnessed the sad days when our hospitals became mortuaries, our emergencies became mourning grounds and our operating-rooms displayed red and its shades . . . . We bore it all alone-no one cared to comfort us. The memory of these events is crisp and killing, why can't I share it I thought. I am a doctor no doubt but I am Kashmiri enough!

My memory is a pomegranate. Shall I open it over you and let it scatter, seed by seed: red pearls befitting a farewell that asks nothing of me except forgetfulness?
(Mahmoud Darwish)

Acknowledgement

I scribbled for some time and when I collected it all, this book was born. All thanks to Almighty Allah for helping me write this memoir. My father has been my greatest inspiration—an intelligent man, he has been my source of greatest information too. My mother—I owe my fearlessness to her. My husband, Nayil, was behind my back in all the odd hours while I was writing this book. He was with me while the book was still in my mind, when it was just a few pages, and when I was stuck up with it, and he is with me when it is a dream realised! My sisters Shagufta, Mudasir, Tabasum, and my brother Gowhar always prompted me to do my best. Tabasum in particular has been a friend, a sister and a mother—all rolled in one. Soayib, my nephew, is tied to my heart and is my inspiration. Thanks to Azka and Baazla, my lovely nieces, and to Sameed, Hasan, and Mustafa, my adorable nephews. I thank my in-laws for their cooperation and help. Thanks to Dr Besina and Dr Aasia for being my constant companions, Dr Naseem for her kindness, and to Dr K.M. Baba and Dr Parveen for their care. Dr Rais was a great help, doing my odd jobs at odd hours. Dr Othman was a timely advisor, a lovely little boy who gave me confidence with his positive thoughts. Dr Saba, Dr Farhat, and other residents too were informative and supportive. I am thankful to Professor Yusuf, ex-head of the Medicine Department, Government Medical College, Srinagar, for his constant encouragement and his care.

Thanks to Dia Mercado from Partridge India for her timely advices.

I thank Mr Irshad Ahmad for typing the manuscript and Dr Farida Ashai for the valuable information she provided. I am thankful to Dr. Mufti Altaf Hussain, for reading the manuscript of an unknown author-word by word. The book would have made some unforgivable omissions-but for his valuable suggestions.

Thanks to my lovely daughters, thoughtful Maryam, naughty Madeeha, and chirpy Fatima for adding colour to my life.

Lastly, thanks to my teacher and guide, who gave me all I possess. I know he wouldn't like to be named here. May Allah give him a long life.

Rumana

Chapter-1

The Blast

I cannot prioritise the episodes I have witnessed. There is a huge gathering, a huge jumble of them in my mind. I wish they would form a queue, an order, so that I can put them forth one by one. But, with disorder engulfing us, no incident can be recounted in a sequence or narrated in an order. No incident has been isolated, and no episode has occurred in vacuum—one incident has led to another and another to another . . . another, a consequence of another. What should I narrate first? What do I recount in detail? I myself wonder. I did not write a note, I did not keep a diary. All those events are nailed in my heart and stacked in my mind.

Kashmir never saw glory. It always saw misery. Was its captivating beauty, or its naive population, responsible for the suffering that it has seen for ages? While I have my own tale to narrate, my father has his and my grandfather had his. My child is building up her account of the trauma on which she will build up her own tale . . . and her children, if we last that long, will have their own tales to narrate . . . . Every crime occurring against humanity in the world gives a feeling of déjà vu. There seems to be no end to the horror we are experiencing, and it seems it's no one's headache . . .

Entry through that Huge Gate

With pride and confidence I entered its gate.
Little did I know what was there in my fate.

Ragging aside, the bustle aside, I entered the gates of Government Medical College (GMC) of Srinagar, with confidence. Maybe I was not following my own dream but was following the dream of my mother, who would get depressed when I would tell her, sometimes, that it was not my dream to be a doctor. But I loved what my mother desired for me, and never did I regret entering that huge gate for the first time.

A simple place with a wide space, enormous lecture theatres, big laboratories, and huge pillars, Government Medical College Srinagar was impressive for a chirpy teenager. Those too many nagging teachers of anatomy were the first ones to snatch your confidence and bring you to level zero, after your admission to the prestigious college made your head resonate in clouds. Those 'finger pricks' in physiology were too painful, and the sadistic staff of biochemistry actually tried to squeeze you through the windows which were, fortunately, grilled. I didn't like them all, but that was the staff of a prestigious institute, I was told, behaving the way they were to enforce discipline. No wonder, Government Medical College of Srinagar was ranked at slot No. 3 in all-India ranking and had the precedence of producing stalwarts who have headed many prestigious institutions in the United States, the United Kingdom and the Gulf States.

It was spine-chilling to flock around that 'dead body' in anatomy dissection hall and remember those 'origins' and 'insertions' of muscles. The subject being difficult to score in and easy to forget, our weekly/biweekly examinations in anatomy, called 'stages' would crush us. Anatomy was exhaustive, boring, and merciless. No guesses would work, no common sense would help, and no wit would guide you to score in anatomy. I hated it—the dissection hall, the dead bodies (no disrespect meant), the unstable stools on which we were made to sit, that horrible formalin odour, and those teachers who seemed unkind and rude. They broke big hearts, depressed great minds, and chopped huge spirits. How many toppers would lose their heads looking for some sense in those difficult-to-comprehend and impossible-to-justify lessons! But most did well under pressure, though some did succumb, never to recover . . .

Physiology was a bit of 'too much information'—long, lengthy, and limitless. The staff was better, though the teachers ran through entire chapters like marathon runners and tried to recover all from us in quizzes and tutorials. Biochemistry—the miniature one—was too symbolic, too bizarre, and too crazy. There were we all, the first year MBBS students, who, after a proud flight, had a free fall in a stuffy anatomy hall and painful physiology and biochemistry labs. God help the confused masses of flesh and blood who had come to the Government Medical College with great dreams and were trying to reshape themselves and reorganise their resources to survive. Was there someone to wish them all good luck?

Our busy academic schedule kept us off the few stray incidents of firing and an odd grenade attack occurring suddenly in the fall of 1989 in Srinagar. The incidents seemed insignificant and escaped our attention, for we were busy with something important—making of a doctor.

Then, an abduction caused a stir in GMC; a doctor from our college who happened to be the beloved daughter of then Home Minister Mr Mufti Mohammad Syed was abducted. I saw the photograph of the ordinary-looking girl on television and recollected having seen her somewhere but could not place her. The girl was possibly too simple and blended with the student population. She walked unguarded; we hardly noticed her. But we were worried for her. A fellow student of ours was being held by people we hardly knew 'who'. After a few tense days, we rejoiced when she was released, and we recognized her worth when four members of an organisation named JKLF (Jammu and Kashmir Liberation Front) were released in exchange. We were unfamiliar with the name of the organisation, but our parents knew it well and knew very well about some imminent disturbance that would jolt the valley sooner than we thought. The organisation, active earlier, had regrouped, and its members had been trained . . . . from across. We were told not to speak it all aloud. We could get killed . . . .

Our first professional MBBS course at the medical college was for 18 long months. After a year of vigorous study, we parted in December 1989 for our winter vacations with a promise to be back in college in March 1990.

Well! Then, came—the winter vacations. We needed vacations after a year of real hard work. Kashmir shines like a mermaid in winter. The snow-clad mountains look like silver tresses as the trembling rays of sun fall on them. The trees, which shed the burden off their shoulders, reveal their anatomy, amusing the onlooker. Falling snowflakes are a treat to watch, and white snowmen in every nook and corner have a story to tell. When snow becomes ice and challenges even Dal Lake, all exercise caution, except the kids who love the slips and the skips. Oh! Yes, we were thinking about all this fun and much more, but this winter had a different face to show, a dirty tale to tell!

It was a tremble that shook us all, an earthquake that never seemed to stop, a volcano that burst suddenly and melted us all, a fire that engulfed every house and kept on burning . . . . We were restless, and we stopped thinking. Our eyes saw death, our hearts felt pain, our ears heard gunshots, and our desperate bodies developed automatic 'ducking' and 'dodging' mechanisms to save themselves from bullets and grenades.

Trouble had arrived.

Guns had conquered the streets.

Young men in *pherans* were there to 'fight' the other men in khaki, who were well armed to 'defend'. And Kashmiris were trapped in a fire they hardly knew the source of. But, was it an opportunity for them to tell the world that 'enough is enough', 'sort out the dispute called Kashmir', and 'give us our due'? A suppressed nation tied in chains and tired of democracy and its riggings had found a new hope in guns, and this was the time to flood the streets, to shout in mosques, and to rise against the liars. Wasn't it so?

A nation of millions became nervous. They thought all that was happening was unexpected. Where was it that the nation went wrong? Wasn't a Kashmiri well integrated with the nation of India? What had happened to him suddenly?

But 'a silly Kashmiri' had thrown a challenge to a great nation.

No time was wasted. The response from the Indian Government was prompt. Military and paramilitary forces were redirected, and Kashmir became their destination. I and my friends, who used to see men in khaki during parades only, saw them in large numbers marching in the streets, plugging the mountain passes, floating in *shikaras,* contorting the hotels, and defacing the Government buildings. No paddy field was left alone, no orchid was spared, and no school was left untouched . . . . All along, a sense of fear was created. Soldiers were put in bunkers in all major and minor streets and bazaars; while they were holed inside, spiny wires were circled around the bunkers to keep the miscreants away.

The harsh winter became harsher; nights were scary and long, and days ended at 5 p.m. The buzz of the day was replaced by the sounds of blasts and the rattle of guns. Snow must have decorated the mountain tops that winter and the winds must have swung the trees, but did anybody notice?

Children fond of snowballs and snowmen lost their space to the men in khaki, young ones clung to their mothers, and older ones thought, thought, and thought . . . . about what they had lost. Each incident left its imprint on their growing minds; each accident left its stamp on their altering psyche. They talked about guns and insisted their parents on having 'toy guns'; they spent their vacation days in 'action' within the bunkers made from pillows. Who would counsel them? Who would help them out?

Me and My Family

We were a family of nine members living in an old-fashioned house in the heart of Srinagar. Our house stood on a 'four way'—commonly known as *chu-voth*—elegantly and beautifully made in wood and mud. It was constructed by my grandfather; my father loved it and never thought of dismantling it. It was cool and airy during summers and warm and cosy during winters. A modern kitchen and a bathroom were constructed as an extension in front of our ancestral home. We lived happily in our home. We grew up playing 'saz long'(Hopscotch) in the lawns and 'hide and seek' in our *dewan khanas*. We were four sisters and a brother. Our uncle and aunt, who had no children of their own, lived with us in the same house. They treated us as their own children. Our house was always full of activity, full of fun, as children of entire *mohalla* would collect to play in our lawns and sing in our *dewan khanas*. We enjoyed our childhood, every bit of it. After my two elder sisters were married, our house was a bit quieter.

And then, the tumult of the turmoil made our house silent and gloomy. Those windows through which we would peep so often were never opened; those *dewan khanas,* which would shake with our jumps, grew scary and haunted us with time. Who cared to play in that fear and uncertainty?

Our parents would caution us as to how we should go about in the turmoil while within our house and outside. Our uncle and aunt—the pair who had known many more raids—talked about the wars of their times, the famines, the accords, the politicians, and the poverty. My father, a sharp-witted gentleman, remembered his own times and talked about all he went through. He remembered all; he remembered the speeches of all those who recited the Koran and quoted Iqbal, taking vows to free their motherland of 'slavery'. He talked about the politicians and their leanings, about their claimed honesty and their much-talked about sell-outs. Never before—had we been so close to each other. Our parents were more anxious and more apprehensive . . . . They had seen harsh times before . . . . And they knew it would be harsher this time.

A Peep into the World of Crackdowns

We were restless for the entire night, whispering, trembling, and feeling nervous as we heard the noise of their boots and those barely understandable messages which they sent across their wireless sets. They were there; perhaps they had come to look for 'gunmen' or their ammunition. We were told by those who had an experience with them that they never believed what people told them and they had been trained to be harsh and unsympathetic.

We spoke in a low tone and waited for the dawn to come.

As the morning broke, we looked out and found them all in their camouflage robes, knocking at the doors of our neighbours and asking all males to be out. A few of them went inside the houses to have a look inside while the rest sealed all the roads leading to our *mohalla*. We waited for our turn. They came and asked for male members; my father, my uncle, and my brother came out. My father and my uncle were spared because of their age, and my brother was asked to accompany them. Two members came inside and searched our house thoroughly. They neither laughed nor talked more than what was required. They searched every *almirah* and every corner of our house. When they were opening one room after another, we knew how much our mother had stored without our knowledge, perhaps for the rainy days that had arrived so soon.

Kashmir's harsh winter blocks the national highway, which is the sole connection it has with the rest of India. Poultry, eggs, and vegetables evaporate from the markets, and Kashmiris rely on their favourite *hokh suin* or dried vegetables. Harsh winter makes them store food and essential items like sugar, pulses, flour, tea, and spices for many months. Imagine a group of soldiers picked up from a hot land of North India and sent to Kashmiri houses in search of arms and ammunition. The storerooms of Kashmiris would surprise the poor soldiers. They would look with awe towards the big bins and tins. 'So much rice, so many pulses, so much tea!' they would exclaim. They would put the butts of their guns or their sticks into the tins, looking for arms and ammunition. They couldn't let go of any opportunity to seize a large cache of arms and ammunition each time they ventured into our storerooms for a search operation. 'Spill' perhaps was the answer to their fears. Spill the bins, and over them, the contents of the tins; tea leaves would get mixed with flour and rice with pickles. The ugly mix-up on the floor was a humiliation a Kashmiri faced each time there was a crackdown; we know . . . how we felt but, did the rest of India know about it?

The soldiers would giggle at their failure to find arms but burst into laughter as they would move out, looking with pride at the mess they had created. Our oldies would see it, our kiddies would witness it, and we youngsters would bear the heaviness those episodes gave us. Should we hate the soldier or the one who had commanded him to create the mess? After the crackdown would be over, the poor Kashmiris would come out with a self-consoling statement: 'Thank God our lives are spared. The mess can be cleared.'

There was no spill in our house though; we were relieved at that. But the thought of my brother who was outside in the shivering cold bothered us. What about his breakfast? What about the identification parade in which our boys/men were asked to walk past masked men and asked to keep their bending necks straight—to show their faces? What about that horrible posture in which a person could neither sit nor stand properly? What about that mouth which had to be shut always? Talking and whispering was never allowed in crackdowns. What would our men do, sitting in an odd posture, bearing patiently the hunger pangs and looking desperately here and there for those long hours to be over? Being a female in this situation was a definite advantage as you could sit inside without facing the trauma called a crackdown, but we knew—outside, our men were worried about the women inside, and inside, we prayed for the safe return of our men from the tense lawns of our local school. This reciprocal worry was unique to us . . . . Our oppressions left us with no option. Technocrats, polite gentlemen, and aggressive students were all queued together in that lawn of the school where sometime back, students danced and played.

As the crackdown was going on, lunchtime arrived. But our men outside were without food or water. What about their lunch and their thirst? How would they respond to the nature's call in front of so many people? Why such a torture? Though we were inside our homes, we too had huge lumps in our throats. How could we eat inside, without our dear ones? From 7 a.m. our men and boys were held up, and we didn't know when they would be set free.

At 4 p.m. that day, a few elderly males were set free and the rest taken to Makhdoom Sahib Shrine and asked to sit on the stairs of the shrine. As night enveloped us, it was difficult to control the impatient crowd that had gathered courage to whisper. To prevent people from running away, the people were squeezed into a limited space and encircled completely. Someone dared to ask, 'When shall we be set free?' 'What do you plan to do with us?'

The soldiers shouted back, 'Only when our boss directs us . . .'

Where was the boss? We women came out of the houses, went towards the stairs, and asked the soldiers guarding our men.

'The boss is held up somewhere and will be arriving soon . . .'

Our men were in pain, their legs might have got cramps, their eyes must have ached, and their mouths must have watered on seeing the soldiers take their snacks and their meals. For what fault were they held up? The identification parade should have been over in an hour or so. What kind of identification was going on?

Where was the boss, why was his presence necessary to set a huge group of starving men free? Was he busy in some party, or was he dining somewhere? Where they planning to kill all in the darkness of the night? The impatient hostages thought.

Our men, the desperate men, and our boys, the angry ones— who could not express their anger—were sitting like thieves facing a punishment unheard of . . . each hour there for them doubled our anxiety and impatience. Whom would we complain to? Who would listen to us? Requesting the soldiers would yield nothing. The stone-hearted, they . . . All pleas were directed towards the Almighty.

Finally past midnight, the soldiers were directed to set our men free. Back from the crackdown, they were freezing with cold. We gave them *kangris* and wrapped them with quilts at home. What had the exercise yielded? Not a single miscreant, not a solitary lawbreaker—so why was there a torture of the entire population of our *mohalla*? If the same episode had occurred elsewhere in the country, wouldn't the Home Minister have gone into hiding? Unforgettable! This first crackdown told me a little more about myself.

For us, each new morning brought in a new worry: a crackdown, a crossfire incident, an encounter, or a fake encounter. The disappearance or sudden appearance of a headless body or limbless body with gouged eyes in nearby *Malkhah* (graveyard) would scare people, and they would chant '*Jago! Jago!*' (Wake up . . . oh people) in mosques. A few shots fired in air would silence them. Firing in a nearby area would push the forces towards our *mohalla* and make them chase youngsters at random or start a crackdown. 'Crackdown' was a tool which cracked our spines and humiliated us. It told us about our weaknesses, about our desperations, and it reminded us about our enslavement.

I remember how my brother was caned, my cousin kicked by men in khaki who were chasing those boys in *pherans* hurling grenades at them. In a flash of a second they would disappear in lanes and by-lanes, leaving the frustrated soldiers with no option but to enter our houses, drag our boys out, and beat them. That shrill 'Ooh' and 'Ah!' of my brother still pierces my heart as his limbs were lashed with canes and butts so many times. What was his fault? Where else would he stay but his home? I wanted to ask someone, but whom would I ask? Many boys of neighbouring *mohallas* were dragged and killed. Could anyone argue as to what was happening and why?

To escape the humiliation, my other uncle, an ex-serviceman in Indian Army, who lived in our neighbourhood, would show his photo in army uniform to everyone who called him out for a crackdown. Sometimes, the angry soldiers would push the photograph aside; then he would show his photograph with Mrs Indira Gandhi.

We were unaware as to which rules were being imposed on us. We heard 'forces' had been given 'all' the powers to do all they desired . . . . Any night could turn into a nightmare; any day could turn into a dreaded black day.

We girls had to be more careful, our parents would advise us. We had to be careful with all our garments, careful about our wardrobes, careful about our personal belongings. We could not leave everything just there in bathrooms or verandas. We had to lock our rooms from inside, whether day or night.

They could come inside any moment.

And, they came in suddenly one night. We were in the middle of our sleep that night when we were awakened by their hits and kicks on our door. In that moonlit night, we saw them moving around in our lawns with their helmets shining! They had already negotiated the wall and the gate leading to our lawns. Since I was sleeping downstairs, I saw them first and raced to inform other members of the household. As my uncle opened the door, they suddenly pounced upon him.

The first one to make an entry inside said, 'Who is hiding inside your house?'

'None,' the trembling uncle replied.

They came inside, beaming torches, and asked us to put off our lights. We couldn't shout, we couldn't scream; all we could do was to helplessly watch them. And follow their instructions. They searched everywhere and came upstairs with my uncle to the second floor. My sister and her husband were there along with their infant son. Seeing a handsome young man there, they started questioning my uncle. They pushed him hard as the old man tried to explain that the man they saw was a son-in-law. A son-in-law is a very special person for Kashmiris. He is respected much and loved dearly. My uncle was worried as to how the special guest who had arrived that very night from Baramulla with his mother to see his child and wife would be treated. No concessions for guests—the 'special guest' was asked to come down. He did so faithfully, asking his wife to do the same. In that fear and anxiety, the sleeping infant boy was left upstairs. Soldiers searched the room again and came down after a while. They found nothing in our home . . . . There was a masked boy with them who spoke Kashmiri, his eyes rolling continuously, perhaps looking for something or someone. He was the one who had brought them to our home, possibly to save himself from interrogation. But why to our house, we don't know.

As the team was about to leave, my sister, who had gone up to see her infant son, came down to tell the leader of the party that Rs. 10, 000 had been taken from underneath her pillow by some member of the search party. The money was gifted to my sister by her in-laws as a part of a custom called *peyav* on the birth of her son, just the night before. The officer, on hearing, this lost his cool. His reply was very interesting. He wanted us to search all the *jawans* for the lost money, and if we were unable to find the money, my brother-in-law, the only young man present in our home at that time, had to accompany him. We realised we should keep quiet and not argue about the lost 10, 000. An argument meant sending our dear one into the unknown.

The currents of humiliation would flow into our bodies and minds each time we were stopped for a check, each time we were searched, each time we were questioned, or each time we were stared at. Sometimes, they would search the buses; ask men to get down and take them for identification parade. The women sitting back would be asked to open their bags-for a checking. How many times women carry certain things which they do not want to show to anyone, and here everything would be laid bare . . . . The modest Kashmiri woman, shy and reserved, was getting publicly exposed . . . how bad!

A Blue-eyed Heart-Throb!

My sister's son—a blue-eyed heart-throb of 3-years—came to live with us in our house amidst all that fear and uncertainty. His parents were posted in a far-off area, where they did not dare to take this boy. He saw it all, the militants, the militancy, the crackdowns, and the firing. He ran when we ran, ducked his body when we ducked; many times when he hugged me in those hours of panic and fear, I could hear the pounding of his tiny heart. Away from his parents, he saw a shield in each one of us; he sensed a comfort in our light touch. He would cling to us, and we would cling to him.

I remember his admission in a missionary school where the school authorities provided no buses and it was the sole responsibility of parents to collect the wards. His grandmother would take him to the school; she would sit in that school garden for 3 hours and get the child back at one o'clock. Those long hours of waiting in the school were better than those panic runs in case there was a disturbance on the way home. No one would trust an auto-rickshaw. Suppose there was firing, what would the *auto-walla* do? Run for his own cover, or look after the child? Risky it was both for the boy and his grandmother to go to and come back from school—such a lovely, tender life and so much of risk? Was it all worth it? Our mother had struggled enough for our education, but again she was risking her life for a 3-year-old. Was life important or education? In that hunt for the answer, our mother preferred education. Wasn't that what most parents did? While most children returned to their homes after their schools . . . some were victims of bullets and grenades. But yes, most lost their childhood to a struggle for life. Alas, for our children!

My nephew had a narrow escape many times. Once when with him at home on veranda, a shower of bullets fell in front of us; we lay down flat. Covering his small body, I dragged myself and him inside . . . . It was a gunfight between some armed men and men in khaki. One was pressing the trigger from inside our lawns and the others were bombarding us with bullets from outside. God saved him and me. I also remember the day when he had gone with his uncle to see his newborn sister in a hospital,

and on the way back they were trapped in a crossfire. The young boy
was too terrified after the incident, and the entire excitement of seeing a
newborn sister was lost in that panic to save his life.

Sometimes on a crackdown day, soldiers would ask about his parents.
'Is your father across for training?' was the frequently asked question. But
the boy had learnt to smile at the forces during those hours which would
make adults lose their senses and cry. He had learnt to adjust to the
circumstances. He had learnt when to smile and when to shake hands. He
had learnt 'what to talk, when to talk, and how to talk'. He matured fast
into a survivor; his childhood remained a mere spectator as he outgrew it
too fast. That innocence and naivety would not help him. He was on his
own, facing and surviving the challenges that we faced. Should we thank
God that he saw no normalcy? For him, all what he was breathing into
was normal.

As Schools Burnt and Colleges Were Lost

We woke up in the middle of that night as we heard a loud noise. I
could see my sister's face clearly as she too woke up with a startle. There
was a blaze, which was reflected in the window panes of our room. 'There
is a fire somewhere,' she shouted.

We left our beds and went up to the *kaney* (attic) and saw the flames
coming from the Girls Higher Secondary School in our *mohalla*. My
sister cried, as this was the place where she had studied. As fire consumed
the L-shaped building within minutes, my sister was sulking; kissing the
sparks as they touched us. Who burnt her school and why? We started
discussing it. 'Don't shout!' We were advised by our parents!

Various theories came up once the school was reduced to
ashes.'Perhaps a military barrack was to be created here. Perhaps it was
burnt by conspirators, perhaps by gunmen, perhaps by men in khaki . . .'
whatever the reason and whoever the culprit, a beautiful structure aimed
at providing education to girls was no more!

Through the same attic, on another horrifying night, we saw another
fire which burnt an excellent centre for science and commerce, namely
Islamia College. Its flames were brighter, its ashes went higher, and its
cracking laboratory equipment deafened our ears. My brother could not
speak for many days. His alma mater was no more!

And then it was my turn to cry. I heard that my school, Vishwa Bharti, was burnt. The fire, they said, was fierce. Cool waters of Dal, on whose banks it stood, could not extinguish it. Thank God! I did not see its flames or feel the bites of its sparks. I never went that side to see how my school looked after the fire . . . . It would pain me, I knew. And I hardly wanted those beautiful memories of my childhood centred around Vishwa Bharti to get tinged with smoke. Those were my assets, and I was possessive . . .

There was so much more that was burnt: the archival Government buildings, guest houses, post offices, plenty of houses and shops, bridges, buses, and Government vehicles. Fire consumed our places of heritage and our places of worship! Fires were almost always mysterious, and the culprits were never traced.

I remember the night when the mosque in the compound of the shrine of Makhdoom Sahib was burnt . . . . The Kashmiri Sufi Saint Hazrat Sheikh Hamzah (RA), popularly known as Makhdoom Sahib, is respected and revered by Kashmiris of all faiths. Why would anyone set the mosque and the adjoining library on fire? The entire *mohalla* of Makhdoom Sahib owed its life to the shrine! Kohimaran, the hill on which the shrine is located, was in flames, and the whole city lost its sleep; women wailed and men cried. Some, in their desperation, carried pitchers of water from their houses to extinguish the fire. The priceless woodwork, the beautifully painted walls, and those shinning chandeliers were all destroyed . . .

We had no control over what was happening. No comment was advised, no criticism allowed—life was more precious! Who was supposed to protect our assets? This query would seem unnecessary in a place where the basic question 'Who is supposed to protect our lives?' could not be asked . . .

When Pandits Left

Fear gripped them, and they ran away in ones, twos, clusters, and thousands. Huge congregations and processions on the streets demanding *azadi* made them uneasy, the loudspeakers in mosques with a chorus singing of '*Jago! Jago!*' made them unsteady. There were targeted killings too and a concern about the safety and security of next generation, which

made them say a goodbye to their homeland. Some carried with them
truckloads, some nothing. After all, how much would they carry? It was a
burden of a lifetime that they had to carry with themselves. Some trusted
their neighbours and handed over to them the keys of their homes, but
some ran secretly in the middle of night with neighbours in the mornings
finding their neighbourhood houses abandoned . . .

I lost my friends, who never called after they went away. Perhaps
they hated us, or perhaps not. I know they hated what we supported, but
we too didn't like what they liked. Our wounds were old, and the new
wounds that were adding up gave too much pain; and their wounds were
just new. So, here we separated! Will there be a union again? Will they
ever love us again?

I remember how they held my hand as I took my first step towards
school, how they taught me my first rhyme, how they listened to the
first poem I wrote, how they corrected the steps of my first dance and
listened to the arguments of my first debate. Will I ever forget them—
and will they ever? By God, they are still the loved ones—we all sense
that after years of separation—even today. Rainawari is charmless without
them, Badamwari is blossomless without them, Habbakadal is scary
without them, and Hariparbat is waiting for their embrace . . . . They
must be missing this all, especially the ones who have seen it all, and the
generation that hasn't, is there a desire to see this all?

Those Pandits kept quiet over what happened to us over the ages . . . .
Those regimes which caned us pampered them. They were powerful,
influential, and intelligent. Their diligence and dedication was their
birthmark. But they were self-centred and dreamt big for themselves.
They made excellent teachers and competitive classmates. They were
Indians to the core, loyal to the cause of India and did well for themselves
till the turbulence pushed them out.

Who was it that eventually pushed them out . . . ? We don't know,
but we know for sure, no one addressed their genuine fears; no one
assured them of their safety; no one . . . . If authorities wanted they could
have prevented their exodus. Secretive and introverts that they were, did
they counsel each other when they left? Did they not think about their
future? Whatever the compulsions, was it wise for the entire community
to leave en masse?

Those worldly-wise and efficient people were deprived of their
motherland the moment they signalled a 'go' to their caravans. Under
whose command were they all going? Where were they all going? Was

there safety across the tunnel, was there peace across the tunnel, and was there 'good future' for their kids across the tunnel? Yes, perhaps all was there, but there was no 'home' across the tunnel—home was left behind, and they were leaderless. The path was not made yet. Nationalism and patriotism would not fetch them food. They had to launch another struggle in another part of the world, in another environment, for food, water, safety, and education of their kids. In this struggle, they forgot all else . . .

Those Boys of My Neighbourhood

That boy, a gentle one, ran a shop in our neighbourhood. One day we heard that he was no more. Shockingly, he was shot in his head. There was a mad crowd accompanying his body to the school lawns where a *nimaz-i-jinaza* would be offered. We saw his father shouldering one end of the cot on which his son's body was placed. The burden was heavy for him and for his weak shoulders. Was he reminded of his dreams while carrying the dead body of his son?

The old man, an *imam* who recited *naat* and *manqabat* at the shrine of Makhdoom Sahib was too innocent to know what had happened to his son. Tears trickled down his face; his white beard was drenched in moisture . . . . No one could control his feelings. Women cried, children were terrified, and youngsters like us tried to console what was inconsolable. The boy was laid there on the stage, where some years back skits and dramas were performed . . . . And that day, we were witnessing a real tragedy as we saw our boy with a calm look, a sharp nose, draped in a white sheet with those spots of . . . blood.

Namaz-i-jinaza was performed by another old man, a friend of the deceased father, who, too, could not control his tears. His words were inaudible; what we heard was no more than babble . . . . *Zafar* (the victorious), as the boy was named, had gone, leaving everything behind. Would his old mother forget the scene ever? Meanwhile, his mother consoled herself by putting a handful of flowers and dry fruits on the body of her son. 'He is a *maharaza*, a groom, let me do it please,' she said.

The boy was not a militant, not one who adored guns, but he was killed somehow while with a friend after a policeman chased them when they had gone for some collection somewhere . . . . Who knows the actual story? Who knows what happened at that site? But this was sure; the boy was unarmed when he was killed . . . . No one gave an explanation as if it was not needed. The mystery of Zafar's death did haunt us for a long time, but how it must have perforated the hearts of his parents is difficult to imagine. While coming back from the funeral of Zafar, accompanying all those who were traumatised, I heard the sobs of another mother who was staggering and was supported by other ladies. 'My Son, where are you?' she cried. She was not inconsolable as she heard our words of hope.

'Your son will come soon,' we said. We knew he wouldn't. We knew he couldn't. It was now quite some time that her boy had left his home . . . to get trained. But he left no message, nor did he come back. No one knew about him. 'Gift', he was named, rather nicknamed. He was chubby, fair, and sweet. His mother was hopeful that he would come some day . . . . . Her 'Gift' would come . . . but would he? She used to speak to him quietly besides his photograph in his room; after, she would clean it daily. Neighbours would whisper, 'He has died on the border,' but she would not care

Many other boys from our *mohalla* left their homes with a promise to be back . . . . Did they have a mania to be the heroes, or were they keen to explore how it was on the other side? Many disappeared, and we never heard about them, neither did their families. Were they in a torture cell somewhere, or were their bodies frozen in that ice on the borders? Will anybody know anything about them ever, or they will be fossilised in the unknown valleys? Those painful thoughts kept on making us uneasy.

I remember the face of each one of them; with some I had played countless games, and some were quite younger to me. Those beautiful faces, those broad shoulders, that wit and that naughtiness—they deserved to live . . .

The tragedies of the kind reminded our neighbourhood of other tragedies that took place on those very lawns . . . . a few months before Zafar was killed. Those four boys brought from somewhere and gunned down there . . . one behind the school's toilet, one in its huge corridors, one outside its laboratory, and one near the dust bins. Who were they and why they were gunned down we don't know. We heard the gun rattle, heard the cries, and witnessed the lull after all was over . . . . Some boys from our neighbourhood went inside the school after khakis had left the scene, they cried and called others. We saw how those boys looked fresh, blood flowing down drop by drop and the body still warm. The police came after a while and took away the bodies. We cried over the bodies of strangers whom we knew were our own . . .

Versions came up in newspapers the next day. They were militants—was the Government version. But, on a corner was the message of a boy's father who appealed to all people not to bring any kind of fruits to his house on mourning days—his son said the message, was picked up in a crackdown and killed in Nowhatta school. Was his story true? Was this the story of all the boys who were killed? We don't know . . . . Newspapers spoke little about such incidents because they had no access to the news. Journalists were not allowed to report, and editors were chocked with raids.

Some boys played games sometimes in the deserted neighbourhoods even when there was threat to life. How long could they sit indoors? The risk was high—a bullet would sometimes find its way into their roaming heads or their moving bodies—we lost a few boys this way. Sometimes, those youngsters would become the targets if there was a firing somewhere. Security forces had to vent their anger on someone, if not the ones who were mischievous, why not on the ones who belonged to the same breed?

I remember that boy who was playing football with his friends in a park of our neighbourhood on a curfew day. He played and played till an involuntary kick on his abdomen by a friend sent him tossing on to the ground. He rolled about and turned pale. The boys took him on their shoulders and wanted to take him to a hospital. No vehicle was allowed. There were too many formalities to be done before a curfew pass could be issued. The boy was gasping, his friends were fretting, but did that make a difference? The hospital was far off and the curfew harsh. Finally, after a delay of more than an hour, the boy was carried by his friends to a hospital, but carrying him to a hospital was of no use—he breathed his last on the way . . . . His spleen was traumatised, and a timely intervention could have saved his life. Our *mohalla* lost a dear son, and the boys were buried underneath their guilt . . . . Were they the killers or someone else? How many times I would curse myself for not being qualified enough at that point to help my brother.

After this episode, our parks were quieter and the neighbourhood was deserted. Our kids left playing and were more often seen staring through the half-open windows of their houses or watching television. *Makhdoom Sahib*, the *mohalla* where I lived, used to be a vibrant and cheerful place in our childhood. In the middle of Kohimaran was the tomb of Hazrat Sheikh Hamzah (RA), the renowned Sufi saint of Kashmir. The adjoining mosque and minarets were elegantly built. Great craftsmen and artisans must have fashioned those exquisite windows and those charming railings. The open space in the middle where pigeons would perch had bluish-green stones that made an excellent dancing floor for pigeons. The library housed extraordinary books. The *hamam* was an architectural marvel—warm and comfortable during freezing winters. The *Zakir Masjid,* a place where Sheikh Hamzah (RA) spent seclusive nights in remembrance of Allah, was a place of peace. In front of this all stood a graveyard, where our kith and kin rested. This boy was laid to rest in our graveyard, adjoining the place where my grandmother rested. Zafar also was somewhere near; an old stone was removed to make a room for his stone . . . . With such overcrowded graveyards, shouldn't we have removed the old stones from our graveyards to keep them ready for the new ones, now that there were too many of them? But, with each stone there was an emotional bonding.

Our common graveyard adjoining Makhdoom Sahib itself told the tale of our common lineage. Those boys buried there were all my relations . . . second cousins or further. We shared a common ancestor and never moved out of the closed *mohalla.* We would see each other many times a day, going to school, going to the market, going to *astaan* (shrine), and going to the playground . . . . and the death of those boys pained so much!

There was diversity all along the Kohimaran. Towards the right of the shrine was a temple, the Sharikadevi temple, and on the foothills was another small Ganesha temple. On the other side (left), there stood a Gurdwara. Kohimaran had a fort at its top. I remember my childhood and the rush of festive days. That *monj goolee* and those *singharas,* those ice creams and those candies, those buns and that bakery—all was unforgettable. Evenings would be delightful; men would collect around the huge chinar and talk about the world. Many would crack jokes, and the evening meeting point was called *Tare-Booni* (chinar of lies). The mornings would break with the tap of early-rising Pandits performing *prakram.* When they would reach near our home, they would turn towards the shrine and give a compulsory bow. Moving on, they would wait near the chinar, look towards the painted stone of Kohimaran, and chant those mantras there. From there onwards, they would go towards the small temple and then towards Sharikadevi, where they would offer flowers which used to grow in our gardens. We fondly called those yellow flowers *Bata Posh* (Pandits' flowers). We would hear a religious Pandits call, *'Moji daya kar'* ('O' Mother, help). With Pandits, the *Tahajud Khans* too would move towards the mosques to offer pre-dawn prayers. They knew each other and exchanged greetings as they treaded steps in their journey of peace. The *muezzins* would call for prayers, and hundreds would throng the shrine, negotiating those broad steps leading towards the shrine. After *fajr*, people would go to the top, *Kastoor Pendi*, a highland park, and get mesmerised by the beauty of Srinagar city. The Dal, Nigeen, Nishat, and those mighty mountains glowed in the morning light. Those vast green lands would shine as morning dew reflection added its own effect to them. The blossoming almond trees garlanding Kohimaran sent an aroma of freshness all through, those sturdy mulberry trees added warmth, and the huge chinars swaying left and right bowed wilfully in that bowl of peace.

There was a fort on the top which housed a tiny mosque and a small temple with *Kali's* statue installed in it. I had seen the fort when I was a small child; I had not gone up for years. It was closed for public.

We would speculate a lot, talk a lot with our neighbours and some hyper-reactive residents of our *mohalla*. Everyone seemed to have his own theory, his perception about the events engulfing Kashmir, and everyone would pronounce his own judgement. We had learnt to suspect, and learnt to attribute all to *challs* (conspiracies). Sometimes, we would overstep, and sometimes the speculations would be really accurate. There were the same discourses, the same discussions, after long curfews, on the disturbing events around *Tare-Booni*.

And then the fort too was occupied. After the fort was occupied, we knew we were chained from above. There were huge lights installed around the fort to illuminate the entire Kohimaran. Though the lights enhanced the charm of the fort and helped people to locate Kohimaran in the dead of the night, for us, the lights came as a problem. We suddenly became conscious of those watchmen during fearful nights. Our privacy—the tatters of which we possessed—was entirely lost. Whether we were in our rooms, in the garden, in the shrine, on its stairs, or walking along the lanes of *mohalla* Makhdoom Sahib, we knew there was an eye on us; a binocular was always chasing us, no matter whether we liked it or not. We kept wondering, were those keeping a vigil on us getting familiar with us as they saw more and more of us? Those faces, who knew us perhaps, were unknown to us, but we feared them no doubt; they could shoot us too!

How did those personnel feel there—on top of the world or not? How did the food reach them? Did they come downhill early mornings? What part of the fort did they use as a lavatory? Was the sanctity of the mosque inside the fort compromised? Did they know about the *Kali's* statue? We would think. The presence of security personnel within the fort kept the people off the shrine and other adjoining beauty spots. Who wanted to risk his life? Gradually, huge bunkers came up within the temples along the Kohimaran. No Pandits would visit the temples. However, pre-recorded *bhajans* would play in the temples, which seemed inappropriate in a setting of doom. The population around the temples became tense because of the bunkers . . . . All was restricted as multiple eyes guarded each individual.

That Wonderful Man and His Orphans

He was our neighbour—a kind-hearted, cheerful man who worked in AG's (accountant general's) office. We would greet him daily as he would park his *Bajaj* scooter in our home as the road to his house was sloped and stony. After he parked his scooter, his two young sons would be seen around the scooter, riding it and doing mock driving . . . . Sometimes they would be seen swaying right and left . . . one behind and one in front of their lovely father, enjoying a *saware* (joy-ride) together.

It was a dull afternoon one day when the sharp siren of an ambulance pierced our ears. We looked out to know what had happened. We saw people shouting and crying, carrying a body on a stretcher. We knew it was a dead body, but whose, we wanted to know. Before we could ask anyone, a mad sea of people was moving with the body towards the gate of our neighbour . . . shouting *Alla-ho-Akbar*. Someone whispered, 'It is the fellow who worked in AG's office.'

I strained my ears to hear it yet again. 'That AG's fellow,' I heard it again—properly. As the stretcher was lowered near that gate, we saw thick clotted blood . . . that clung to his neck. It was the same angel who would care for everyone in the *mohalla,* the same angel who helped my father and many other retirees of the *mohalla* with their pension papers. We would miss him . . . his warm morning greetings before he raced to his office; we would miss him and his mandatory evening chat as he would quickly tell us all that had happened around Lal Chowk and in his office . . .

This death tore our hearts, blew up our senses—it was a depression which encompassed the entire *mohalla*. Oh! That lovely man, that father of two lovely boys, that caretaker . . . was no more. His mother was old and his father ailing . . . terminally. His father would not, I was sure, accompany his son to the graveyard. Obviously, he was sick enough waiting for his own day; but on his day, for sure . . . his son would not accompany him. His two naughty sons . . . did they know the magnitude of the tragedy that had befallen them? And that woman, his wife who had gone to see her parents living nearby, had been recalled . . . to witness the devastation.

That scooter in our parking space was missing and was in police custody . . . he had fallen down from it after having been hit by a pellet at Lal Chowk. His two young sons played cricket in the nearby lawns the next day and his father mourned the death of his son for a week . . . . On the eighth day, the old man was laid to rest. The two little boys cried bitterly that day!

Memories and Memorials

Red was never the colour I hated; however, I hated it once there was too much of it in our lives. We saw all its shades—the muddy red, the dark red, the brick red, and of course, the blood red. Those flakes of red on streets . . . would make the hardest amongst us to cry. As a mark of respect, people would encircle the pools and spots on the roads with bricks and stones. The canines never dared to go near those pools but passed off the cordoned area quietly. A shower would wash the flakes away, or a fresh massacre would relocate them. It happened in Gawakadal, it happened in Khanyar, it happened in Handwara, it happened in Sopore, and it happened in Hawal . . . as hundreds were fired upon. They were all mourners, mourning the death of their leader and carrying the body for its last rites. He was no ordinary man. He was a *waiz*, a *Mirwaiz,* one last candle of a constellation blown to the other side. So many died with him. Curfew was harsh—we could not break our own silence . . . We wept inside . . . . Those who broke the silence died mercilessly.

Moulvi Farooq's assassination was a shock to us. My mother was deeply upset. She was from *moulvi* family incidentally. She recalled *Mirwaiz's* childhood, his adulthood, and his brave leap on to the pulpit of a *Mirwaiz*. In the past, she would always recollect the night when *Mirwaiz* Moulvi Yousuf Sahib left Kashmir. That night, when he had to leave, he had come to see her father. She would recall their whispers and their last hug. That night, when she woke up, surprised to see the two together, her father told her that her uncle would never come again. And that the future of Kashmir was grim. Moulvis had to go into hiding somewhere. Her father, too, had cried that day . . .

My mother would always go to Jamia Masjid on Fridays, listen to the *waz* of *Mirwaiz* and come back satisfied. The presence of *Mirwaiz* in the mosque would always reassure her. *Mirwaiz* had read the *Nikah khutbah* for many of our relatives. So the day brought a feeling of emptiness to a woman with the strings of her heart tied to *moulvi's*. But the massacre at Hawal made her forget a single man, and she was submerged into a marsh of sadness, from which she did not raise her head for a long time.

A young boy in his teens was nominated as *Mirwaiz's* successor. We saw him on a Friday at Jamia Masjid, delivering his first sermon to the people who loved his father and his family. He spoke in a croaking adolescent tone made harsher by the frequent hiccups from his uncontrolled sobs. I felt sorry for the gentleman. Losing his father at such a young age was a big loss, and getting pulled out from the playground of his youth and pushed into the dirty world of Kashmir politics was a bigger tragedy. No option for the young boy but to proceed ahead.

A triangular memorial was erected in Hawal, inscribed with names of all those people who lost their lives on that dark day. The memorial just gave the names and nothing about the lives of all those who lost their lives that day . . . nothing about the struggle of all those who tried to escape but couldn't . . . nothing about the fright and flight of those who witnessed the horror and still lived . . . . that day (while their companions died). The blood spots told the tales, the jumbled chappals spoke it all . . . . They could not be described. No one asked for the justice to the victims; they knew it was something that could not be granted. Another massacre happened behind the mighty Himalayas, and the world remained silent.

While death became common, memorials became commoner. A tap with an attached chain and a tumbler was a part of many memorials. There was an adjoining washbasin decorated with beautiful tiles. The name of the deceased was inscribed on the front tile, it was written so that people after quenching their thirst would pray for peace of the departed soul. But memorials were not there to stay. A day or two after a memorial was erected, the tap would be no more, the chain would be broken, and the tumbler would become invisible. The pretty-looking basin would be broken, and the tiles would be smashed. The dear ones would repair the basin and the tap and re-fix the tumbler and the chain . . . . They would do it again and again, and finally, they would give up. By and by, the memorial would disappear . . . . Who was it playing with the emotions of the people, destroying their connection with the dead—an outsider or an insider?

Our vacations were extended. I had seen my college a long time ago and wanted to be there again . . . but couldn't. I spent a part of my day reading, and my evenings, brooding over our fate . . . waiting for a better morning. We would speak to ourselves, silently and loudly. Sometimes those mirrors would be our companions, where we would pose and broadcast our thoughts.

Teacher of the Wounded

As the schools and colleges were closed, it was difficult to see our kids at home—eating, sleeping, and watching television. We couldn't afford to send them to playgrounds too . . . it was risky. To impart some kind of education to our kids, a makeshift school was raised in the lawns of Makhdoom Sahib Shrine. The educated people from our *mohalla* volunteered to teach children upto class 10th. I too volunteered to teach science, though I was asked to teach history and civics also. It was a great experience to teach kids from different backgrounds and different schools. The love of our kids for studies was apparent when I would see them there before time—sitting on the ordinary flooring, waiting for the classes to start, and attempting to learn. We had converted a wooden '*Dab*' in the lawns of Makhdoom Sahib into a school and put temporary partitions to separate the classrooms.

Sometimes, the shots in nearby areas would frighten us, but the kids were brave . . . they would never run away from the classroom for cover, never panic. Their steadiness in the midst of trouble was encouraging.

All those kids were lovely . . . . There was a sweet boy whose comments in the class were always crisp and stimulating. I heard one day that his father was shot . . . while accompanying the funeral of Maulana Farooq. We were saddened to know about the child. The boy attended the school after a few days, but he was quiet and depressed . . . always thinking. He remained in this state for some time, and we were happy to see smile returning on boy's face gradually. We heard that he and his younger sibling were looked after well by their uncle.

A few months later, his uncle also died . . . They say, he was pulled out in a crackdown after an episode of firing in a nearby area and shot . . . dead. After this episode, the boy never smiled. He had a lot to think about, a lot to care for . . .

Teaching science and math was easy—these subjects could not be challenged—but teaching history, civics, and social studies was difficult. We were confronted with so many questions. We could not explain 'independence' to children who saw their entire population besieged on Independence Day. We would not talk about the auspicious character of Republic Day as terror was spat on us on that 'auspicious day'. The pain of celebrating Republic Day and Independence Day was suffered most by the people living around the stadium where the National Flag was hoisted. Frequent checking, closure of lanes, and unpredictable crackdowns had made their lives miserable. Students would ask, 'For celebrating a national day, was it essential to terrorise the population of Srinagar?'

And there was civics with its outlined rights . . . right to equality . . . and other rights. Why wasn't it mentioned as to who were not equal in the eyes of law? What was the nature of their deficiency? Why were some inferior and others superior? What could we do? What could we say to the queries which seemed so relevant in our settings? The definition of 'democracy' was not understandable even . . . 'Government of the people, by the people and for the people'—this popular phrase was irrelevant for us. We never saw anything happening for the people, about 'by' and 'of', I was not sure.

Many times, the young boys and girls studying in our school must have thought as to what was wrong with them. Why were they in a makeshift school and not in regular schools? When the world was moving about so smoothly, why was the piece where they lived a disturbed area?

Back to College with a Hope

The decision to keep the college going was a bold one. When we reached our college after a 6-month-long break, our soft-spoken principal told us that the college and hospital would remain open. This delicate lady was determined to fight the circumstances. Curfew passes were arranged for us, and special passes were issued to the vehicles which carried the students and the staff. As this new announcement came, I knew now that someone at least in the turmoil-ridden valley had a positive thought in mind, a thought of making doctors out of us. This woman held the hospitals together when everything else was shattered; the college re-lived amidst death. She kept the hope alive . . . . A woman of guts, Dr Girja Dhar, I salute your courage.

A day later, from the foothills of Kohimaran, I started hesitantly with heavy steps and a trembling heart towards my bus stop. Some distant shots were heard on the way—the shots to the sound of which our ears had got used. Some shots appeared to echo from a nearby area . . . . In spite of fear, I continued to move. I knew that amidst those deserted streets, a 'messiah' would come to take me to my destination. In fact, he did arrive—like a king on a lonely street. His name was *Badshah*; the name suited him, and he pulled a long blue bus with the words 'Government Medical College, Srinagar' neatly painted on it. My stop, Shahampora, was hardly a few yards away from the primary troubled area of Nowhatta. The skinny, tall fellow greeted me as I boarded the bus. I forgot my worries as I saw my friends' chuckle, smile, and chatter. The bus moved on . . . picking up the students along Khanyar (also called *'Khoonyaar'* because of the bloodshed it witnessed), going on towards Baba-demb, Fateh Kadal, Syed Mansoor Sahib, and onwards towards Government Medical College. We knew we were the only ones on the roads . . . . All along the way, we saw deserted streets, dusty shutters of the shops (the shopkeepers had not pulled them up for months), and the men in khaki. Badshah was hypersensitive to their whistles and their gestures. He stopped when they would hint, and would race when they whistled.

Sometimes they stopped us and checked our curfew passes, —and sometimes, they just would stare at us . . . . We learnt to obey them, and Badshah and his deputy—the conductor of the bus—learnt to convince them.

Well! Inside the Government Medical College, life awaited us. The college was open when all else was closed. We rushed to our classes. Amidst all that uncertainty, we were taught physiology, anatomy, and biochemistry. There were teachers we admired, and amongst them was one soft-spoken gentleman, who taught us anatomy using an accent which would leave us wonderstruck. He stimulated us to appreciate God's perfection in creating a human being with all his levers, pulleys, hinges, soft parts, and subtle organs. We saw him there outside the college gate . . . just the moment we reached the college. He waved at us, and we smiled, knowing little that we would never see him again. That day, he had come to pick his things from the college or perhaps to say a goodbye to his colleagues. And, anatomy was never the same without him . . . . We knew we had lost a guide and a communicator between our mind and the dead body. He belonged to Jammu and was all set to go home . . . . We could not hold him back; safety of his life was a concern . . .

As the Pandits left, a void was created in our classes. We missed them, and some of us missed them badly. We were now studying in classes which had a homogenous population; the diversity was gone. Those who had visited Jammu and other parts after the turmoil told us about the pitiable condition they were in. Some were in tents, some were in rented one-room sets, and some made use of makeshift arrangements. The student community of Jammu Medical College protested and did not allow Pandit students to use the facilities present there—not even for a day. Most Pandit students of Government Medical College had left without any batch having appeared in the exams. Their examinations posed problems. Would they be examined by Jammu University or Kashmir University? If by Kashmir University, then how would men and material flow to Jammu to do the desired? After lot of difficulties ultimately, we heard that all those who migrated wrote their exams in Jammu and were sent to different colleges of India for studying medicine.

The race of Kashmiri Pandits . . . like grains, they were tossed to medical colleges located in various states of India, and thus began their life away from us. Most preferred to have no contact with us; occasional acquaintances exchanged hollow greetings.

Some Pandits, in spite of the odds, stayed back, and a bold girl from our class also preferred to stay back while her family left. She stayed in a Muslim friend's home, who extended all the warmth and affection to her. The family never bothered about their own safety but looked after the Pandit girl as their own daughter. The Pandit girl looked like our own, and almost the entire college knew about her. In a student population of more than 500, there were a few miscreants too. A hefty girl, two batches senior to us, a girl known to trouble freshers and bother teachers, had threatened the poor Pandit girl and the family who sheltered her.

One morning, we found the Pandit girl missing. We were told that she had left—to be with the likes of her in Jammu. Meanwhile, the hefty girl terrorised us all. She ordered us to cover our heads, and wear a *burka* the way she wore. At whose behest she was doing this all we hardly knew, but the fact was that we were scared of her. We did what she told us; disobeying her meant an open invitation to death and who was interested in dying at her hands?

We lost the colour and the crispness, but we were ready to be 'doctors churned out in adverse circumstances'. They taught us medical studies but not how we should go about in the turmoil. Nothing was written in books; there was no tutorial for us . . . . We kept wondering, what happens to medical studies when a 'war' envelops a nation?

Downtown and Uptown

Srinagar is a dream city—a city of lakes, gardens, and streams—green and vibrant in summer, dazzling red in autumn, and white and humble in winter. It has a rich history, a rich culture. Some time back, they say, it was on its own—proud and prosperous. But then came the Moguls, who gripped it tight, though enriching the city with beautiful gardens and monuments. And thereafter, there followed a chain of aliens, who plundered, conquered, and captured the city, squeezing its population which tumbled from one punch to another. The last few decades have seen too many disasters and tragedies, and too little of prosperity.

Turmoil divided Srinagar into two segments—the 'Uptown' and the 'Downtown'. Before the turmoil, it was just 'Downtown'. Downtown is the old Srinagar—an intertwined, closely packed portion of the city, which—abounded with life-before turmoil. Its lovers called it '*Shehr-i-Khas*' (a special city). Special it was (and still is) for it housed a vibrant, sensitive, and creative population of Srinagar. It is garlanded by beautiful mosques and *khankahs*. It was the intellectual hub, the economical hub, and the hub of creativity. Many tightly packed colonies here kiss the banks of river Jhelum on either side, and some *mohallas* are named after the names of the bridges on Jehlum as Zainakadal, Habba Kadal, Safakadal, Naidkadal, Aalikadal, etc.

All artisans and craftsmen of Kashmir lived in specific pockets there; some areas were named after the profession the group had. Barbers occupied *Naidyar*, butchers occupied *Puj Mohalla*, carpenters occupied *Chan Mohalla,* dyers occupied *Rangarstop*, leather workers occupied *Gunz Khud* . . . each pocket represented a distinct clan of hard-working workers who created marvels with their hands. The beauty of Kashmir—its fruits, birds, and flowers—got reflected in their artwork. The mountains, the chinars, and the breathtaking landscape got immortalised in the art and craft coming from Downtown. Those civilised and lovely people represented the heart of Kashmir. They lived with each other and lived for each other.

Missing Badshah's bus meant losing hope. If the bus that would take you safely to your destination was gone, it meant you had to go there all alone . . . through the narrow alleys and lanes of what had become a 'death trap' called Downtown.

On a day without Badshah's bus, I had to tread it all alone. As I moved through its listless and lifeless lanes encased by wires and blocked by huge bunkers, I remembered my childhood. Those were the days when my parents would take me around the node of activity and the station of creativity. The huge houses with their marvellous woodwork and clay work would buzz with men, women, and smiling youngsters who would watch with curiosity all that was going on in those lanes and by-lanes through their '*Dabs*' and '*zoon-e-dabs*'. Who would have imagined that someday those glittering streets would fall vacant?

I remembered that *harrisa* which was made there, that *kandkari* copperware which was carved there, those ethnic *namdas* which were fashioned there, those minute *guls* and *badaams* of priceless shawls which were designed there, those *wazaas* who would roll those balls of meat called *rista* and *goshtaba* there; that calligrapher's den was there, that *tildooz's* chinar was there, that carpet weaver was there, that poet was there, that barber was there, that 'leather-man' was there, that 'fur-man' was there, that buzzing *khankah* was there, and that ringing temple too was there . . . Nostalgic memory, I can never get rid of it. I remember the fishy odour of *gada kocha* (the fish market) and the bite of its chillies, the echoing voice and shrill cries of the fisherwomen, and that muttering of the *mutter-walla*. Those shops had tiny verandas, *wani paennd,* on which people would gather to discuss politics and cricket.

That was past.

How much had the Downtown changed now; how much had it been choked?

Nowhatta Chowk—the chowk that has become a seat of resistance is actually a chowk where pledges and promises were made. On a curfew day it is strangulated. On other days, the chowk hosts a bunch of angry youth. A death in Palestine makes their blood boil; a blasphemous word in America makes them stage a protest. These guys, good-looking and great ones at heart, are known to do good—beyond their means. They dress the wounds of people they know not, shoulder the burden of unknown coffins, arrange food for those stranded, and yes, they are most respectful to women. They are mad for cricket, love the likes of Nana Pathekar, and hate the ones who try appeasing them. They are driven by rage and anger against most politicians who lied not to them but to their fathers and forefathers a hundred times on the podiums which were erected in this very chowk. Those politicians were liars; they bred liars . . . they sold out an innocent herd and made a comedy out of their miseries. The handsome bargains they got were all for themselves, and the generation next and next . . . . How could they forget? How could they spill out their anger, vomit out their frustration? These innocent boys took those Russian-made toys in their hands and lost the control of their being. Some went to avenge, some went to take revenge, some went for the excitement, and some were taught to be warriors—the *Islamic Mujahideen.* They were told the tales of Arabs—how a few of them fought the pagans and came out victorious. But no one concentrated on the 'character' of these young boys. No one told them about the Prophet's (SAW) exemplary character and his (SAW'S) message of peace. Islam and the gun were seen as synonymous. Islam became a casualty, and its message of peace was shadowed by the gun and its might.

As I passed through Nowhatta Chowk that day, I remembered this and seemed to call out to them, 'O you, the sons of the soil, you were too precious to be lost to these winds!' I still wonder, was death the only answer for all what they believed in? Did they not deserve to be counselled, to be hugged, or to be understood? Did a week's training in operating a lethal automatic machine make them a real threat for a well-equipped army of a big country?

They became autonomous. Some were caught and taught bitter lessons in prisons and lock-ups, and some murdered . . . . Whether meticulously done or mercilessly executed, murder is a murder. They left behind unprotected tender families who struggled for survival. Some got it all for what they possessed, and some got it for just being the passers-by. A youngster of Nowhatta and its adjoining areas was always at the receiving end. Whether he knew it or not, did it or not, he was always seen as a suspect and loathed, tortured, humiliated, and kicked. He was angry at what was happening to him, and willingly or unwillingly, he bred another generation of anger!

In this boiling pot, there is a cool spot. A spot where minds are freshened, hearts are solaced, and sins are washed. A witness to the trauma, this mosque of Downtown called Jamia Masjid lies humble and low. Its lovers thronged it always. Made in a distinct style, all it did now was to stare at the helplessness of the people of Downtown. I remember my childhood when I used to go there with my mother and sit besides the pure waters of its fountain. I remembered how there in the open I would gaze at the beautiful sky and dream big. I remember how my mother would sit in the 'marked' space for women and listen to the *waz* of the *Mirwaiz*. I remembered those pillars I used to hug, those jars I used to admire, those doves and pigeons that fluttered about its minarets . . . those stories my mother would tell about angels descending there. I remembered all as I passed by it.

'O, Allah, why is the place of solace too closed?' I ask the Almighty. Sometimes, they say, 'its gates open and an occasional sob is heard.' It must be some man crying in some corner, praying for a respite from all that we were witnessing. 'Will Allah listen to his prayer ever? Will the mosque be full again—some day?' I thought as I went past it.

Onwards from Nowhatta and Jamia mosque, as I walked across the lanes of Downtown, I became tense—no sound anywhere, no tap, no shout . . . . The narrow lanes had been blocked by bunkers and by-lanes barbed. Noise you could not make; race you could not run. If you did that, you could die . . . . The *panjra* windows of those huge houses were closely shut. No holes were apparent; perhaps paper and plastic had been pasted on inside to make them opaque. The doors made from thick wood were tightly closed with tough latches on them. The ones that opened towards the roadside had been shut closely with a hard rock called *kanz,* used for crushing chillies.

Men in khaki were there in lanes, marching or walking briskly one after the other. They would stare, question, or frisk the passers-by, unaware, however, about what they had done with the population of the Downtown. Did they know who had been caged inside? Did they know who had been frozen in their four walls? Those artisans of repute, those craftsmen of high calibre, those thinking minds, those feeling hearts, those guardians of our culture . . . those pillars of our tradition who did not have freedom to move, to talk, to listen, leave alone to argue or to question? The sound of television would irritate the 'masters on the road'; the flush of toilets would make them furious as the flowing dirt in the open drains was offensive!

How was that population surviving in that oppression? Why won't they burst someday? Why won't they be ever able to overcome those restrictions? Will they melt down under the heat of this humiliation, or they will smash it to get back their identity? I kept on thinking as I moved deeper into its deserts.

With tears in my eyes, a prayer on my lips, I seemed to shout, 'O, the dwellers of the town! Where are you? Does the world know that a civilised population is in a collective grave? Young and old, men and women, why are you all are imprisoned inside?'

I couldn't help but think as to what thoughts they must be having. What ideas must be striking them? What must be happening to the psyche of their young ones who are keen to peep outside? What must be happening to the energy of those youngsters who were fond of playing cricket on busy streets . . . ?

Towards Becoming a Doctor

Becoming a doctor anywhere is no easy work, but becoming one here was equivalent to a squeeze—a tightness which would grip and render one motionless; there would be an interruption by a series of violent jolts which would shake your interior and exterior. There were those parasites and bugs to be memorised, that death and disease to be classified, that drug and the dose to be calculated, that organ and system to be identified, and those muscles and nerves to be tested . . . for their function. There was so much of fear and so much of confusion. How would you do all that amidst so much tension outside? How does it feel when you study anatomy, physiology, and biochemistry in a place which is besieged and caged, where fear thrives and uncertainty prevails, and where indoors are trapdoors and outdoors death traps? Why does it go on like this? We always heard with interest about the past of our college—how it was fun to be there, how the bubble and charm of the medical college made it the place of envy for those who could not make it there.

But for now, we were like a herd of cattle, driven to college in queues and made to study medicine.

Examinations were unwanted. Could we memorise Guyton and Snell's when our neighbourhood was mourning the death of a handsome boy who went out to play cricket? Could we remember those 'reactions' in biochemistry when our entire area was under a crackdown? But yes, there were no short cuts; whether we liked it or not, our examinations would be held .We were told, there would be concessions for us and the examiners would be lenient and blah, blah, blah . . . . But nothing of that sort happened. Examinations for the first professional were tough; no help came from any quarter. Burning midnight oil did not help too for our minds were out of focus. Bearing pain and panic, we made it to college on every examination day.

Sometimes there were difficulties; I remember how my class fellow made it to college from the Downtown Srinagar on a day when no one was allowed to move out of his locality as there was a crackdown. I can imagine how he must have got up from the rows of people sitting in an odd posture. I can imagine how he must have pleaded with the khaki guarding his group. I can imagine how he must have reasoned with him to set him free—for appearing in his exams. I can imagine how he must have convinced him . . . . We saw him outside the examination hall. We witnessed his tremble and tremor. We saw his parched lips, heard his cracking voice . . . . And he showed us his hand, drenched in sweat with marks of faded ink on it . . . . It was a 'pass' he said, written by one of the officers on his hand; it had helped him negotiate various layers of security as he moved towards his college . . . . He dared not go back; 'the faint, faded pass' on his hand would not be accepted, and he preferred to stay back in the hostel but still hesitated to wash his hand . . . . Maybe he would need the pass some day, so he let the imprint last till it would . . .

No one would dare to come to the 'Paradise on earth'. Not even the examiners. But then how could the examinations go on? Internal arrangements for examiners (from the same university) were permitted to let the academics continue. The internal arrangements were, at times, annoying for the students as the same old faces would be there on the other side of the table, torturing the already tortured beings. With restricted enjoyments and the burden of the turmoil, who would feel like reading or working hard? But in spite of unwillingness, in spite of a noticeable disgust, the classes continued and examinations were held—though never in time; postponements and cancellations became routine . . .

Some professors were sadists; no matter what happened inside or outside, they would torture the students. I remember a professor who would call five or six of us into his room, make us line up, and shoot questions at us. Our utterings would become public. Those were painful times when the other one got the question you wished you would get and the chapter you had memorised the entire night was skipped altogether. This exercise made you feel low, saved the professor's time, and gave him an opportunity to 'laugh out loud' at you!

First professional passed off. Many students failed, but they could join new classes with us while preparing for a supplementary examination. It pained us to see their depression, but we couldn't pause for them. They had to bear it all—memorising, practising alone during those fearful nights, doing everything that would push them across into the second professional.

That night I remember, there was a gun battle in a nearby *mohalla,* we all lay flat and put off our lights. Our asylum that night was a tiny storeroom which had no windows. There were too many of us in that tiny room and it was mid-July; the temperature high and the air motionless. As there was a lull after the rattle, I was in a fix, wondering why I couldn't crawl back and go to my room. There were those parasites to be learnt, their life cycles, their hosts—the intermediate and the permanent, for a 'stage' the next day. I wondered, what should I do?

I was trying hard in that choking place to memorise those bugs. I was making circles in my mind—connecting the hosts with the diseases they caused, and yes all seemed to fall apart as I heard a piercing shot perhaps coming from a rifle. It was too close and too sharp to disturb everything that was in my mind. Safety first! I thought, as my sister pushed me inside further into the darkness of the storeroom.

Recitation of the *kalima* came as a solace. There is no God but Allah, the forces personnel with his rifle and his furious mood was not Allah, neither was that Madam of parasitology who was to examine me the next day . . . . It was past midnight when the rattle stopped; my mother lit a candle in the kitchen, and we hurriedly had our dinner, not knowing the contents—just attempting to pour something into those bellies which were sucked in with fear. We wrapped ourselves with sheets on those mattresses put haphazardly on floor—no beds to be used, they could prove dangerous!

The morning broke; we removed our heavy curtains to look through the windows. Nothing outside, no activity. We knew, all of us, how we had spent the night, but someone had to go outside to see how things were outside. After some time, a gentle morning breeze blew, the silence was replaced by the flutter, and we heard a stir coming from outside. People had started to move on the roadside; the rustle of a few cars was also heard. This population had survived another nightmare, and thank God all had survived!

What happened to me should not bother anyone. It was an isolated incident. The 'stage' had to go on . . . whether I failed or passed, no excuse would do . . . . All I would be asked would be about bugs and nothing about the previous night's misery . . . . Badshah would come again and take me to the place where I had to be . . .

Third-Year Syndrome

The third year was the year when we went across to the hospital. We felt like doctors in the white coats with stethoscopes hung around our necks. The wards of SMHS (Sri Maharaja Hari Singh) Hospital were huge and dirty too. The odour of flint and Dettol prevailed over the stink of pools and puddles present in closed spaces nearby. The windows were hazy, some opaque, because so much had collected on the meshes guarding the windows. The corridors looked like kitchens with lined up stoves, and lifts were dangerous like jolting see-saws. The hospital was old, but it was a goldmine producing a class of doctors with a strong clinical sense who had made a name in the East and the West

Standing next to patients was exciting. We surrounded them and asked them questions. Most patients loved to unwind and spoke about the unwanted and 'wanted' details of their lives; they uncovered happily, letting each one of us palpate, percuss, and auscultate. Sometimes it hurt them when we tried to elicit those signs . . . but they still cooperated. I don't know how they felt when we all surrounded them. They knew it was a class going on and we were learning, but they still obeyed our commands and did what we asked them to do. We were callous; I know we never told them the truth about ourselves, never told them that we were just students in the initial phase of our learning. We exhausted them with all that we did to them, too much of talking, questioning, and too much of handling by too many of us. In our set-up, no consent was needed; no permission was required for all that we were doing . . .

There were patients who had braved the bitter tragedies of their lives, now braving an odd disease. We never were there to take care of their tragedies, but yes, about their disease we wanted to know . . . though in third year, it was yet too early.

The professors taught us how to take history and how to examine the patients, and cautioned us not to be in a hurry to make a diagnosis. They stressed on small things like standing on right side of the patient, positioning the patient for the examination of nodes, eliciting tendon reflexes . . . and so on. They were well-known physicians and surgeons with big Indian and foreign degrees, some with preserved values and some with a dilutional effect, but nonetheless, wise and committed. People respected them, and we loved it when they taught us.

There were those teachers we admired like that priestly head of Medicine who had an enviable memory and sharp clinical sense, the doyen of medicine, as he was called. Dr G.Q. Allaqaband was a high-ranking clinician, very popular with patients and very high on the academic front. It was a dream to be in his unit; externs, they said, learnt a lot of practical points when on rounds with him. I remember having envied all those students who were posted there. There was that handsome Dr Yousuf, nicknamed 'Marshal' by the students—perhaps out of admiration for the way he marshalled and managed the classes. Admirable! No one could parallel his teaching skills! The calm and composed Dr Durrani, too, taught with commitment and passion. These doctors were followers of legendary Dr Ali Mohammad Jan, who was considered the Luqman of Kashmir. People held his laminated prescriptions decades after his death and would try to get the medicine he had prescribed from old stores—the medicines which are no longer available. Dr Ali Jan was trained in the West, but he practised his skills in Kashmir. One of the brightest in medicine, he became an icon for Kashmiris, an ideal doctor for them, and an inspiration for those pursuing medicine or aspiring to pursue it.

That skinny Dr Khan was a class part. With his English hat and his unique overcoats, engrossed in himself and his subject, he gave life to pathology. What a diagnostician, what a pathologist, and what a lovely human being! No one liked to disturb him, not even the men in khaki who, on a crackdown day, would leave him in the company of his slides, his microscope, and his books!

There was still another tall professor, Prof. Syed Zafar Mehdi, professor of Medicine, heading Unit IV. I remember the crackdown in the college and the hospital, when the entire hospital was sealed and studded with short and stout men in a green camouflage. They had broad noses and puffy eyes and belonged to a regiment of the Indian Army. They moved about swiftly, in lines, and dispersed everywhere at the blow of a whistle. The SMHS Hospital was under their rule for one terrible day. They pulled out all doctors, paramedics, and nurses from the wards, theatres, and OPDs and made them sit in that horrible posture, facing the wall. All were sitting and squatting in the corridors where they used to walk like kings, for they were the elite ones—respected and loved ones who never shirked work and treated beggars and kings alike. We, the students, too were bundled and brought out into the corridors. A tiny lane in SMHS Hospital, the Professor's Lane, housed great names in medicine. It surprised me that they too were paraded one by one in the same corridors as we were. They were in despair; their faces depicting anger and disgust, their heads were held low. One head refused to bow down, one neck refused to bend, and this perhaps irked a soldier who shouted at the tall professor, 'Face towards the wall and sit down.'

'No way,' the professor replied. 'Go and get a chair for me. I cannot sit like a criminal,' the professor shouted back.

The soldier was angry; he called for help and hit the wall with a huge stick. He put the butt of his gun on the professor's chest. A few of his men arrived at the scene to sort out the mess, but the professor refused to bend. His next reply silenced them all. 'Get your officer. He will understand what I say.'

After this, the professor was unmoved, the soldiers too stood still, and we all watched with fear and apprehension—the struggle of a tall professor for his honour. An officer was called, and he negotiated to resolve the crisis . . . The tall professor stood 'taller' amongst all the dwarfs. Had he been beaten, shot at, or hurt, would we have called him insane? Had this all happened in other part of the country or any other part of the world, would it have made a big story and would the professor have become an instantaneous hit? But yes, here in Kashmir, the news was gulped down. We all who were a witness to the entire episode forgot it too; our minds preferred to give space to more gruesome episodes! Was it this humiliation or the fear of being humiliated which made our professors chase dreams for their children in the West? Was it their short-sightedness, far-sightedness, or selfishness which made most of those so-called 'giants' send their wards for higher studies outside the country?

The Mourning Dal

Summers would come and winters would go. I and my friend, tired of those boring theory classes, decided to breathe some fresh air on a day of hartal when not a soul walked on the streets. We boarded an auto and reached the Boulevard—a long stretch of road along the banks of Dal Lake. As we walked together, two lonely girls—holding each other's hands, we cast glances towards the serene surface of Dal, which was glowing with the blue reflection of the mountains; the rays of the sun played on its swaying and circling waters. There was quietness all round. We watched and watched, walked and walked till we noted the presence of khakis who were marching and looking with suspicion towards us. We slowed down our pace to decrease the pitch of our taps; we were scared, no doubt because the tap of our shoes was the only sound audible. As we walked a few steps more, we found a lonely *shikara* man on a *shikara*, facing the harsh sun, perhaps searching for an even customer on an odd day. We saw a hope in him, and he perhaps saw a hope in us. He was the one who could possibly take us out of the odd situation we were in, perhaps away from those chasing glances, away from that fear . . .

We stopped for a while and asked him, 'Can you take us around?'
He smiled and said, 'Sure, please come.' We jumped on to the *shikara* without a second thought. As we were passing slowly across Dal, hearing the gurgle of its waters, a feeling of uneasiness gripped us. Were we enjoying, while the rest of us were mourning . . . ? We did not know where we had to go; we did not know how far he would take us . . . . Could he take us somewhere, from where we could walk down to our homes? There stood Kohimaran with its huge reflection in the Dal, and we remembered our destination and could obviously point towards it. 'Take us somewhere near that fort,' we said, pointing our fingers towards it.

It seemed to lie too far, but *shikara-walla* smiled again and said, 'No worry, I will take you there.'

I and my friend on an outing were uneasy on this adventure . . . . What would the *shikara-walla* think about us? Two young girls . . . on a lonely trip to Dal . . . on an odd day! He paddled his *shikara* slowly and steadily across the lake; through the narrow channels; around the floating gardens; through its pure and impure patches, it's clear and muddy inlets, its broad and beautiful outlets; underneath the staggering and smart bridges . . . . But all was quiet. Not a child was visible on what used to be its busy banks; not a man was seen on *shikaras,* which were abandoned and kept aside. Paddling across the unknown lands, the *shikara-walla* talked about Dal and its admirers, about Dal and its history, about Dal and its glory. He talked about *shikaras* and their making; he took us along the narrow pools where houseboats were once made and showed us the arts and crafts showrooms which stood vacant along the banks. We listened to him as he compared his 'now' with his 'then'. His 'tomorrow', the thought of it even stirred him, was a liability, and his 'today', like ours, an uncertainty. He cried and sang . . . We thought about him. We thought for him. What made him go out with a *shikara* when everybody else was home? What kept him going? Was it his desire to feed his family, or his desire to be amidst his love—his Dal? He was an old man. He could have sent his son for work and rested himself, but this he could not do. He feared for the life of his son. He told us about the stories of young boys and young men who were lost in his precious Dal . . . forever, boys who were killed or chased till they drowned.

He paddled slowly as he saw a few men in khaki on a *shikara;* this he did so that they would not suspect him. He gave them a broad smile and said, 'To Pokhribal . . . *saab.*'

'OK, OK,' they said. He lowered his voice as he reached a huge bunker in the heart of Dal on a floating garden. He repeated his statement 'To Pokhribal . . . *Saab*'. This time there was no response from the khakis.

He moved on towards somewhat familiar surroundings . . . . Jogilanker, he told, we were heading towards. I saw a building drenched in smoke, black as tar, and closed my eyes.

'Oh, it is my school, my own Vishwa Bharti!' Wounded and blackened, a victim of circumstances, a target of someone's madness, it was too humble to yield anything. Would I find some of my memories there in the rubble? Those charts, those boards, those swings . . . I grew impatient and asked the *shikara-walla* to move fast. We heard a few shots as we were moving . . . faster. We knew those were gunshots, but we pretended not to listen. I murmured to my friend, 'Where will our parents find us, if we cannot make it alive to our homes?' So many guesses people would make, people would talk about us. 'Oh God!' We panicked.

Thankfully, we reached Pokhribal—a still pocket of water afflicted with dirty weeds—where a hospital for lepers stood on a raised landscape . . . . The lepers have lived there together in a colony for decades like untouchables, away from city dwellers, away from all that which consumed the city. They were there atop, staring towards their own sky, waiting there for their own dawn . . .

We got down and handed over some money to the *shikara-walla*, thanking him; he kissed the notes, telling us that they had come to him after many weeks. We waited as he turned his *shikara* . . . . The thought of him going alone, paddling all along, smiling at khakis and saying it aloud . . . 'Back from Pokhribal, *saab*' was disturbing. We prayed for his life, prayed that he reached his destination safe, with all that he had earned. Did he reach home alive? We didn't know, but yes, he managed to help us reach Makhdoom Sahib from where my friend went to her home and I to mine. Though we reached home a bit late, we remained quiet about all that we had done—bunking classes in the midday and going across the entire city in a *shikara*. We knew we would be killed, so we remained quiet . . . . It was an adventure we vowed we would not repeat.

The Examination Hall Terror

The second professional had to be overcome; except for clinics most students did not like anything about the second professional. Pharmacology made it boring, pathology made it lengthy, and forensic medicine made it irritating. Curious we were to become doctors, but examinations were tough. Sometimes, examinations were unwanted too. It was a terminal examination for pharmacology that day. We were shaking outside the examination hall, murmuring and cramming those dosages, toxic effects, and pharmacokinetics of hundreds of drugs. . Some of us had prepared well and some had not; somehow, second professional exams meant the beginning of an escape . . . . When we sat for the terminal exam, the head of the Department of Pharmacology, who was fond of choosing unusual questions for the examination, went on reading the paper and a Demonstrator wrote the paper on the board with chalk. There were no formal question papers then; the questions had to be written on the board. We sat quietly as we heard the paper from the Head; the paper, as expected, was mostly based on postscript notes and pharmacokinetics of unusual drugs. The paper included questions from the tiny jottings which we always ignored. We felt miserable! But we would try to do what we could. No one we knew could do 100%. When we were about to start, just then there was a bang, a shout, and we all trembled.

'Get up all of you! No exam today!'

Some of us rose from our seats, and some were still seated. The one who had shouted was a fellow student who was actually our senior and had left his studies for many years but had rejoined the second professional with us. He was creamy white, short-statured, and bald—looked like a Dad of most of the boys who were with us. The bald man was joined by two more boys, who too shouted. They all screamed and asked us to leave the examination hall. It seemed they were strangers, as if they never knew us. We quickly started moving away from our seats with our answer papers in our hands. A boy, thin and skinny, however, refused to move. He wanted to do the paper, he said. In spite of repeated threats, he remained glued to his seat. And then I saw something that I had never seen before. It was a black piece of metal, with a trigger and a nozzle. It was a pistol, yes, directed towards the frail boy . . . . The bald man held it firmly, and it seemed he knew how to operate it. I couldn't scream, but other girls did and some bold ones begged the bald man to spare the skinny, studious boy. The boy got up and we all ran towards the doors of the examination hall. The bald man and his friends were the last to leave. They left with a bang. The glass panes on top of the door came down crashing onto the ground. Surprisingly, our teachers and the Head had left the scene quite early.

All of us on that fateful day rushed back to our homes. The next day, no one spoke about the incident. The bald man was missing from the class. All of us had queries which we kept to ourselves; no one could be trusted. The bald man could have planted his own men amongst us. Who knew, our friend could be a bald man's loyalist. We kept thinking about the bald man and our pharmacology terminal. Would the bald man let us ever sit in the examination? Would the Head be irritated that bald man was our fellow student? If the examinations were held again, would the Head set a tougher paper and take revenge from the entire batch? Or would the scare make him set on easy paper?

We don't know if the bald man and the Head ever met or ever talked to each other after the incident or reconciled with each other. But the incident did not make news. No one complained to any authority. The bald man escaped, and he knew he would. Perhaps the only reason he had rushed to rejoin medical studies with us was to take advantage of the circumstances and to become a doctor. Circumstances were definitely in his favour!

After a week, a new date for examination in pharmacology was announced. We couldn't study for it as we were unsure whether it would be held or not. As we sat in the examination hall, we looked for the bald man. He was there, seated, confident and wearing a broad smile. He and his associates sat through the entire exam; they did not copy . . . . Did they know all that was asked in the repeat exam, or had they played some other game to get through? We don't know. Though uneasy, we were relieved to solve a better question paper on a better day.

Then onwards, we knew that besides the external environment, our exams depended on the mood of bald man and his weapon . . . because we were appearing for exams at a time when no police would guard the examination centre and when the invigilating staff was non interfering . . . . In such times, only silence helped. Many teachers hated us, and they called us 'devilish batch', and for some of the examinations, we were left to ourselves without invigilators, without any check. To copy or not to copy was up to us.

Board and University examinations of the 1990s were just token examinations, where all passed, thousands got distinctions and first divisions . . . . The terrified and threatened invigilators and superintendents ignored what the students carried: guns, chits or sometimes, entire books. So with such a scenario outside, why would medical students stick to decorum and values? Why couldn't they, too, cheat? Why couldn't they use guns like they were used elsewhere? About what you did in the examination was a matter between you and your God, and most students thankfully did respect the sanctity of examinations when they could very well be a part of the bald man's team!

The bald man had done something that no other medical student of GMC had dared to do in those times. But we all agreed that 'no matter who cheats, doctors should not' . . . . We deal with human lives, we thought, but never uttered it to the bald man.

The Loot

I remember seeing that handcart with a huge pile of books. It seemed those books were on sale. People flocked around the cart, turned the pages of the books, and quickly dropped them back. My brother too went to see what lay there on the cart. He came rushing home with a huge book in his hands and asked me, 'This is a medical book, do you need it? It is for sale, Rs. 100, can bargain if you need.'

I took the huge, somewhat familiar, book in my hands. It was old and torn, but the pictures were fresh and real. I knew it was a book of anatomy—the so-called 'Bible of anatomy'—*Gray's Anatomy*. The binding was in shambles, but on one of the corners of it was an indelible mark of its owner . . . 'Dr *Kaw*'. '*Kaw*', meaning 'crow' in Kashmir, had flown away and left his assets and memories here.

The book belonged to a doctor who had fled . . . Kashmir. He must have preserved that book for years and finally when he left, he must have thought it to be a heavy and a hefty companion. I hastily returned the book to my brother telling him that it was old and haggard and that I didn't want it. Though we preferred smaller and smarter books in anatomy, having *Gray's Anatomy* at home would have been wonderful. But the thought of it being someone else's property was irking. Was it a book stolen? And if so, was it proper to acquire knowledge from it, and would that knowledge be helpful? On the cart, there were many more books.

'Were those all books on the cart medical books? Were those ordinary ones or there were some rare scriptures too?' Who would ask and why? Who would buy all that stolen wealth? I don't know if there were some takers for those books or whether the books were sold off to a *masala-walla* to pack the *masala* into cones-to be made from the books on sale. In retrospect, I keep thinking about those books and their owners; I keep on thinking as to why I didn't buy the entire lot to give them off to a library at a later date. But I didn't; I knew I couldn't. It was a difficult responsibility, and I was too scared to bear it.

I remember those stools which, too, were for sale in a nearby *mohalla*; the stool I saw carried a distinct number on one of its legs and an abbreviation GSN on the other leg. It did not take me much to understand what GSN meant after I saw people purchasing those tough steel stools for Rs. 30 only. Those stools belonged to Girls School, Nowhatta, and were stolen on the very same night when the school building was set on fire. Those who purchased the stools knew well wherefrom the stools had come; some preferred to repaint them, and some did not mind the abbreviations on the stools. After all, they had purchased the stools—no matter from thieves; if they would not have purchased them, someone else would have. So where was the problem? The school deserved to burn! Was it because it belonged to the Government and the stools too deserved to be looted? Who was selling whom and who was selling whose—and why? Could we ask?

Did it happen for each school which was burnt? Did it happen for each college which was lost, and did it happen for each office/ Department that was burnt to ashes? Were there other items from the school for sale elsewhere? Were we a party to this destruction just to fill our own homes when someone else had set our common asset on fire? Was it a tale of all failed communities or was it the beginning of a doom? Who would tell . . . ?

Bad times, they say, expose a human being's inherent nature. Turmoil is a physical trauma, a psychological trauma, and it exposes a human being. Where does life go into hiding when turmoil strikes? Where do sympathy, good nature and good morals go when people are tested? An individual who lives amidst hopelessness, why does he become selfish? Why does he want to be the only one to survive? Is it because his foundations are weak, or is it because his heart has hardened?

It seems strange that in an attempt to curtail the unrest, all else was ignored. Health, education, agriculture, and environment—all was plundered. The watchdogs, conceivers, implementers, and planners shut their eyes to let the plunder happen—the faster the better. Was militancy the only issue in Kashmir? Years after the stool episode, I saw a photograph in a national daily of a woman carrying on her head the stolen items from a Government building after the fall of Saddam Hussein in Iraq. It reminded me of how my assets were looted and sold. No one took a picture of our assets being stolen for it was happening in a shielded well of a democratic country.

The Sher-i-Kashmir Institute of Medical Sciences (SKIMS) . . . Loot!

A breathtakingly huge structure on the banks of Aanchar Lake, a brainchild of Sheikh Mohammad Abdullah, was erected with care and caution. A state-of-art tertiary care centre, one of the finest in India, it was a class apart. Kashmiris had not seen anything like that before. Only he could dream SKIMS—no Kashmiri ever dreamt so big. The neat, clean, smart, and sweet place had it all—hi-tech machinery, dynamic workforce, and an organised set-up. All that was latest was shipped to SKIMS; people were trained from within and outside the country to kindle a hope for the hopeless . . . . An electron microscope was brought to SKIMS when there was just one in North India. SKIMS worked well; its doctors and scientists loved the new-found environment and worked to transform medicine from an art to science. SKIMS brought Kashmir on the international research map. The job was well done.

Turmoil spoiled it all—the refractile corridors, the shining walls, the clean bathrooms, the hi-tech machinery, all would have been well had the doctors stayed well. They fell—some to bullets and some to pressure, some fled, but the brave ones gave their best in the most testing times. The clever ones took all they could in the worst of times. They managed promotions for themselves and their dear ones, took away the benefits they never deserved, and worse—manipulated the rules to suit themselves. This 'take-away group' functioned autonomously and misused power. They tampered with the records, manipulated date of births, got important assignments, and became all powerful. They drove the skilled ones out, pampered the unskilled and chased the chairs they never deserved. They did the institute a great disfavour by staying back. And this the cunning ones called a 'favour'. Many people were employed at SKIMS at gunpoint. Some people who were not suitable for Government service were inducted into SKIMS—to complete the loot. The institute became a more notable place . . . . Perhaps it saw more of death and devastation, or perhaps it contained young blood which would boil too often at the sight of too much blood spilled in its corridors. There was so much suffering that SKIMS witnessed. It's Emergency Department and its wards and operating rooms were overcrowded to accommodate patients of trauma, trauma, and just trauma . . . . How many young boys left their mothers wailing and pounding their chests, how many young boys and girls witnessed the death of their fathers here, how many sisters lost their only brothers here? Who wouldn't cry here? Who wouldn't lose his wit here? Who wouldn't feel suffocated here . . . ?

Conscious and energetic employees organised many rallies in the very campus of SKIMS . . . no one stopped them, but no one cared about what they did. Some people emerged to be the *pech-i-dars* (wish I could translate this Kashmiri word meaning 'something of a ringleader'), speaking against the injustice and the excesses and challenging the powerful Government from the stages erected in its campus. A few employees lost their lives, including the topmost Cardiovascular and Thoracic Surgeon Dr Abdul Ahad Guru. A senior faculty member at SKIMS, a head of the department, a conceiver of a medical college, a great human being, and a capable doctor was abducted and murdered— for a sin that each one of us had committed or are committing even now. Did not all of us come out in rebellion? Did not all of us ask for our due? Then for what fault was he murdered? We were upset, though we never knew who he was; he belonged to our fraternity, but for a fear that was there, all kept quiet.

I heard he had a family too. His son of our age was pursuing medicine in Karnataka. Who broke the news about his father's death to him? How must he have taken the news? What happened to Guru Sahib's widow? No one knew, and possibly no one was interested as time passed.

The death of this dynamic doctor terrified the entire doctor community. The top ones moved out one by one . . . . The *pech-i-dars* too fled, running away from the chaos and their own pledges . . . . They told the naive ones, whom they used to address in huge gatherings, that they would go out of the country to 'talk Kashmir' in bigger halls and more effective forums. Those selfish ones left SKIMS with a promise to return soon; meanwhile, they had to make some money!

With time, the institute became a thoroughfare. No one enforced discipline, nor was it desired by anyone. Rooms were used as sanctuaries by people who couldn't go elsewhere. The faculty rooms, the resident rooms, and the rooms holding sophisticated equipment were occupied. Who would complain, to whom?

The institute was looted by all who could. Machines, laboratory equipment, mirrors, taps, washbasins, and even latches and locks were not spared. The rooms were plundered, microscopes and endoscopes were stolen. Threat and fear conquered every nook of SKIMS. A desperate plea written by a conscious Kashmiri on the walls of one of the bathrooms at SKIMS read: '*Aol Gol! Tas Mari Bab Mol—yus yath bathroomas choor kari*' (Round round, let his guardian and father die who takes anything from this bathroom).

The graceful mounts and gardens, the beautiful flower beds and charming trees were all lost. The lawns housed tea stalls and sellers of cosmetic items, and on festival days, huge merry-go-rounds were put up. *Masala-wallas,* balloon-*wallas,* hawkers, and newspaper vendors ran their shows efficiently in its lawns. Trucks and load carriers used a part of its lawns as a parking space. Who cared about what was happening to the 'dream' healthcare institution?

SKIMS became a shelter home for the homeless; an upcoming bazaar for buyers and sellers, a dumping space for all that was useless, besides being a place where fierce wars were fought with death and her associates by those who valued human life, irrespective of caste, creed, or religion . . . . Great work was being done each second to save a life . . .

But tell me why the people didn't understand the sanctity of SKIMS? Why did the people of adjoining areas of Aanchar, Soura, and Bohlachipora take non-stop electric connections from SKIMS? Why did they enjoy hot showers in hostels meant for postgraduate and resident doctors? The height of things was when the local residents occupied the paying ward block and put their own locks on the doors of its rooms and mini-wards.

And tell me why were those corridors on laboratory side used by the likes of quilt—and pillow-makers? Agreed, no security was relevant, no administration was functional, but why didn't anyone stand in defence of SKIMS? Why did destruction prevail over preservation? Did it matter whose dream SKIMS was? Why didn't anyone think what 'dream' SKIMS was?

All was not well with our psyche. We should have cleaned instead of spitting, given our own things and our own resources to keep the work going, encouraged the staff instead of criticising them, and helped to maintain the system instead of derailing it. We were not selfish even. Selfish people think about themselves and work for their own benefit, but we cared not to care for ourselves even. Somehow, it never occurred to us that we or our near ones could gasp some day in the very institution which we were trying to destroy.

The loot prevailed everywhere. In those circumstances, there were people who thought just about themselves and their families. They purchased when people sold, they snatched what was public, they broke the rules, swallowed the roads, gobbled the graveyards, and made kingdoms for themselves. They utilised guns for what could not be done 'officially'. Encroachments in the form of slums and colonies came up everywhere. Srinagar began to expand disproportionately; it began to shiver and lost all its sheen. The countryside lost its farms, its paddy fields, its orchards, and forests to the people who were ready to construct their own dream houses when all else was burning . . .

The Suffering Villages and Towns

Srinagar was locked from all sides. We hardly went anywhere; for the male members, the restrictions were more as sometimes they got caught in painful crackdowns and identification parades away from their homes. 'Guest crackdowns' were more humiliating—both for the guest and the host.

I remember those two young girls who had come to shop in Srinagar for their marriage. Simple countryside girls were caught in a crossfire at Lal Chowk, and the easiest way out for them was to rush in an auto to a nearby relative's house. We were surprised to see them at our doorstep. Hesitant they were to come inside, but there was no way; they could not go home—home was in Baramulla, far away. There were some deaths because of firing on a mob, which prompted the authorities to impose a curfew in Srinagar. The girls could do nothing but be a part of the suffering with us. They ate what we ate, drank what we did, and they slept with me and my sister in our bedroom. As we told about our suffering to them, they told about theirs . . . . It was impossible now to tell who was a bigger victim. They talked about the occupied orchids and paddy fields; the empty farmhouses and meadows; the young men in fields who were shot for no reason; the people who disappeared, leaving behind 'half widows' and orphaned kids; the gutted schools; the plundered Government buildings; the half-burnt bridges; the roaring streams, which became torture beds; and the still lakes, which had become the dumping yards for unknown bodies killed elsewhere. No one was immune; we knew it, but the dimensions of tragedy in towns and villages surprised us . . . . While we comforted each other, a cousin of mine showed us photographs of a few young boys . . . the boys who had ventured into unknown lands out of emotion or excitement and were caught in a trap of death. The photographs showed calm innocent faces drenched in blood—some with neat holes in their heads and some with pouting brain matter. Who could bear those scenes? My cousin had taken those photos from a friend who was a journalist working for a local newspaper. He had heard that one of the slain boys belonged to Baramulla, as our guests were from Baramulla, he got the photographs to us to see if by chance our guests would recognise any of the boys. The girls saw the photographs one by one; we could notice strange expressions on their faces. As they saw the last photo, they gave a shrill cry . . . . We wanted to know what had happened. The last face they saw was of the boy who lived in their neighbourhood, the one with whom they had spent their childhood. They recalled their childhood and their days with the boy. They remembered him as a naughty, gullible, and cheerful boy, and yes, inquisitive and adventurous too. That is perhaps what took him to the lands where he should not have gone—the land where his head rested on the rocks and where he bled to death. They say fate takes you to the spot where you are destined to die, and thus the naughty boy of our guest's neighbourhood was taken by fate to die in the highlands along the Indo-Pak border. 'Why did he go there?' The girls asked each other. 'Who must have killed him and why? Was he killed for trespassing or in a gunfight? What must he have murmured when he was shot at? Did he plead for his life or did he get no chance to speak?' They began guessing .Our guests, it seemed, shed all the tears they had as they talked about the boy . . . who was their childhood companion.

The girls became restless and informed their parents on phone about the slain boy. The parents had a huge rush of people in their home who wanted to know more about 'their boy'. The body had not reached the home, and all wanted to know what was the status . . . but how could we tell? All we had was a photo . . . . The rest was a mystery. Next day, newspapers carried the photographs of the youngsters we had seen the other day, the caption was clear: 'Militants killed attempting to cross the border—a large cache of ammunition seized'. The story following was the same we had read umpteen times: 'Militants trying to sneak in . . . challenged by forces, started firing . . . were killed in cross-encounter. Large quantity of arms and ammunition recovered'. The story was the same; only the characters had a different name.

Today's boy was known to our guests, yesterday's boy was known to someone else, and whose boy was it who died the day before yesterday? Do his parents or dear ones know about him? And what about tomorrow and the coming days? Whose boy will die on those highlands next?

Those photos crippled the two girls, who had come to shop in Srinagar for their own weddings but they were lost in the mourning of someone else. The moment curfew was relaxed, they leapt back into a *shikara* to Lal Chowk from where they tried reaching their destination. God help them, was all we could say.

Weddings Continued

Kashmiris love to eat; their feasts, especially their wedding feasts, are famous all over. The meatballs they roll, the meat they fry to give it a unique brown look, and the long kebabs they mould decorate the large plates called *tramis,* which four people share. But the times of mourning did not qualify for *wazwan.* Uncertainty compelled people to observe austerity. Who would risk the lives of hundred-odd guests in case there was firing on the wedding day? Who would have his guests humiliated in case there was a crackdown? Who could eat *wazwan* when a neighbour was mourning? Who could relish the aroma of *wazwan* when the odour of human blood spilled here and there was too strong . . . ?

But even in the disorder, marriages happened, though they were not celebrated; children were born, and some youngsters romanced, though majority remained indoors within the confines they didn't like. *Barats* were restricted to one or two people who would accompany the groom .Many grooms have nothing great to remember about their weddings; the dress, the feast, or the journey to bride's house all was worth forgetting. But was it all worth forgiving?

This is no tale, but an incident depicting our helplessness and our care for one another. It happened in the heart of Srinagar, the Downtown. A groom draped in fear moved in a car with his companion of life, his beloved bride whom he managed to get from her parents' house after a simple ceremony in that curfew which was too 'tight'. His vehicle was allowed, however, and a curfew pass was managed for him, his bride, and the driver. Fears were troubling them on the first day of their life together as they moved across the slim lanes, showing off those pink slips of paper known as curfew passes to the security fellows stopping them at intervals. As they moved deeper into the Downtown, the bunkers they encountered became bigger, the lanes slimmer, and the population of those interceptors in khaki . . . stronger and stronger. As the vehicle pulled inside into the Downtown . . . the interceptors became more irritable and they were charged with hatred and suspicion. The bride, supposed to keep her gaze low and supposed to lower her veil over her face, had to repeatedly look into the eyes of the strangers she did not want to look at and to answer uncomfortable questions which she did not want to answer. There was that pain of losing her home, her parents, her backyard, and there was that fear of going to an unknown place. How her in-laws would behave with her and how her husband would treat her?

And then there was an uncertainty on the day of her wedding. Wasn't this all enough to make her tremble?

Before they could go further, harsher people they encountered had nothing to do with the curfew passes they were flashing. They were ordered to 'stop, do an about-turn, and go back'. How they would manage, they didn't know. Could they make it walking to their home if they sent the driver and vehicle back? They thought they should just try out that option. Just as the couple stepped down from the vehicle, the interceptors stopped them. They couldn't walk down to their home as an encounter/action was going on inside. As they were pleading for help, they heard a window creak, a compassionate head peeped out to see what was going on, and just then a woman opened the thick door of her home and called the couple inside. The couple had no option but to move inside. It seemed the woman knew all what had happened. No more speaking was desired. In those deeply interwoven clusters of houses God knows from where all those women came, arranged themselves in groups, and sang . . . the songs meant to be sung for the bride and groom. They braved the threat and broke the silence, and there was rejoicing, there was celebration. They gathered the best food to feed the couple . . . . And how was it at the groom's house, celebration or mourning? It was a crackdown there-no celebration! Perhaps the news had sneaked in that the couple had been received elsewhere and their wedding celebrated elsewhere.

The bride and groom spent the first three nights of their lives together away from their home, though in a home. After 3 days, the curfew was relaxed; the couple went to the groom's house and prepared themselves for another warm reception. Would they or won't they remember this episode for their entire lives? Would they narrate it to their children? Lucky fellows they were still; they had halted at a place where love was showered on them, and they still needed to be thankful to Allah that they were together in their first hiccup. And thank God, both survived!

How many more weddings have been and would be celebrated this way . . . God alone knows! We know about a young bride who was detained and raped on her way to her husband's home. Her aunt, accompanying her, too was raped. The incident was reported for a few days in the press but later on, all were silent, as the young bride started her new life with an injury that would never heal [1]

Years later, it happened in Tujjar, when Tahir, a 22-year-old boy was taken away by security forces at 4.45 a.m. He spent his first morning after marriage in the company of army men. He was neither a militant nor a sympathiser, but 3 days after he was taken, they brought back his dead body; 19-year-old Afroza became a bride and a widow in the same night. Afroza's marriage lasted for 10 hours.[2] She had, poor girl, a long life to lead . . .

Chapter-2

The Chaos

Abductions

Abductions became a sad routine of our lives. Prof. Mushir-ul-Haq, the vice chancellor of Kashmir University—his abduction and subsequent murder was a slur on our hospitality for which we were famous the world over. We cried when it happened. A humble soul, a non-political personality who had nothing to do with all that was happening or that had happened to us in the past, his case weakened our cause. My sister had been his student in Jamia Milia Islamia. Though I don't remember, my parents and others in our family remember when he dined in our home on a trip to Kashmir earlier. I can't forget the scene when his daughters were shown on television crying at the airport, 'O, Abu,' when his body was flown to Delhi and handed over to them. I felt sorry that Kashmir had struck so many lives—so far away! We did not want to be associated with all that had happened. We wanted to tell the world that we had taken due care of our guests, and in fact, a Kashmiri too had laid his life for Professor Mushir. God bless the souls and expose the culprits.

Intellectuals; people with high connections; the rich, famous, and notorious ones; businessmen, and Government officials too were abducted. Some were abducted to secure the release of people in jails, some for money, and some to serve petty interests of the abductors. Many doctors, too, were abducted, including some senior professors and consultants. Some doctors were abducted to get the desired patients treated, some to get a difficult work done, and some were abducted for money.

Torture

The governors chosen by the Centre to rule us were known for their skills of bulldozing and gagging people. They had all the qualities that would make them efficient managers of military operations. They gave the forces a free hand to deal with the situations the way they desired. They worked on a one-point agenda . . . of curbing the militancy by whatever means and silencing people. Inaccessible to people and indifferent towards their plight, they fanned the flames of hatred that had enveloped Kashmir. Under those tough regimens, torture centres were promoted as the 'centres of excellence'. These were the places where innocents were tested for their levels of tolerance. Name a torture technique, and our boys have tasted it. It was in these very centres that people confessed for the crimes that they had not committed.

Going back to the night when we had a crackdown in our home—I remember the boy who had shown forces the way to our house. I remember him as a frail, thin boy with a sharp nose, his face covered with a black handkerchief.-. What had brought that boy to our house? I had thought that day. Was the boy tortured so much that he pointed to our house, just at random, or did he point to us for any other reason? Don't know. Was he a boy from our neighbourhood who had played with us in our *dewan khanas*?

Many boys of our neighbourhood were routinely taken, and if fortunate, they were let off after a few tough sessions of grilling and grinding lasting a few days. Many boys never returned . . . some died and some disappeared. No one owned the responsibility of having taken them in the first instance. As men became soft targets, they could never spill their anger, never go out to protest. Women from our *mohalla* and neighbouring areas would go down to Nowhatta or Hawal holding placards and calling for an end to the atrocities-and asking for the release of their boys. I don't know if anyone noticed them .But as so many boys were every day taken away, it was a routine affair for the women of Nowhatta and adjoining areas to stage protests. People learnt to avoid Nowhatta and use the by-lanes instead!

Though not a doctor as yet, I got to see wounds of some of our boys. They showed me the ones on their shins and calves. I would sense their discomfort when they would sit and moan . . . . Their postures told me that their wounds were more private. Torture victims, they were kicked everywhere, and one who has been hit himself knows how it feels. Sher-i-Kashmir Institute saw a huge patient population of renal failure caused by excessive lysis of the muscle (rhabdomyolysis) occurring mostly in boys and men subjected to torture. The data was presented in national and international conferences, and some of the papers were published in leading international journals of nephrology. Following is the abstract of an article published by Malik GH and colleagues from SKIMS, describing the pattern of hurt caused to our people and the unique renal failure resulting from torture.[3]

Abstract

Thirty-four males aged 16-40 (mean 25) years in the period from August 1991 to February 1993 presented in acute renal failure (ARF), 3-14 (mean 5 days) after they had been apprehended and allegedly tortured in Police interrogation centres in Kashmir. All were beaten involving muscles of the body, in addition 13 were beaten on soles, 11 trampled over and 10 had received repeated electric shocks. Patients were studied in three groups: group I those with evidence of only myoglobinuria (n = 21); group II those with both myoglobinuria and haemoglobinuria (n = 10); group III those with evidence of only haemoglobinuria (n = 3). All had varying degrees of ecchymotic patches on the body and patients in groups II and III were beaten on soles ecchymosis of soles. Hypertension was present in 11 and pulmonary oedema in five. Mean haemoglobin, BUN and serum createnine were not significantly different in three groups. All cases had metabolic acidosis, 20 had hyperkalemia, plasma haemoglobin was 11-48 (mean 26 mg/dl) in group II and 26-56 (mean 35 mg/dl) in group III. Urine test for haemoglobin was positive in seven cases in group II and two cases in group III. Pigment casts were present in 10, 8 and 2 cases in groups I, II and respectively. Evidence: only those who were beaten on soles had evidence of haemoglobinuria.

In an earlier study by the same authors on ten cases of acute renal failure following physical torture authors observed oliguric renal failure in all cases except one case. Besides a history of physical torture two patients gave history of electric shocks and one patient was put to sit and stand exercise for three hours[4]. These papers on the cause of renal failure affecting Kashmiris did not evoke condemnation from any quarters or any world health forum.

The interrogation centres were spread all over Kashmir. The infamous ones like Papa II, where most of our boys were taken, would put Guantanamo Bay to shame. As our boys would tell us, conventional and unique techniques were used to make the boys confess for something they had never seen or done. Those who have been that side always would hear the voices and sobs of young boys saying, '*Mojai* . . .' (O! mother).

On the lighter side of it, the torture and hurt caused to a group of eunuchs staying together in Batmaloo by security forces made them sing, '*Azadiyai Azadiyai, aesey kehay koruy azadi*' (O Azadi, what have we done to you?).

Gun—the Other Side of It

'Gun' was a revolt against a broken promise, a rebellion against a mockery called democracy, and a reaction towards the rulers of a suppressed nation. We purged our feelings on streets—in unison.

But that sentiment of raising a voice against the oppressor and a cry for a dispute called Kashmir was lost too quickly. 'Gun' prevailed, and sentiment took a back seat. It brought us uneasiness, it disturbed our peace of mind, it terrorised us . . . it traumatised us. It was used on familiar heads, soothing souls, and beautiful minds. 'Gun' was no longer a deity but a curse. The curse called 'Gun' made us fight each other—for no reason. Initially, we knew only two or three parties, but they multiplied; we had them in hundreds, each issuing a separate roster, a separate calendar for people to follow. They fought and fought bitterly with each other, little remembering the sacrifices people had given. A handful of them could have done nothing; it was the people who came out—lakhs of them to Chrar-i-Sharief and to UN headquarters, asking for a settlement to Kashmir issue. I remember that 'victory sign' that the old and the young would show as they marched towards Chrar-i-Sharief or UN headquarters during those massive demonstrations. Those old women too did not resist as they shouted for *azadi*.

But now another memory of another sad day . . .

I remember the day when they collected near our home—with those clicking Kalashnikovs. They had a prey at hand—a smart young boy who was being interviewed and interrogated by each one with a Kalashnikov. He was pleading for his life. My mother cried when she heard the pleas of the boy. After a while, they knocked at our door and asked for tea—for all of them. We faithfully prepared a samovar of tea and gave it to them—my mother took it as an opportunity to speak on behalf of the guy they held. They sipped the tea happily, but refused to let the boy go. They called him a traitor, a person belonging to the rival group. But the boy was pleading repeatedly, 'I am an M.Sc. I am a gold medallist. My mother has raised me with difficulty. Let me go please!' The boy was crying, and my mother was repeatedly pleading for his life. Fearing the drama might reach an unwanted climax . . . they all left the scene along with the boy.

Next day, an unidentified body lay in Malkhah; it was the same boy who was held near our home. He had been shot early morning. Some early risers had seen how the boy was asked to run for his life . . . further and further till a bullet pulled him down on to the ground. The Bollywood-style drama . . .

The 'Gun' had let us down. My mother didn't eat for days. We couldn't raise a voice; we knew we couldn't. It was not worth recalling even. For what had the boy been killed?

Those boys who held the gun for a cause were dying, getting caught, or decaying in prisons. There were other people called *soyaths* (wicks), so-called 'yes men' who were happy to occupy the seats of their bosses. They spread terror. They were mad after money. Businessmen, Government officials, small-time traders—all were made to pay, weekly, monthly, or quarterly. You had to pay them to get your work done. You had to pay them to stay alive. You had to pay them to avoid abduction. Smaller in rank than *soyaths* were the so-called *tuchs* (kitchen cloth, a rag), who were louder, smaller, and pettier. People were disheartened to see them. This was not what should have happened to a mass movement. This was not why people had come out on streets. This was not why people had shed their blood. And this was not why . . . people confronted a huge nation. There were women too who did all what was alien to us. Burka-clad and wearing *Action* shoes, they would threaten women to use the veil, and at times, they threw paint on the ones who defied . . . . But we knew for sure that they were the hijackers of a movement; they were not the ones who would represent us, ever. But then who would represent us? Gunmen had been silenced, and intellectuals—the scary lot—were getting killed. Then who would tell the world about us?

Some known faces of the past who used to sit in assemblies, known to argue there, sat together and formed a conglomerate known as All parties Hurriyat Conference (APHC) with young Mirwaiz to control the movement and to give it a proper direction . . . It was, however, difficult to imagine how people with different mindsets would work together.

Change of Guard

How long would a democratic country keep a state under Governor's rule? So there was a need to change the drivers. In that desire for change, politicians who had left for London and away were recalled to cook another curry in Kashmir. All along, they rested elsewhere while we all were dying. Never a word of comfort for us, never a consolation! They came here to fight elections. Elections meant just filing the nomination papers. No extra effort was needed for them to be the members of honourable assemblies.

I have not seen a gloomier day in Srinagar than the day of elections, the first one after the turmoil began. Not a single person came out to vote in our *mohalla*. As the polling was drawing to a close, men and women from a nearby slum were picked up to vote. I remember how those women too were shouting, '*Azadi! Azadi!*' as they were being led by the forces to the voting centre.

There were ultimately the declared winners. They took the oath. It was a day when our politicians were told, 'Sky is the limit.' It seemed there was another hidden line written . . . 'But know your limits.' It was an opportunity for our politicians to ask for the resolution of the Kashmir issue, ask for a breather for the people, ask for some ease, ask people for forgiveness. But they did nothing, just enacted a drama . . . shed tears at the reunion with a chair that they feared had been lost. People did not forget the day and will not forgive and forget the politicians who took another oath of loyalty that day!

At that stage, I wondered, what was it that India was doing in Kashmir? Why was it practising time-pass politics? What was this selection and election business? Redoing all the misdoings? Re-winding the wrongs, reshuffling the rejected ones? . . . . The Indian Government was aware of the hatred Kashmiris had for its policies and politics. Why didn't they address the hatred part of it—ever? The politicians promoted by the Indian Government and crowned as authorities over us compounded the hatred Kashmiris harboured. Why did India avoid talking to Kashmiris . . . ? It should have concerned them as a nation that Republic Day and Independence Day had to be forcibly celebrated in Kashmir—to keep the flag fluttering. Militancy did not provoke, nor ignite the anti-India sentiment but exposed it and revealed its depth and dimensions.

While hospitals and essential services worked, rest of the employees were not wanted. They sat in their homes and were handed over the salaries at the end of the month. This did not go well for the health of the departments. Working people were made idle, corporations started collapsing, and various departments became defunct. The opportunists utilised the concessions and took up foreign assignments while keeping the jobs back home intact—double benefits!

The Barbaric Species

Those barbaric species ruled the city and rocked the countryside— terrorising and killing. No killings were reported; no demons were ever stopped. They were called *Ikhwanis*—the brothers; various other names were used for them—*Sarkar Nawaz Bandook Bardar, Nabied,* or renegades. The press referred to them as 'unidentified gunmen'. They were above law—serving the cause of a great civilisation, conditionally. When the services they offered came with heavy conditions, they were silenced. And another crop-in-waiting was recruited. They and their patrons gave us convulsing memories. They caught and killed—why and for what, no one could ask them.

For a small benefit, they changed their loyalties; for a petty sum, they changed the direction of their guns. They hunted for 'others' with the gun and killed them mercilessly. We helplessly watched as they took away our boys in night raids and killed them publicly. They were ruthless, heartless, and harsh. How cleverly had they been planted with the boys who took to the gun for freedom? They woke when all slept, looted homes, snatched away breadwinners, and killed them by deceit. They spoke Kashmiri—the nude form of it—the brutal form, and were well built and stout. The areas where they predominated, they brought about devastation. Why they hated human beings so much, I still cannot understand. What was it burning within their hearts that kept them away from every emotion, every sentiment? They hated humility, disliked mercy, and liked an open display of their arrogance and power. They were powerful before us—but how powerful were they before their own chiefs, God only knows. They were not alien, but we would wonder how come so many of us were like that?

A few boys of our *mohalla* were taken by them in the deadliest nights . . . . The boys cried for help, and I remember that no one dared to say a word. It gives me goose pimples when I think about those boys who were pulled out from their beds, and next morning were thrown with their eyes gouged out and limbs mutilated into the unfilled pits at Malkhah. It was never easy to forget those incidents because these incidents rendered us mute, we never spoke a word against crimes which occurred in our neighbourhood.

They took that red-faced smart boy nicknamed 'Shining', who lived in our neighbourhood. 'Shining' had just gone to his bed when he was dragged out. His parents shouted for help. We heard their cries, their calls for help—but such was the fear that none of us came out. We spent the night in pain but were getting buried underneath the guilt of not helping our neighbour.

Early morning next day, 'Shining' had left to be in the company of other boys who died. He was brutally murdered. And his body, too, lay in Malkhah. 'Shining's' face was pale and indrawn, and there was fresh blood on his nose and mouth. The same scene followed—crying, wailing, and shouting. But I could not even cry for him. With what right could I do that? I did not open my mouth . . . when he was shouting for help, '*Mey bachevtavu* . . .' (save me). It was the last I heard from him. 'Shining' too was buried in our graveyard in the lawns of Makhdoom Sahib.

His parents perhaps were aware of the helplessness of the entire *mohalla*. They never complained, never held a grudge against anyone, but shed their tears . . . silently. When they would pass by, I would bow down my head in humiliation and regret. They would stop and answer my hardly audible '*Asalam-o-Alikum*' . . . (peace be with you) with a warm '*Wa-Alikum Salam*' (peace be with you too).

Those men murdered a junior of ours in medical college—chased him and killed him. Our batchmates told us that the boy tried to flee but was captured and killed. Elsewhere, students would have staged violent demonstrations . . . but here in Kashmir no one asked the authorities about who killed the student and why? And we too mourned his death silently. What else could we do? Anyone who raised a voice would meet the same fate. It was a sad day for the boy's parents; they had brought him up—exceptionally, he was admitted to the medical college, was ready to be a doctor, and then died an unknown death. Some say he had friendship with people who were 'trained', and some say he was himself trained . . . . Whatever the truth, a doctor in the making was silenced.

Their grip was always deadly firm. Not many boys could escape. I can recall the story of the escape of my neighbour's son—an 18-year-old lad, who jumped on to the rooftop of his house in an attempt to save his life. I remember how he cried and shouted . . . . We did not save him nor did we attempt to save him, but he held on to the rooftop—till the 'would-be killers' got tired and gave up. It was a dawn of a new life for that boy. He escaped, and we never saw him again. His mother, a widow, lived alone and faced a new crop of gunmen every night who would enquire about his absconding son!

With a Government in place, things became more difficult, more complicated. A 'Task Force' and a 'Special Operation Group' came into being, and *Ikhwanis* received patronisation. They killed thousands. They painted the saffron fields red as there were too many of them on that side. They killed too many in Pampore, including a relative of mine. That boy was a darling named Raja, the only son of his noble parents, the only brother of his three sisters. He was dragged out of his home one night and killed. His father didn't know how to cry, and his mother didn't know what to mourn. And the fault of the boy . . . no one knows.

Some of the dreaded *Ikhwanis* occupied honourable seats in the honourable assembly. Some were chosen for National Awards and some for special deals.

Respectable citizens were abducted and never let off. We lost a human rights activist, Mr Jaleel Andrabi, to abduction and later on, found his mutilated body on the banks of Jhelum. Dr Abdul Ahad Wani, a professor in Kashmir University, was abducted and murdered. His son was our junior in MBBS and his other siblings were younger to him. We saw how that headless family was looked after by that young medico. The noted human rights activist Mr H.N. Wanchoo was also silenced. He was a respected Pandit who documented human rights abuses in Kashmir.

Those abductions and mysterious killings . . . were like slow poison to us; young boys, old men, intellectuals, human rights activists, lawyers, and doctors were taken at gunpoint. Some were killed and some were lost, leaving behind sad and waiting womenfolk . . . hopeful mothers, unwed sisters, shy brides, or lovely little daughters. Even foreigners were caught in our misery.

Those five gentlemen who wanted excitement and adventure in our meadows and our slopes were abducted. We felt pain for them as we felt for our own people, especially after one of them was left headless in one of the meadows he loved to dance in. Their mysterious disappearance left us guessing. Who was it who wanted to lower our image in the eyes of the West? Not that they ever cared for us; the abduction and killing of foreigners was against our cause! Don Hutchings, Keith Mangan, Dirk Hasert, and Paul Wells were never traced, and Hans Christian Ostro was beheaded. The poor fellows too were sucked into our turmoil.

More Challenges for the College

No fresh appointments were made in the college; there were just temporary adjustments. The college functioned with difficulty. The staff was inadequate, but those who were available took up the additional burden. Basic sciences like physiology, pharmacology, pathology, and biochemistry suffered the most. The faculty shrunk. Adhocism became operational as an emergency measure, but no long-term solutions were sought. We, the students, did not bother about what happened to the faculty strength. All we were bothered about was our own studies which, thanks to those awesome and bold people, went on regularly, non-stop. I remember those teachers in para-clinical and basic sciences who took our theory classes while they were just graduates. They taught with the confidence of professors and knowledge of exam-going postgraduates. Was it their love for us and their concern for us which stimulated them to do so much, or was it their love for their respective subjects which made them the torch-bearers? These adhocees never received a medal or an honour, not even a word of acknowledgement from the Government which was focused on curbing militancy, only militancy. The Government at the Centre too cared little about anything else. They pumped in money and pushed herds of men and women to silence a nation. They heard nothing about their woes and overlooked their bruises, but yes, militancy had to be curbed!

As the college and hospital came down from 'exceptional' to 'ordinary', it was now a turn for us to witness just the 'basic' and 'mandatory'. Each new retirement was seen as an 'old' pillar falling with nothing concrete to rely on . . .

As the postgraduate guides were depleted, the postgraduate programme operational in most of the departments suffered badly. When a cry was raised about the depleted faculty, a few new recruitments came up. Newcomers were inducted from across the tunnel. They joined the departments and went back to the places where they came from—for security reasons. The posts, the guides, and postgraduates were transferred in a hassle-free manner to the other side. What was meant to serve the interests of Government Medical College of Srinagar turned out to be a blessing for the other Government Medical College—overfilling it? The promotions also went the fresh recruitment way. All those who were promoted to higher posts ran back to Jammu with promotions and posts. Government Medical College, Srinagar, remained miserable and relied on the adhocees who delivered . . . amidst odds . . . without an incentive. Was it also a policy decision to rob Government Medical College of Srinagar and to extend special treatment to the other Government College?

No sincere effort was made to address the issues related to Government Medical College Srinagar. But yes, there was a principal with a vision who kept the hospital going and the college functioning. Dr.Girja was known as a good clinician, an able surgeon and a tough Head of the Department. At a time when she could have left Kashmir and looked for better options outside, she kept the candle of hope burning. We owe it to Prof. Girja Dhar that the college survived the worst tumult of the century. With her commitment, vision, and will, the bold woman did the job that would have made 100 men jitter!

But then her exit was not trouble-free. She survived a shower of bullets on her last working day at Government Medical College Srinagar. We were all humbled by the incident. A destructive psyche and disturbed mind must have been behind the incident. The principal of the Government Medical College Srinagar, was a high-profile public servant, but surprisingly, no one looked into why she was attacked. Why was the administration too not bothered? After Dr.Girja, Dr Allaqaband took over as the principal of the college. He did not have security guards to guard him—he was accessible to all people, with and without guns—which strongly interfered with his work pattern. A man whose very presence in the corridors of college would send everyone somersaulting, he too was abducted, humiliated, and not allowed to work without interference. At one point, he was troubled so much that he left his chair for 3 months.

Those Strong-willed Women—in Medicine

A Kashmiri woman knows her business, whether it is driving a *shikara*, manning a bakery shop, selling fish, spinning pashmina, or purifying her soul in the outdoors of a *khankah*; she fearlessly performs her task to perfection. She has been doing it for ages. When elsewhere in India, women were burnt in the name of *Sati,* Kashmiri women were doing poetry and practising mystics. So much was the influence of women on poetry that even men would use the lyrics of *waseiy* (O friend, used in context of females) in their songs. Medicine, though a challenge, was never impossible for Kashmiri women. They sought admission in medical colleges, excelled there, and came out as successful gynecologists, pathologists, ophthalmologists, and pediatricians.

Departments, where hectic and heavy work was done, too had many women doctors. There were women doctors in medicine and surgery too. One beautiful doctor, known for her surgical skills, was Prof. Mehmooda Khan. A delicate woman, a meticulous surgeon, an efficient clinician, and a strict disciplinarian—this foreign-returned surgeon headed the Department of Surgery for a long time—a woman leading a caravan of men . . . . Looking at her commitment to the subject, young doctors (males and females) would idolise her.

Women's Hospital and Other Hospitals

Passing second MBBS was a tough job, really. But most made it, thankfully. And passing it meant going to many more clinics, touching patients too often, and dangling a stethoscope regularly down your neck. We had to know ENT (Ear, Nose and Throat), ophthalmology, Preventive and social medicine, and pediatrics. We concentrated on eyes which were red, noses which bled, and kids who fled while we tried examining them. Preventive and social medicine spoke about calories and food values—something hard to remember and boring to recall again and again. The arrangements for clinics were flawless; buses took us to all the corners where different hospitals were located. We were received warmly everywhere and taught with care and affection. The teachers criticized less and taught more. Perhaps this was what set aside first MBBS teachers from other teachers who taught us in clinics. We loved the teachers and the clinics too.

We had a posting in pre-final, which our seniors called 'fun'. It was a posting in the only maternity hospital of the state named Lala Ded Hospital or LD Hospital. During that posting, we were off our classes and we had to stay in specially allotted rooms at LD Hospital for a month to learn the basics of obstetrics. It was like a hands-on workshop. We loved to do practically all that the doctors at LD did: monitoring patients, conducting deliveries, resuscitating babies, and yes, the best part—learning and doing episiotomies ourselves. Those curved needles, that vicryl and silk, those needle holders, and those blunt scissors—I remember how I trembled and shook when for the first time I gave a cut to a patient who was crying aloud with pain. The patients did not know we were 'learners' learning on 'dummies' who were alive and conscious. Sometimes we did well, sometimes we did not. But the poor patients saw 'saviours' in us, and we liked the applause we got from the patients' family after our job was done. We fought with each other for primigravidae for those were the patients we could test our surgical skills on. The house surgeons and postgraduates readily gave their cases to us; it was possibly a relief for them as there was a huge rush of patients who needed to be attended and what better way could they think of than to hand over a good number of them to us.

We ate our food at the canteen, and sometimes our parents sent for us a good food preparation. In our batch, there were twelve of us—four girls and rest were boys. The four of us stayed together, worked together, and talked a lot—about ourselves, our families, and our ambitions; we preferred not to talk about the surroundings. During those 'hectic' nights, sometimes we sang together and laughed together . . . . It seemed that after years of sulking and tension, it was a moment of fun for us and perhaps a moment of our release from all that which occupied us. LD Hospital buzzed with activity, and we wilfully ran from one end of it to another. And if the entire city was going topsy-turvy, LD Hospital was still working—uninterrupted.

Turmoil or no turmoil, children were born, and there was LD Hospital to care for the rest. As peripheries were collapsing, the rush to the LD Hospital was increasing. There were too many patients and too few doctors. The facilities were minimum, but the work done was voluminous. The work done by doctors at LD should find its place in the *Guinness World Records*. Having children in the trouble-torn vale was not easy. I remember how difficult it was for women to 'carry that burden' and to 'give birth'. With 'fight', 'fright', and 'flight' so common, miscarriages became a routine. Pregnancy, they say, is itself a 'stress'. Add to this the stress of all that we were experiencing, and the results are not good. The antenatal care of the would-be-mothers was subject to the conditions in the valley. If there was calm, women would come for the check-ups; if not, they would stay back home. We would see women with severe anemia in advanced pregnancy, who would need transfusions at the time of delivery. These women could have been better with proper antenatal care. I remember a case of firing in *Malkhah* area when a couple from Alamgari Bazar, who had boarded an auto to see a gynecologist, were fired at. The couple died on the spot. The woman was pregnant, and the man was an employee of J&K Bank SKIMS, Soura Branch. Here was a couple who went to care for their unborn child and came back as corpses. Was that incident ever probed?

We liked our work, but we hated to be mere spectators to all that was happening in LD. Posted in the LD labour room were a good number of female and male *dais*. Their job was to assist and support the patient and doctors at the time of delivery. They would take the baby, clean him/her, and hand over the baby to the attendants. Who had entrusted them with the job of handing over the baby? We did not know. But this is where they played their foul games. They handed over the baby in exchange for a good amount of money. The birth of a child, whether a boy or a girl, called for celebration, and those who conducted the delivery needed some money, which attendants had to provide. It was a gang working together. One *dai* would assist the other in extracting the money. They would refuse to hand over the baby to his/her parents unless the money which was demanded by them was supplied. They didn't care if the baby born was dead or alive, with or without an anomaly, or of wealthy parents or paupers. They did their business efficiently but collectively. As evening would set in, they would count their day's catch, and all you could hear was a flutter of notes. We hated those faces, but we knew their power. No one dared to challenge them . . . . We kept wondering, what was it they possessed which scared the administration? It hurt us deeply that they were on their own . . . fleecing the public, extracting from those who were already depleted . . . . Sometimes, we heard them tell the attendants that they needed money to share with the doctors. Were they demonising doctors also for their petty bargains? We, the idealistic new entrants to LD, were warned by our seniors not to say a word to 'these' elements; otherwise, we would be in trouble . . . . Though these *dais* were notorious, some nurses, laboratory attendants, gatekeepers, and a few people from the staff who worked in the theatre also refused to do what they were supposed to, unless their pockets were warmed by bribe.

No single human was spared, not even a doctor who would deliver there . . . . With shameless faces, they would ask, 'Doctor *sahab,* we expect more from you. We want to celebrate your child's birth.' the poor doctors would have no option but to give . . . to the greedy ones they hated.

This apparent bribe aside, there were so many scandals going on within the hospital: the scandal of baby exchange, wherein male babies were exchanged for female babies against a good sum; exchange of babies with anomalies for normal babies; or baby thefts . . . . Why was this all going on within the hospital? Why were those miscreants left on their own? Where was the administration? Was law and order the only thing important in a troubled state?

It was a surprise as to how the hospital was running when so much was in disarray. The post-operative ward was an insult to the entire institution of health; there were no facilities for monitoring and no concept of cleanliness in it. It looked like a busy fish market where everybody was running after a 'sister' to do the needful—set right the intravenous line, infuse a fresh bottle of Dextrose, give a parenteral antibiotic, or check whether the patient was alive or dead!

They say that before the turmoil, LD was neat and tidy, everything was well organised and well planned, the patient management was exemplary, and academics was an order. But what the turmoil did to this hospital was too apparent. The hospital situated on the banks of river Jhelum had two main gates. The two gates of the hospital opened on to the two streets—Gonikhan and Jawahar Nagar. The selfish 'we' converted the hospital into a thoroughfare. All those who needed a short cut from one street to another used the hospital corridors. Sometimes, bicycles would be seen racing along the corridors, carrying on them tiffins, and those people who sold those petty cosmetic items in the busy lane of Gonikhan would carry all that they had to sell through the hospital corridors. And the poor patients and their attendants would be lost in that rush!

The corridors were also decorated with stoves; the areas which were not used as a thoroughfare were used by attendants who would sit together on rugs and blankets and share the food, happiness, or grief. A formality-eaten Kashmiri would get livestock too inside the hospital— sheep or goats too would hop inside the hospital corridors—for celebration. The birth of a son or a daughter required their presence too. Beggars abounded inside as they paid the hospital staff a few bucks to make money from the attendants who were in panic. The administration was responsible, we know, but how about the people? Why did they not ever care for the hospital?

We never saw an official on rounds in the hospital, never heard about this all in the news. All what was happening at LD was too small and too insignificant to make an impact on the administration. Curbing militancy, chasing suspects, and spreading the threat was all that was important.

The nights at LD terrorised us. The roaming dogs, the loitering beggars, the suspicious masked men, the opportunistic policemen—all would be looking for their own safety, their own targets. We, the naive ones, passed by everything we saw, as if noticing nothing. We tried to be focused towards our jobs . . . without looking here or there!

With so much of rush, so much of chaos, the status of sanitation was understandable. Patients threw food everywhere, which blocked all the pipes, the drains, and the bathrooms. The taps which leaked once were never set right, and they kept on leaking and leaking . . . weakening the foundations that had withstood the turmoil.

The noise and screams generated within the hospital masked the noise of grenades, bombs, and firing in the nearby areas of Tagore Hall and Lal Chowk. Unless there was a sudden gush of people through the gates of LD, which caused sudden splashes of panic within the hospital, we did not know what was happening outside.

The maternity posting let us taste the real working of a hospital during the days of pressure and pain. We felt proud to be a part of the group that was working when all else was at a standstill. We felt happy for those patients who benefited from our presence and sorry for all those who did not make it to the hospital in time . . . . There was so much we wanted to do and so little we were doing, but, little or more, we were doing our bit. We heard the bitter tales of crackdowns within the hospital—the tales when doctors and hospital staff was manhandled, the tales when doctors were stuck up for days together in the hospital because of the disturbances outside, and tales about doctors who were beaten in ambulances. There were brave ambulance drivers too, who were beaten when they fetched doctors or moved patients from one hospital to another. One ambulance driver who had gone to collect a gynecologist from home was shot in the wrist and abdomen and was hospitalised in a critical condition for a long time. He never received a certificate of merit or a medal from any source.

Lal Ded Hospital was a great place to get trained in . . . but not so great a place to be treated in . . . . The pain of waiting, the distress of overload, and the discomfort of unhygienic surroundings would haunt you . . . . Once in, those opportunistic pests, who took bribes for every word they spoke or every movement they made, made the place all the more distasteful.

Adjacent to the maternity hospital was an old wooden structure which sheltered sick neonates and children. The hospital was called the Children's Hospital. We were told that it used to be a *sabzi mandi* which was later converted into a hospital. Those hospital doors and windows were never mended, never painted. It was here that our 'future' was gazing at our helplessness. The rush was tremendous; dehydrated children, children with bronco-spasm, children with fever and jaundice occupied all the space that was available. There were open doors, narrow corridors, and uneasy stairs . . . . People were in plenty everywhere, colliding with each other and cursing each other and the place. The wooden ceiling had huge gaps and sheltered a unique population of rats—big, brown, and dangerous. They surfaced on to the floor in intervals and took away everything available. They nibbled with ease at the tiny faces of those who came there to get cured. They ate an infant's nose once; it became a news item, but no one disturbed their havens. They roamed about in critical care units, and were a party to all the procedures going on there, and no one bothered to get rid of them. I am sure no traps would have trapped them; special ones would have to be made. And in a land of turmoil, who would bother about those rodents when there was so much to be bothered about?

Pre-final, though mostly clinical, was not easy. We rolled from one hospital to another, watching sickness and its varied forms.

We went to a hospital where bones and joints were treated, and my God, what a horror we witnessed—broken backs, severed limbs, and horrifying wounds; those victims of a conflict, those bystanders, and those helpless attendants who were there for months attending to the patients who never seemed to get well. The victims were not the ones we did not know; they were our own ones, our neighbours, and our friends. A friend of mine was a panicky attendant one day when a bullet pierced the leg of her smart younger brother. Nothing could save her brother's leg. That young boy was maimed for the entire life, and his future was distorted and deformed. And the pain the family bore only they can describe. It didn't matter whose bullet pierced him.

Orthopedics was interesting—a satisfying branch where everything was too apparent and a cure was a possibility for almost every case. The teachers were exemplary and taught with heart. I remember that great man who taught us the Green stick fracture, the tennis elbow, the frozen shoulder, and all that we ought to have known about orthopedics as MBBS students. How he caught our attention and how he mesmerised us with his powerful oratory skills in the very first lecture he delivered! I cannot believe that he, a bespectacled and frail gentleman, an expert orthopedician who liked to play the harmonium, liked to touch the chords of musical instruments would be silenced so soon . . . . No, we did not get to hear him again. He fell to a bullet or to a shower of them on the evening of 18 February 1993. He was driving his car at 5.30 p.m. and returning to his home in the campus of Barzulla Hospital with his family. It was apparently cool; there was no curfew that day. His wife heard three shots coming from a nearby bunker on Barzulla Bridge; one bullet hit him, and he collapsed that very moment. His wife held him in her lap and asked her daughter to drive. With what heart must the daughter have driven her gasping father to the hospital where he worked? And how difficult it must have been for a woman to carry her companion to the same theatre where he operated upon patients and saved many lives! The courageous woman intubated him to pull him out of the slumber someone brutal had pushed him into. That elegant body was drowned in a pool of blood and could not be revived in the theatre where he, a skilled surgeon, had managed thousands of such victims and, in fact, headed the management team. As Dr Farida pointed out, the troops on duty that day recognised Dr Ashai's car. The car was moving slowly with inner lights of the car on so that those seated inside the car could be easily identified and questioned if required. There was no crossfire, so why was the car fired upon? I talked to his wife about the incident, and that was how she narrated it.

An orthopedic surgeon, a leader, an academician was killed so easily; the bullet did not know what it pierced. While a hospital lost a leader, the faculty at GMC lost a dear friend, we students lost a teacher, and a family lost a head. While we could endure the loss, we watched (another teacher of ours) his wife, Dr Farida Ashai, struggle through the odds of life—alone, looking after her kids and herself under that constant hail of fear . . . . We miss you, sir, we miss you Dr Farooq Ashai. Who would know your dream for us and your dream for the college you belonged to? Alas! A great life was cut short. Generations of doctors graduating from GMC Srinagar had known him and loved him. A multifaceted personality, a talented human being was killed, and no one ever probed how a doctor who was looking after such a big hospital in such critical times—leaving his home and staying within the campus—was killed in cold blood? Why were the doctors of the world silent? Dr Ashai, it was alleged, talked to press and foreign correspondents about the victims who would be admitted at Barzulla Hospital[1]. Was it a targeted killing then? So much time has passed, and Dr Ashai and his family have yet to get justice. There has never been an apologetic note from the authorities, never a word on who killed him and why.

There was another hospital in Srinagar up above on a mount which was a leftover of Britishers who had constructed a sanatorium there for patients of tuberculosis. The concept was beautiful, but with the advancement in medicine, tuberculosis no longer needed sanatoria and the hospital was converted into a chest disease hospital. The hospital had a few old-fashioned beautiful buildings overlooking now what was left of Dal Lake, seated firmly in the lap of Shankar Acharya Hill. The hospital was visited by sick, spitting patients, who had to negotiate a tough slope to ascend up. The wards were warm but housed many chronic patients who were abandoned by their families because of the stigma associated with the disease they had. How could patients of chronic obstructive pulmonary disease, asthmatics, patients of pneumoconiosis or patients of pulmonary tuberculosis move up such a slope for treatment? Wouldn't they feel breathless? Why this hospital was converted into a chest disease hospital is still an enigma to me.

We students were welcomed by the staff and patients of this hospital—such a gesture was there perhaps because the hospital was too isolated and hardly had any communication with the medical college. The bazaar in the vicinity was congested and on the top were those human beings in those dull uniforms, sitting and guarding the hill in many tightly packed bunkers, which had circles of wires encasing them. Some would be seated inside, and others guarding each inch of the hill with their huge guns. We all preferred not to look up. The skies too had been blocked for us!

Did those soldiers ever enjoy the beauty of Dal? Or did they just stare at the landscape, focusing on their prey and ignoring all else? The road from Dalgate onwards towards Gupkar was guarded heavily. It was here that our elite lived. We never saw them but would hear the siren of their vehicles the moment they raced past this road.

We continued with our studies through the pre-final into final, the killings continued, the grenades continued, and the blasts never really stopped. And we the 'doctors in the making' did not stop . . . for anything or anyone. There was an uneasiness amongst fellow students and an urgency too, urgency to complete the course. But there were those fellows who wanted the exams to be postponed. Because of the happenings earlier, no one wanted to risk his life and the 'postponement group' always had the last word. They stretched the pre-final from 1 to 1½ years. The postponement group included the weak ones, the meek ones, the fearful ones who could display guns, and those happy-go-lucky ones who left their studies for the last week.

Those Painful Sieges

Those painful sieges stretched for months together. Dargah Hazratbal, the place housing the holy relic of Prophet Muhammad (SAW), came under siege when armed men held the place and the people hostage. What a pain it was for entire Kashmir. Hazratbal shrine had become a victim of designs in the past as well. Kashmir was swept by emotion and agitation when 'Moi Muqadas' was stolen. Our parents had witnessed that chaos in their days. Why and how it was stolen and retrieved no one ever found out; but then for decades politicians used Hazratbal shrine for their own speeches and their own interests.

We were scared—scared for the people holed up inside, scared for the bloodshed which could occur or for an unpleasant happening that would hurt the sentiments of people. But a suffering calm prevailed amidst long hours of curfew and sporadic protests. Despite a keen eye on the happenings at Hazratbal, we don't know how the siege was lifted, how people were let off, and how, eventually, the culprits were silenced. All happenings were bizarre, beyond the understanding of a common man. Who would dare to be uncommon and predict what actually happened there?

The happenings in Chrar-i-Sharief, the shrine of Sheikh Noor-ud-Din Noorani (RA) left the entire town devastated—the shrine included. The woodwork and the artwork were charred. We were told that an outsider was holding the entire shrine hostage, but when and how he escaped and how the shrine was gutted was not understandable. The population around the shrines suffered for no fault of theirs—those sieges left the populations starving for days together, and once, a mysterious and unkind fire consumed Chrar-i-Sharief and the structures adjoining it, the neighbouring houses too were gutted. It was difficult to assume how a siege by militants could occur when the entire Kashmir was under siege itself. The security of shrines should have come about at the start of the turmoil. The sieges and fires were prevalent, but no one cared to apply proper preventive measures which would ensure the safety of the shrines.

It was again a sentimental issue for Kashmiris. No asset of theirs was safe. Even the places of their worship were being snatched away from them. Those lonely women shared their pain with their Lord in those peaceful places called *astaans* and were losing them . . . . their places of solace.

During those sieges when we were jailed inside and caned outside, we were isolated from the rest of the world. Even our college was closed; the exams were postponed, and we lost many vital months. MBBS was getting stretched, we thought, indefinitely.

My dear little nephew while playing with his friends surprised me with his heroic narration to them. He told them how upset he was with the siege at Hazratbal and how he, on his bicycle, went inside the shrine under siege and delivered *biriani* to the people holed up inside, how he was welcomed inside, and how the people praised his bravery and courage. We laughed amidst desperation at his imagination and his will to do something to change our state of affairs. Obviously, these were the situations which called for an intervention from a 'superman', and my nephew had become a 'superman' that day.

The Final Call

In spite of postponements, final year sounded like a final call. We laboured hard in clinics and sweated in operation theatres. The rounds with the head of the unit were interesting and demanding. Those huge books of medicine, surgery, and gynaecology got memorised automatically. Registrars and postgraduates taught the theory, and 'clinical skills' were transferred to us from those experienced men and women who often noticed the unnoticed, saw the unseen, and elicited what seemed to us—impossible to elicit. They included the professors, the heads of the departments, the senior consultants, and those underdogs who had no ranking in the departments but were 'moving books and manuals'. We salute those unsung heroes who would join the rounds out of academic interest but were posted as 'Assistant surgeons' in our hospitals as there were no apparent slots where they could be fitted. Those great teachers taught us even when they were never paid to teach us. Dr Tajamul of medicine was one such genius.

As the final MBBS examination drew close, the tension mounted. We started preparing for the 'send-ups', the exhaustive examination which was tedious and tough; it nearly killed us. But most survived it and appeared in the final theory examinations with comfort and confidence. Final year university examinations were easier and more manageable. While this all was going on, we noticed many boys and girls carrying different books and studying them secretly, hiding the books from fellow students and teachers. Our friends were preparing for other exams—the ECFMG and PLAB, the exams required to gain entry into United States and the United Kingdom. There were those boys whose parents wanted them to leave, and there were those who thought they had enough of the torture named 'Kashmir'. Passports were hard to get—but all those who could, managed them and prepared for a better and a more peaceful life in another country, or was it another world?

Too many wanted to go out of the 100-odd in our batch. Were they doing it out of their will to excel or out of a will to survive elsewhere? How about all those who did not prepare to go? Was it because they could not afford to go elsewhere? Or was it because they liked to be glued to their homes, not wanting to leave, not wanting to leave their parents and relations? Or was it that they knew that leaving Kashmir meant leaving a home forever? Students were fast turning into mature adults, trying to make their own decisions, trying to shape their lives themselves. They had every right to do so; who would question?

And, finally, the celebration of having made it! That degree— Bachelor of Medicine and Bachelor of Surgery, that is MBBS—that we had so long struggled to dream, we had it. It was a dream come true in the most taxing circumstances. And yes, we lived to see the day. The bullets fell close by, but fortunately they did not touch us; the grenades seemed so near, but we escaped, nonetheless. Our male counterparts survived hundreds of identification parades and crackdowns; many survived those smashing canes and the force of rifle butts, but the beautiful degree we got in the end was worth it! Thank God for it.

Young Interns

And here again after our results, we separated from the herd and came together in groups of twos and fours. We were on the track towards becoming doctors, and for a year, we were supposed to rotate from one department to another to learn 'something of everything'. This period they called internship.

An intern was an onlooker in allied faculties of medicine and surgery but a slogger in major postings of medicine and surgery. They knew that they had a lot of knowledge, but were keen on a practical experience, a hands-on feeling, and this desire rendered them susceptible to exploitation. House surgeons/physicians used them for every odd call at every odd time. Registrars sucked them too; they needed their signatures for the certificate which they would get at the end of the year and also for that meagre sum which they would get at the end of a month. This petty sum was incidentally the first salary that a doctor got; one felt proud about receiving it. Most of us were content during internship because practical learning was more important.

There was a sense of pride in accompanying the professors on rounds, watching how the scary questions skipped interns and landed up on different targets—the final year students. It was only a few months back that they were the susceptible ones, but thank God, they didn't need the shields now to cover themselves during the rounds. That period of questioning and torture was over. There were final year students lined up to be told how to prepare for the final professional; they had to be told about the frequently asked questions, about the methodology of preparation for the practical exams, etc. As interns, we were coming closer to becoming doctors. We were minnows but important; we walked the way we were asked to, carrying messages and calls, forming communication chains from one hospital to another. We were taught the tricks of the trade—which patient to attend to, which one to be avoided . . . . 'Turco' or tactful avoidance of an impending problem was an art the house surgeons and registrars had mastered, and they passed on the skill . . . to us. Some of us were idealists who practised their own methodology; they caused irritation to the 'immediate' seniors but were anyway respected for their attitude. In our MBBS, we were designated as 'brilliant', 'average', and 'dull' but as interns; the classification was more simple: 'workers' and 'non-workers'. 'Workers' were loved, taught the practical procedures, and given an opportunity to 'do' them; and 'non-workers' were reserved for 'painful calls' and accompanying the patients as they were shifted from one hospital to another.

From dermatology to psychiatry, from orthopedics to pediatrics, from ophthalmology to radiology . . . it was an interesting rotation . . . . We fell in love at each doorstep and wanted to be the specialists in every branch that we were posted to. How interesting was the work in each discipline! How difficult it was to tell which branch was more interesting than the other! The major postings of medicine, surgery, and gynaecology were tough. We learnt to work under pressure, to manage the rush, and to run the outpatient departments (OPDs). Learning skills there was a necessity, and dealing with a disaster was a requirement. We worked, committing blunders but creating hopes as well. Those so-called 'genius' brains were no longer sought or given special attention; the ordinary ones pushed them aside where skills mattered. How difficult was theory from the practical exposure we were getting as interns!

But many of 'us' were not noticed. They had gone into hibernation of some kind . . . . They skipped this compulsory training, but they could well afford to as they prepared to move to better places. How they managed those signatures without actually working—the same signatures for which we were made to fret—we don't know.

Our medicine and surgery postings as interns were challenging. We were posted in OPDs—which were crowded and unmanageable; it was here that our patience was tested. We were posted in casualties/ emergencies where our presence of mind and our wit was tested, and we were there as little extras posted in operation theatres where we would long for a 'chance' to hold a retractor or to close a wound. The department of Surgery at SMHS hospital was doing a great job-managing trauma, managing emergencies which had become super-emergencies because of the late arrival of patients to the hospital. Unforeseen conditions caused patients to rely more on painkillers and short-term remedies. When the situation got out of hand and a full-blown emergency emerged, patients would come to the hospital—toxic, in shock, or in extreme pain.

We interns loved surgery for the relief patients got with intervention. The house surgeons, postgraduates, and registrars had an excellent exposure and managed all emergencies with competence and confidence. Those grenade blasts would be sudden. Many times, innocents would become targets, and many times grenades would burst in the midst of a crowd, causing widespread destruction. The patients arriving in hospitals after a blast seemed to come from a battlefield—tattered clothes, bleeding bodies, and a feeling of panic and anger. Most patients would be brought to the hospital by strangers.

The consultants were good, but some worked too little in the hospital and too much in private . . . . They came to hospital in style and left in style in their huge cars coming out of their private practice. There were many conscious souls who would bother about those for whom nobody cared. Surgical wards were overcrowded after 1 p.m. The nurses were usually invisible and had to be carefully hunted for.

There were patients with odd wounds at odd spots—usually the torture victims with their gaping and oozing wounds. Their pain and embarrassment shattered them and their families. Who can be so cruel to give so much of pain? Who can be so cruel to inflict so much of trauma? I had not known that rods could be put per rectally as a torture method, causing perforation and peritonitis. A schoolteacher from Tral was taken into custody and tortured with electric shock, and an iron rod was inserted into his rectum and pushed through to his chest, rupturing his lung. He was found by the side of the road and taken to hospital, coughing up blood and showing signs of peritonitis. He was operated upon in the hospital; a part of his rectum was removed. His diaphragm was perforated, and his lung too was pierced. Bile was confirmed in his pleural cavity as his liver was traumatised. Such a gruesome punishment for a schoolteacher! The man was interviewed by many international news channels. But this case too was collected into expanding bellies of cover-ups.[1]

So many other victims did not reach the hospital or went to other hospitals. Their pain and helplessness did not reach us. Should we have rejoiced or felt sad? Sometimes there were crackdowns in the hospital to nab the militants-the patients and attendants would have a tough time then and in search for the 'suspects' sometimes drapes and dressings were removed from critical patients.

There were other sad cases occurring as a result of something that was beyond our control. There was disruption of electricity at odd hours in the hospital. A young boy was being operated for an elective lobectomy (resection of a lobe of lung). Suddenly, the electricity went off and suction could not be maintained, which led to the boy drowning in his own secretions.[1] One of the worst tragedies we witnessed in surgery was when Dr Malik, one of the senior professors of surgery, was hit by an army vehicle and killed in Lal Chowk area in broad daylight. No probe was ever ordered into his killing, and no culprits were ever punished. A gentleman and an excellent surgeon's life fell before the arrogance of a military driver.

As interns, we were put on a duty roster for the night. Managing the wards all alone . . . having evening rounds, checking and cross-checking the blood pressure of patients, administering subcutaneous heparin, setting right those oxygen cylinders, and most horrifying of all . . . declaring a patient 'dead'. What a difficult job it was, looking for the pupillary reflex—trying different angles to check—checking the pulse and trying to hear that lub and dub . . . The first one I 'declared'—I went to the nurse's room to ask her to check what I had already checked. I remember how I trembled, how those things were falling from my hands—that torch, that stethoscope—but the nurse was an expert; she declared the patient 'dead' but not even once checked all that I had already checked.

Those Days and Nights in Casualty

The Casualty/Emergency area of SMHS Hospital was small, but it was smartly managed. It was very well planned with two main divisions, one each for Medicine and Surgery. There was an adjoining emergency operation theatre, a laboratory, pharmacy, an X-ray room, and a room for the Casualty Medical Officer, who managed the medico-legal cases. There was a room for drivers too, who would, on a duty, day smoke *hukka* there and sleep on a nearby bed to be available when we needed them. Those drivers were well behaved and well connected; any problem in the Casualty would be OK with their intervention. Those fellows were perhaps the boldest in the entire medical and paramedical community. They never let us down. They would always ferry doctors and patients through the deadliest parts of the city in the darkest hours of the night. The ambulances they drove told the tale of all the dread they faced on each trip. Their broken bones and bruised bodies from canings and beatings made them stronger. Once, an ambulance driver, Mr Ghulam Nabi Bhat, went with an attendant of a patient in his ambulance to collect antiserum from Badami Bagh Hospital for a patient suffering from gas gangrene. The soldiers there shot the driver dead, and the attendant

was injured. Ghulam Nabi Bhat was buried in hospital grounds.[1] After
that incident, drivers hesitated to move during the night.

There was a driver with a shabby beard, always burying himself in the
pheran he wore; with a pathetic look, he would request you for something
that he needed desperately—it was fortvin injection, the injection
pentozoscine that would make his body calm and cool. Without it he
would be in pain and agitation. We would resist giving it to him, but he
knew of a second place always wherefrom he could have it.

Working in Emergency meant working against the odds, making
quick decisions, and saving one's own skin. We learnt to deal with
hypochondriac patients from our immediate seniors. First gastrointestinal
bleed would go to Medicine and second to Surgery—but when in
Medicine, we would put the pressure on the patient to confess that it was
his second bleed and not the first, but when posted in Surgery we would
do the reverse. But in spite of these minor wrongs, we worked in unison,
managing sick patients in the surgical and medical wards of the Casualty
to our utmost capability.

All tragedies were managed together. The difference between senior
and junior, on-duty and off-duty medicos and paramedics would dilute
when tragedies struck. While female interns and house surgeons were sent
to the ward rest room after midnight, the male interns, house surgeons,
postgraduates, and registrars toiled hard for almost the entire night—
managing colics, operating acute abdomens, managing bullet and pellet
injuries, or treating acute exacerbations of chronic ailments.

I remember him and his overcoat—light brown—as he was brought
to the hospital in an auto; the auto raced up on to the ramp of the
Casualty and three young boys carried him inside. We were terrified
to see an auto in front of our eyes—that racing bug-like vehicle inside;
when trolleys and stretchers were absent, it was perhaps the quickest way
to deliver a patient inside the otherwise narrow alleys of the Casualty.
Anyway, a pale face with open eyes was facing us. He was motionless,
cold, and pulse-less. A registrar raced up to him with a stethoscope; he
put it hurriedly on to his chest and separated his eyelids further, and there
stood his widely dilated pupils, which had stopped their oscillation. The
registrar said it aloud . . . 'Brought dead.'

The three boys accompanying him began to search his pockets. We
were wondering why they were doing so, but responding to our curiosity,
they said, "We don't know who he is. He just fell down, when there was
firing in Lal Chowk. We are looking for his identity card." We too needed

the identity of the person to fill in the hospital papers, but we were concerned that the man in front of our eyes, nearly 50 years of age must have left his home with a promise to be back in the evening. He must have gone out to earn a few bucks, or maybe for something else. The boys couldn't find the identity card but pulled out a few hundred rupees from the inside pocket of his overcoat . . . . The notes were wet and had an altered colour. We knew after we saw the notes that the man had received a bullet, deep there on his left—a place where his spleen rested. The wound was small, obscured by the ooze, but it was enough to kill him.

The dead body was handed over to the police. God knows what happened to him next . . . whether his legal heirs located him or not . . . . But there was yet another precaution to be taken in the land of turmoil we were working in—carrying an identity card. At least carrying it would ease the burden you could be on others—in case you died . . .

In the Emergency, there was a tiny doctors' room nearby where doctors would take a short nap somewhere after the midnight. That time, the scare in the city was too much, and patients would not dare to move out and come to the hospital. Most patients would land up in Casualty 'early mornings' . . . having fought the pain and discomfort all night. But that nap was always interrupted by patients, hysterical females, anxious attendants, or all those desperate souls who would go there in search of a bathroom . . . and an odd patient would sometimes piss on the poor doctors sleeping in dark. No fault of theirs. There was no bathroom in the Casualty!

Disturbed Minds

After a long battle in my mind about where I wanted to work as a house surgeon, I chose a hospital which had lately emerged as the busiest hospital of the city. The hospital close to the lap of Kohimaran, tasting the cool breeze of Dal Lake, was ideally situated to refresh a tired and agitated mind. I had been there earlier in my short posting during internship, and yes, in my childhood, too, I used to go there, accompanying an uncle of mine who had a seizure disorder. The hospital in those days provided free medicines to patients of seizure disorder. I have a beautiful recollection of how the hospital looked in those days. The hospital was all wood and stone, rectangular, barrack-like, facing beautiful lawns. The neatly manoeuvred evergreens, the all-embracing

umbrella trees, and those sweet-smelling flowers gave the lawns the look
of a Mogul garden. There were a few doctors there, but that beautiful and
elegant Englishwoman was the most conspicuous of them all. She was a
darling—loved by all the inmates and the outpatients. They called her
'Miss Hawk', and they say the creation of a psychiatric hospital in what
used to be a barrack of central jail was her brainchild. She nurtured it till
she was there.

I witnessed how the psychiatric hospital lost its place as a hospital for
psychiatric diseases and became crowded and congested, where people
would queue up for medicines and an immediate cure to their disturbed
state of mind. Cows, stray dogs, vultures, and crows would venture into
the lawns which were previously a hub for koels, hoopoes, and sweet
singing nightingales.

I came to the hospital with a hope—a hope to do something for
all those who were forgotten in a tragedy that had made us miserable.
I came here with a desire too—a desire to attend to all those who were
too traumatised by the events to lead a normal life. The inpatients were
the ones we had forgotten, and the outpatients, the ones with a bleeding
psyche, climbing desperately to crutches for support.

I worked there for a good 6 months, trying my best to understand
what was going on within those huge halls which they called 'wards' or
in those overcrowded rooms—the OPDs. There were a few competent
psychiatrists working here.

And yes, there was a doctor who talked much and showed an
odd behaviour at times. He, I came to know, was a patient of chronic
schizophrenia . . . . The fact that he was picked up by Miss Hawk and
brought here to work was a surprise. But a thorough gentleman—well
behaved, doing his work effectively, writing and asking the histories of
patients, diagnosing the patients of a particular psychiatric disorder and
treating them also—he was an asset to the hospital. A patient had become
a doctor of his patients!

The inmates were hard to describe, but they were the ones familiar
with the hospital staff. Some of the aggressive ones were in cells, and
some violent ones, tied in chains. Some were talkative, and some never
talked. Some sat besides the windows, and some wrapped themselves in
sheets. They were dirty; sometimes they would be in rags and sometimes
in a crumpled hospital uniform. I didn't know if they knew what was
going on outside. Somehow, the inmates were never terrified by the
bullets, never shaken by the pellets; no blasts would make them run, and

no tragedies would make them cry. The women would sing, shout, and taunt each other. I remember a Pandit woman, a chronic schizophrenic, who was there in the ward for many years. Her family had migrated to Jammu, leaving her behind. No one, the hospital authorities told me, ever enquired about her . . . since the turmoil struck the valley. She would sing melodious Kashmiri songs at times and call out the names of her sons and daughters, never forgetting to add a suffix '*ji*' to their names—that peculiar Pandit style of addressing a dear one. Sometimes, fellow inmates would taunt her calling her '*batni*', '*batni*'. God knows what was going on inside her mind, or what was happening to her heart . . . . Would the psychiatric hospital be her home forever? Some other patients who could have led normal lives after their acute illness was over were again trapped in the wards as their families disowned them. Rehabilitation of the mentally sick—who would think of that in a place torn apart by wars? Sometimes, there would be sporadic violence in the hospital—the inmates would hit each other, bite each other, or abuse each other. There were people in the hospital who would separate them; somehow they had the knack of making them quiet.

Brushing, combing, or bathing was not in vogue. The authorities must have employed people to help the inmates maintain some sense of hygiene. But I never saw anybody in the ward help any inmate. Obviously, those poor fellows who were unaware of their own needs would not complain against any employee. Some of the females had their hair trimmed to prevent entanglements and parasitic infections; also, having long hair for an inmate meant trouble—it would be pulled during a fight . . . .

Interestingly, all of them were always barefoot—I don't know why? Their soles were thick, black, and cracked. As they roamed in the lawns which were full of filth and dirt, pieces of glass, thorns, or nails would find their way into their soles, letting loose the speeding showers of blood. The other smaller and sharper bits would be lost in the thickness of their soles. No one cared for their wounds. The inmates had learnt how to stop the ooze—tear their dresses and seal the wounds. Seeing their repeated physical pain, I decided that I should arrange slippers for them. I discussed this problem with my sister, who helped me get some eighty pairs. The thrill and excitement which the slippers brought to the inmates was unimaginable. They readily put their feet forward and slipped the slippers on to those huge, ugly feet. The caretaker staff made faces 'Ooh! Aah! *Hinh*!', but it was a day of celebration for the inmates. I slept peacefully that night!

On the morning rounds, I was keen to know about the inmates and their slippers. But I noticed the gloom and was surprised to see them all quiet. I enquired, 'Why, what happened?'

A sobbing young man said, 'They took the chappals away.'

'Who?' I asked.

'Those men and women,' he said, pointing his finger towards the people who had made faces the other day.

I complained to a senior doctor, who remarked, 'It won't change here, don't worry.'

When the sanes were getting chopped like carrots, why would you bother about the insanes?

I would watch them and their pale faces and wonder, did they have anemia? I got a few of them evaluated at SMHS Hospital for anemia. I remember how I took one with me in the ambulance to SMHS Hospital and how he ran away in the OPD there. How I ran after him to get him back. My friends posted in other specialties at SMHS laughed at me that day! But, even before I had the Hemoglobin (Hb) of the patients done, I knew the cause; the cause was their food. The food served to them had no trace of hygiene or nutrition. They would gulp the food without ever chewing it. We would watch with disgust their horrible food; the vegetables served to were raw, and their rice was full of big and small stones, which would produce screeching and penetrating sounds when they rolled between their teeth. Swallowing the entire morsels was the only way to avoid the unpleasantness which the rolling stones gave. A few wise ones would pick the stones from their plates before putting the food into their mouths.

But sometimes, an odd guy would have a visitor just near the umbrella tree—a caring mother would be seen feeding her son and watching him lovingly gulp down the food he so much longed to eat!

My heart would cry on seeing this all. It was a murder of innocence, a torture of innocents. The inmates would never complain, never say a word in resistance. I know their complaint cell was located higher, higher than we all could imagine, and unfortunately, their 'Master' had reposed a trust in us for their custody. We know well how we failed in our jobs, in our trust; we played a foul play with the innocent souls, least fearing our 'Master'. God forgive us!

Looking at the stress and pressure that a common Kashmiri suffered from, you would wonder as to why the entire population was not suffering from extreme psychiatric disturbances. Perhaps their trust in destiny helped, perhaps their unwavering belief that 'All good and bad is from Allah' helped, or perhaps their belief that miseries of life will be rewarded handsomely in the hereafter helped. I had heard that 'faith saves'. For the faithful, it was a panacea; whereas for the faithless, faith was a paint, a paint of the exterior which cracked in heat, shrunk in cold, and was weakened by moisture.

But still a large population did succumb to the pressure of turmoil. Depression became common, and stress-related disorders came to the surface. With time, there was an epidemic of depression, conversion disorders, and post-traumatic stress disorders. From young children to old, a huge population was affected by the disorders that maimed the society. The psychiatric hospital, which was seldom visited by those who thought they were normal, became a second home for city's women. These were the women who would previously visit shrines and mosques to seek solace . . . but the unfavourable situation in the valley had made the shrines dangerous places. The hospital, like other associated hospitals, suffered from severe staff depletion and was being over-utilised. Long queues in the OPDs left the doctors exhausted.

The doctors were doing a great job, and yet not doing it. They were taking care of the acute crises and doing nothing about the real disease. But they were justified when they said, 'The root cause of the problem cannot be removed. The problem will manifest somehow.' Mentally fragile, sensitive, and caring ones fell sick in large numbers and landed up in our psychiatric hospital, which was ill equipped to face the onslaught.

But in spite of such a major catastrophe affecting our population, no remedial measures were sought. The doctors—many of them on stopgap arrangements—were just trying to touch the tip, and the entire cake of diseases remained submerged. Poor fellows, what more could they do?

Imagine such a huge population suffering from psychiatric disturbances and no guidelines from Health Ministry, no plans outlined to tackle the problem, and no manpower available to manage the hospitals. Working in the psychiatric hospital was giving me more pain than pleasure. There was so much I wanted to do, so much I wanted to change, but then how would I change anything? How could I? Maintenance of the psychiatric hospital was nobody's concern. After all, of what use would those people be? As happened everywhere, so it happened in the psychiatric hospital too. You could not 'order' anybody to do anything; the subordinates did not remain subordinates and the bosses could not act as bosses.

For the higher-ups, the tensions were more. . The psychiatric hospital should not become a 'miscreants' den. No one should take shelter there pretending to be mentally unstable; no one should use it for the purpose it was not meant to be. How would they ensure that?

Then on one still day, perhaps a Sunday, the hospital caught fire. I remember the fire of Mental Hospital, the ugly one, the smoky one. It consumed a selective portion of the hospital. The poor inmates were smoked out into the nearby market outside, where they jumped with excitement on seeing the open space for some time. The fire was believed to be a conspiracy; someone within the hospital had done the evil deed, it was said. The fire had to do something with the store where too many items were gobbled, and the fire, they said, was there to set the records straight. It would cover up the misdoings of a few people. Don't know how true it was. No one would dare to dig out the reason. It was the best time to set the hospital on fire; so many people could be blamed. As expected, people at the helm kept quiet—out of fear they felt, it was better to keep the mouths sealed to avoid an uncontrolled aftermath which could follow if the fire at Psychiatric hospital was probed. The fire took away the only asylum the inmates had. Limited space was limited further.

The morning round following the fire was a torture. Grumbling and trembling inmates were shivering. Piles of burnt files which carried in their chests stories of life were fluttering in the form of blackened bits and dancing like mad whirlpools. The smoke choked the senses and blocked the minds. Who had benefited from the fire? An accident it was not, an incident it was that lay bare our selfish self. Whoever it was, he was answerable to all those men and women who had lost a home. When the psychiatric hospital burnt, I knew this was not the place where I should be. I needed to bother about my own self, the stability of my own mind. I was feeling those features of depression—that disinterest, that unaccounted fatigue, and that disgust. I compliment the doctors who were working there and are still working there. They had a strong will which I perhaps lacked!

It was time I left the hospital. And I did so. A petite me could not cope up with the challenges there, and my presence, anyways, was not making any difference. Six months' house job and I bid psychiatry goodbye.

Medicine and its Challenges

I returned after being away for 6 months to the place which was like a second home to me. As a house physician in Medicine, I was posted in Ward 11 of SMHS Hospital. Circumstances had turned SMHS Hospital into a busy Indian railway station where there were too many people, twitchy and anxious, tripping and spitting, shouting and screaming, and making the corridors turbulent. Burning stoves decorated all the corridors. Many anxious attendants would utilise the corridors for sitting and waiting outside the theatre or wards—or for eating and chatting.

Ward 11 was a big ward with two connecting limbs—for women and sick patients. The ward was managed by Unit 1 which was headed by a gentleman, a soft-spoken angel of a man who was labelled as the 'best teacher' of medicine. He loved all and believed all, never lost his temper, and never stopped learning. When he talked, no talk was important. Handsome, articulate, and smartly dressed—he was none other than Professor Yousuf. His deputy was a doctor with a sharp clinical sense. The two made a good pair. Ward 11 was very close to my heart—the effect of the head of the unit was apparent on everyone and everything belonging to the ward. Though a happening place, it was a place of learning. The atmosphere was cool, the consultants were good, and the registrars were friendly and cooperative. Each *dai*, each sanitary man, and each nurse was well behaved and hard working.

But the real life of Ward 11, its real core, was a senior consultant. Humble, meek, humorous, and committed, he was an epitome of hard work and dedication. He was never late for his job. He would start his rounds in time, whether there were people available or not. He would examine each patient meticulously—all systems. He would do the examinations most of us skipped—a thorough neurological examination and an unpleasant per rectal examination. His examinations many a times were non-contributory, but his findings sometimes embarrassed the seniors and juniors. He picked up a node in a neck we always wrote as normal, picked up icterus in the eyes which stared into our faces every morning, picked up a rare complication of a rare disease, or diagnosed a life-threatening adverse drug reaction.

There was something else he did. He stopped the stoves in the corridors, chased the hawkers who ran freely in the ward, and stopped the newspaper vendors who would be shouting in the ward in his absence. The hospital administration was non-functional, but he . . . was functioning . . . efficiently. When he entered the hospital, his presence would scare the attendants away; all stoves would fall silent as he snatched away their pins. Those who knew him would hide their stoves before his arrival, and the fastest hawkers would run for their lives as he was ruthless with them.

Was it worthwhile to do all he was doing? His bit was miniscule, but would it have been different if each one of us would have done 'our bits'?

His strong human values would jolt your conscience. When there was no threat of accountability, no fear of job loss, how did he stick so strictly to the code of conduct? When no law was being obeyed, no rule was being followed, how come he behaved as if he was under constant surveillance? Who had trained him to be mindful in that mindless, chaotic world of ours?

With all the dedication and all the commitment he had, he deserved much more than he was given. He served at a junior post, stuck up on an adhoc appointment, for years together. No one pleaded his case; no one spoke for him. But he never complained about his status, never pitied his state. In our hospitals, it is a common practice to see doctors talking about the injustice that has been done to them, the favouritism that has marred their career, and the conspiracies which are being hatched against them. But this man never talked about anything that had happened to him. He did not bother about the type of dress he wore, the type of bag he carried. But a patient's condition would trouble him; the condition of Ward 11 was his worry. We would sometimes walk down together through Downtown on our way back from our work. He would amuse us with Rumi's poetry and Sheikhul Alam's couplets, and we knew—he cared for all that was worth caring for!

This great man was no genius, was not a roaring practitioner, but he had patience . . . patience to examine a patient, patience to assess him, and patience to understand him. He was someone who was never tired of seeing a patient. For him, there was no dearth of time. He Dr Abdul Majeed Ahangar—a great human being, an excellent physician—God bless him wherever he is.

I was the only female house physician working in Medicine at that point of time. The job was tough, but I was happy—each moment was a moment of learning. The OPDs were hectic, the ward rounds were exhaustive. Although I had come from Psychiatry to Medicine, not much was different in medical OPDs. There were the same patients, same complaints, and same worried faces. Here, too, women outnumbered men. Our prescriptions in the OPDs here were not much different from those in the psychiatry OPDs.

Our patients needed an ear to listen to and a heart to understand them. We couldn't afford to talk to them for long . . . . There was always a rush, a push on our door from outside. But women would sob and talk about a pain in their hearts; they would show us the long strips of a graph of their hearts, called ECGs. And we would interpret them as normal! What more was there to be done? We were tired of writing prescriptions for anxiolytics, painkillers, sedatives, multivitamins, or antacids. If the previous records indicated that such drugs had been used earlier, we would just change the brand of the drug. What more could you offer? A huge population of patients had no apparent disease; there was just a feeling of anxiety, a feeling of pain, for which there was no apparent organic cause. Sometimes, patients came for a follow-up and sometimes never . . . . The patients would roll from one OPD to the other.

Our emergencies too were hectic. We would receive females with fainting spells—what we called in psychiatry as 'hysterical conversion reactions'. We managed them crudely, sometimes slapping and striking their soles and sometimes attempting to put in a Ryle's tube. The moment they were revived, they would sob. We didn't have time to listen to all that they had to tell us. But on an anxiolytic and a painkiller, we would send them off, to follow up later with the psychiatric OPD. No patient wanted to acknowledge that his ailment was because of psychiatric disturbance . . . but that is what the truth was, unfortunately, for most of our patients.

Other patients with more serious diseases would reach us late . . . curfews, hartals, and restrictions would convert minor medical problems into major emergencies. Some would survive with difficulty, and some could never make it back home—alive.

Ward 11 was the ward where a great doctor heading the Department of Psychiatry breathed his last. They say he came here with fever and a feeling of being unwell. The head of the unit, seeing his condition, advised him to be admitted. My colleague house physician was on night duty. He saw Dr Beigh sinking and called his boss, who came online to advise. The Registrar too was in a panic. The Head of the unit could have come to see his friend. But how could he? He lived far away. No ambulance driver could risk his life to go that far, clearing the dens of security and getting him to help his friend. A referral to the SKIMS, too, couldn't be managed. Beigh Sahib died in his friend's ward, without his friend being at his side. What a pain for the friend! Did those memories of his friend make him uneasy? I know how depressed the house physician was after Beigh Sahib's death. There was a feeling of guilt, a feeling of depression; he blamed himself, his own inexperience for what happened to Dr Beigh. But then no one could have done better in the circumstances we were trapped in.

Night duties constituted the most challenging job . . . of working in medicine. On an emergency day, Casualty and the ward had to be managed together. The Casualty was miles apart, connected to the main hospital by a thin strip of a long corridor, which was scary. It was a resting place for canines and homeless humans. You never knew whom you would meet on the way to Casualty in those dark nights. There used to be posters pasted on its walls—calling on people to do whatever was desired i.e strike, protest, shouting in mosques, or anything else. There were imprints of sadness too; someone would write ballads, someone beautiful couplets of Iqbal and Faiz on those walls of a neglected corridor. The calligraphic reflections in coal and colour would often end with the title of the artist, G.R. Gamgeen. Who was this man writing on the walls? He must have been a sad man—thinking too much and using an outlet like the connecting corridor for the display of his emotions and expressions.

SMHS Hospital was a place where too many people would come and go. Restrictions on the duration of the attendants' presence and their numbers were hardly ever seen.Inside the ward, outside our room, I used to see new faces every day. There were people in *pherans* leaning against the hot radiators of the ward, talking about the familiar and unfamiliar happenings of our lives. There used to be some tense faces too, possibly looking for an asylum. Some unusual noises and flutters underneath their *pherans* would make you alert. But pretend ignorance and you are saved. You don't disturb them, and they wouldn't disturb you! The hospital was functioning because of a few overburdened souls—most of them were doctors. People shrugged duties and remained off for months together, but no one had guts to question anyone. Many employees became liabilities, happily turning out to take salaries but otherwise never worked. Some junior employees were the ones who took maximum advantage of the situation. They would spread a scare around the hospital and in the wards. You had to attend to their patients first. You could never say 'No' and that was an 'Order . . .' I had some horrifying experiences in Ward 11 with the employees.

I remember the night of *Shab-i-Qadr* when I was on a night duty. A hospital employee knocked at my door and politely asked me if he could do *wudu* in the bathroom attached to the house surgeon's room. The night of *Shab-i-Qadr*, a night better than a thousand nights, when blessings are poured in tons—how would I refuse his request? He used our bathroom, and I don't know when he left as I was busy . . . . After an hour or so, I too went into the bathroom and was surprised. The guy had opened the geyser, taken out the element, the anchor, the wires, and everything else. The body of the geyser was hanging lose . . . . Such a deed on such a great night . . . I was dumbfounded. I couldn't open my mouth. I didn't know what to do, whom to complain to. The geyser in our bathroom was a massive one; it supplied water to all the adjoining rooms. The next morning, the doctors using the adjoining bathrooms enquired about the state of the geyser, and I narrated the entire incident. Everyone wanted to know who it was, but I didn't know the employee by name; I could recognise him, though. Next day, I saw him vividly yet again and called my seniors—to take action against him. He, an orderly working somewhere else, would come around into any ward and steal everything that was handy. The damaged geyser was not replaced for all the months that I was there, neither was the employee punished! That was what the turmoil did to our wards . . .

A harsh knock at the door by the attendant of a patient having COPD (chronic obstructive pulmonary disease) made me rush out from the room on a post-emergency night, leaving behind my Littmann stethoscope and my little black watch. I looked at the patient; he was a bit breathless. I adjusted his posture, reassured him, asked for the oxygen cylinder to be changed, and went back to my room to collect the stethoscope. But I could find neither my Littmann nor my watch there. I loved both, the watch and my Littmann. And I was sad. Not knowing what to do—suddenly, a hospital employee clad in a *pheran* came to my room to tell me that he had changed the oxygen cylinder of the patient and that the patient was doing fine . . . . As he was about to leave the room, a little black thing fell down from inside his *pheran* at my feet. He stooped down to pick it, and I stopped him.

'Don't! It is mine,' I said as I recognised my watch. 'Where is the Littman?' I shouted.

'I don't know,' he said.

I picked up my watch and called the attendant of the patient whose oxygen cylinder the employee had changed. The attendant grabbed him and started beating him. We had caught a thief . . . red-handed; the artificial hospital lights could not hide his paleness. Many more attendants collected to recover the Littmann from him. I was requested by all those who caught him not to complain against him. I knew no complaints would be effective, so why to waste one's time. All I wanted to know was his name, his designation, and the place he was working. Surprisingly, he was posted in Casualty, about a kilometre away, and there he was supposed to help patients with oxygen pipes, catheters, etc. He was cleverly escaping the duty there and making his way into the wards as someone who was supposed to set right the oxygen pipes and catheters . . . . He would steal from all—the patients, the attendants, and the doctors. He had been caught previously also, but no action was initiated.

One lesson learnt—patients don't cheat, attendants don't steal . . . poor fellows, they are already in distress, fearing God, trying their best to please Him. It was our own men who had deviated.

Though some of the paramedics were dedicated many more were readily escaping their duties. Those nurses posted in different wards managed their own routine cunningly putting each one of us in trouble. Each ward was supposed to have a nurse on night duty, but the nurses would tag up with each other—one would replace four, and two would replace eight. And they would take night off for 2 days without actually performing the duty. On our own duty when we required a nurse, we had to trace nurses from one end of the hospital to another. If the task was so difficult for us; how difficult would it be for the patients and the attendants to locate a nurse? There must have been a few nurses who worked well, but in that sea of deceit, where would we find them?

On a night duty, I and my intern were inside our room taking a little rest after a heavy emergency duty, when loud jerks on our door shook us. They were looking for 'sister'. We told them that the 'sister' was not in our room and that they should look for her in another room. After some time, there was another knock—a fierce one that burst the door open. The latch broke, and the door got cracks. Two men came inside and started hitting us with chairs and stools lying in our room. The two scared females could hardly resist the onslaught . . . . 'Oh my God!' There was no one to call for help. But the attendants of patients admitted in our ward rushed in to help us. They drove the violent ones out.

Perhaps the miscreants thought I was a nurse hiding in that room . . . .
The attendants called the police, and an FIR was lodged against the
miscreants. The policeman asked the two of us to narrate our story. I
cried bitterly that night. What was my fault?

Next day, I talked to the Head of the department about it, who
assured that the matter would be investigated and formed a committee
to do the same. The committee questioned us and found out the truth.
A patient had expired and patient's party wanted the hospital personnel
to take out her Ryle's tube, catheter, and the fluid lines so that the dead
body could be taken home. They looked for someone in every corner of
their ward, and when they failed, they turned to another ward where they
saw a nurse, who said, 'I don't belong to that ward.' They came to our
ward; on hearing our reply . . . they taught us a lesson. It would have
been the end of my life but for the attendants. The nurses were adhering
to their own roster their own schedule in a ratio of 4:1, the higher
authorities were aware . . .

But nothing happened. No one was punished. On the other hand, I
was made to feel uncomfortable. That policeman who had come to my
room on the day the incident occurred kept coming again and again. He
wanted to know the odd details about who had hit me and how . . . .
When I would come to the ward, people would tell me that a policeman
was looking for me. It seemed to be an odd mess into which I didn't
want to fall. I had a few restless nights and uneasy days when I would
be running away from police and the so-called investigation. I went to
the Head of the unit with the plea to rid me off the mess. He called the
SHO, who asked me to sign a statement saying, 'I didn't identify the
people who created violence in Ward 11.' I quietly signed everything
without regrets. A rash attendant whose mother had expired wanted some
help from a nurse, and in spite of trying his best he couldn't locate her.
Unfortunately, I came in their way and received their wrath. Whether I
deserved it or not was not his concern, but by hitting me, he was at least
doing something. I forgive him and his companions—but not the nurse
who was not on duty . . . . Administrators too had let us down—they
needed to be more vigilant in the tiring circumstances; they forgot that
they were the 'caretakers of so many lives'

Small things kept on happening in Medicine . . . . Supplies to
the hospital were blocked because of continuous shutdowns and
curfews; those which managed to reach the hospital were not in the

hospital. Small things kept on disappearing, and I learnt that gauze, bandages, syringes, and cotton were stolen . . . . And I learnt to keep on ignoring . . . the small things. There must have been bigger scandals also; I don't know. The lack of those essential items ensured our primitively functioning health care. It held us back firmly to the 'basics' without any advancement, without any improvement.

A friend of mine, while in SMHS Hospital, had to attend to the delivery of a patient. Since Lal Ded Hospital was quite far away, she tried to conduct the delivery herself. She wanted some thread to tie the cord . . . The main theatre was closed, and the Casualty theatre was on the other end. Seeing her discomfort, the attendant asked her what she wanted. 'Thread,' my friend said.

The man hurriedly went to one side of the ward and got the thread— one, two, three, and many in hand from the tie which held his trouser in place . . . . The doctor perhaps used the thread . . . she had to; there was no other option . . .

The inflow to the SMHS Hospital was not checked. Anyone could come inside and do whatever one wished to do. Besides small-time robbers and pickpockets, drug addicts and beggars, too, found SMHS Hospital to be a safe haven. The patients in OPD and Emergency were continuously exploited. Touts circled the hospital corridors . . . . Specific drugstores and laboratories planted their own men within the hospital corridors and hijacked the patients to their own lairs. We would ask the patients to get one drug, and he would get the other one . . . . We would ask for one investigation and patient would show us a series of investigations. Who would nab the culprits sucking the blood of innocent sufferers?

We asked a jaundiced patient once for some investigations . . . . The patient surprised us when he returned to us with a whole battery of investigations in record time. We were surprised, but when we saw the reports, the reports seemed unpalatable. We asked the patient to go again and ask the technician to reconfirm the tests . . . . The patient returned to us with a different report showing different parameters. We enquired from the patient about the laboratory wherefrom he had got the investigations done. To our surprise, he told us that a man in the corridors of the hospital had taken his sample from a nearby shed and handed him over the reports within 5 minutes. When asked to reconfirm, he had torn the previous report and written a new one. The patient had each time been charged Rs. 100. We looked carefully at the report; the form bore a laboratory name and address. We sent someone to confirm where the laboratory was. As expected, it was a fake laboratory, and someone was moving about in the hospital, looking for the innocent patients needing investigations and taking samples in a nearby hospital shed. That person would give assurance to the patients that latest and modern technology was being used for performing various tests in their laboratory, making it possible to get the results in minimum possible time. He would also assure them that they need not come to the laboratory; samples would be collected and reports would also be delivered to the patients within the hospital. So much service for just Rs. 100! When we went to look for that man in the shed, we could not locate him. Perhaps he had changed his hunting place. How low we had stooped!

Some more people would pretend to be hospital employees, and for an investigation like ultrasound and X-ray, they charged money from the patients, pleading with other employees to give the patients an early slot. In a house of misery, how miserably was a patient treated!

I had not heard about 'knowledge' being stolen. In Ward 11, I learnt that it could also happen. In a batch of fresh interns, a guy joined the ward, telling us that he had been directed to join Ward 11. We were happy to have him there. He could at least help us with our work we thought. But the boy was a bit weird and confused and could neither write nor talk properly. What kind of an intern was he? We were surprised. But in spite of being uncomfortable working with him, we used to give him an opportunity to work. Whenever we asked him from where he had done his MBBS, he would say, 'Outside', never naming the college or the place where his college was located. We were pulling on with him with difficulty; once a student (extern) recognised him, telling us that the fellow was pursuing some course in 'alternative medicine' in Hyderabad, and after having failed many times there, he had got fed up and had returned to Kashmir. How he had sneaked in, quietly in our ward, and tried to become a doctor, no one knows. What he gathered in our ward, he was ready to sell . . . . Who would question him? Passed or failed, it did not matter; allopathic or alternative medicine, it did not matter . . . . What mattered was that he could treat the poor patients of the valley and extract money from them as a doctor. As soon as this *'Munna Bhai'* came to know that the news about him had leaked, he ran away—never to be seen. Maybe, he practised medicine somewhere as doctor 'so and so' under registration no. 'so and so'.

Soon, bunkers were erected within the hospital premises. With bunkers inside, walking around the hospitals became difficult and attending calls during nights became impossible. Those suffocating muddy structures, through which the forces would peep to locate a miscreant, spoilt the beauty and peace of our institution. It did stop the movement of some people within the hospital—but the other mischief-makers, who would roam about in the hospitals to loot the public had no fear; a bunker or no bunker, they would loot!

As the World Disowned Us

Documentaries were made on us, movies also—some tragedies and some full of patriotism. That is what sold in an India blinded by the media which never told the truth. We preferred not to watch them; it hurt when we did. All characters were dubbed with lies. They called us 'patriots' when we were not. They called our youngsters 'misled youth' when what they spoke was truth and nothing else. Their lies and our lives were running parallel. On watching the television and on hearing their versions-we would cry out-*Apuz Apuz* . . . . (lies . . . , lies . . .). *Apuz* was the arm that had been used consistently in Kashmir. The media used it, the administration used it and the commentators and anchors used it. The good old days of Indian cinema, when Bollywood heroes and heroines danced on the waters of Dal Lake and hopped about in the meadows of Gulmarg—were seen as pleasant pages of Kashmir history. As tourists avoided Kashmir, the hoteliers had fled and locals had moved to congested sites for more protection; but the meadows had a new habitation. The forces occupied the mountain tops and were down there, guarding each crevice. We know about their insecurities; the buzz of a bee would make them alert! Meanwhile, horses and mules were having a merry or was it agitation? They danced when it was quiet but ran for their own covers when they heard a shot. When they danced too much, a frustrated shot in the air by a frustrated one on the ground made them gasp and run—some odd shots would hit them to incapacitate them for life . . . . Our miserable life disabled them too.

Our own intellect froze, so froze the poetry and the prose. No one spoke; no one wrote a line about what was happening. There were disturbing accounts of torture, men were being sawed, women were being gang-raped, and entire families were being wiped; and we were helplessly watching, fearing a loud word might kill us too. Automatic shutters fell on the mouths wanting to speak; automatic handcuffs twisted the hands which could write. Writing in papers was not easy, but there were some brave ones doing their duty passionately and fearlessly. Widely read local Urdu press, which had successfully overcome 'Punjab Urdu Press' and its unpalatable views on Kashmir and Kashmiris, was working against the odds, reporting amidst threats of all sorts. Experienced editors of *Daily Aftab* and *Srinagar Times* gave up their homes and lived in their miniscule office spaces to give up-to-date information to Kashmiris. While veterans were spared (by pure luck or otherwise), promising journalists were abducted and some killed, including the editor of Urdu Daily *Alsafa*.

English press was non-existent in Kashmir; national newspapers reached Kashmir after days together, but the national press ignored Kashmir. Kashmir Times was perhaps the only newspaper that reported with some degree of honesty the events happening in Kashmir. This paper too, unfortunately, reached us a day later. Although Kashmir Times was published from Jammu, the paper lived true to its name, bringing in the truth from the remotest corners of Kashmir on to its pages.

We grew sick with time seeing all those mutilated faces, those tearful eyes, and those words of sorrow in newspapers. Sometimes, entire pages would be full of photos of dead bodies, and sometimes, old memories were recycled . . .

Kashmiris were desperate for a local English paper. An effort made by civil society resulted in the start of an ordinary English daily named Greater Kashmir, which, at a later date, went on to become a leading newspaper of Kashmir.

But in that chaos and fear, a scrupulously honest reporter from BCC Urdu Service, namely Yousuf Jameel, would update us about every untoward incident happening in Kashmir. His courage to speak the truth in world's most dangerous place made him risk his life so often. We loved his voice on radio when he spoke truth so loud and clear. I do not know if a non-Kashmiri ever heard what Yousuf Jameel had to say . . . but it eased our burning wounds when we heard the echo of our own words on BBC. Did English services also air those views? We didn't know.

Yousuf Jameel lost his colleague Mushtaq Ali to a parcel bomb meant for him. They reward reporters for fearless reporting—posthumously. How about those who report and live?

And then there was Agha Shahid Ali, a Kashmiri poet in the United States crying for Kashmir. He put his tears for Kashmir into his poems and made the world cry . . .

I kiss your poems Shahid,
garland your words.
Who was ever so open,
so straight and so true about Kashmir?
You died so early.
Didn't see you alas!
Would I bear if I would know about your pain,
not the painful crab who was eating your conscious mind,
but that beautiful land faraway—beyond Himalayas glued to your heart.
Those needles of separation,
those cries of desperation pricking it.
Wish I love Kashmir, the way you loved Shahid.
Wish I feel its pain, the way you felt.
'O' God! Change our fate,
let an Agha be born here again.

The Saviours

Somewhere in Government Medical College Srinagar, where there was a large population of youth, sanity prevailed and a few noble souls spread the true message of Islam. A few faculty members, who were enlightened with the knowledge of Islam and applied it to their own lives, started a steady transformation of youngsters and presented them with the pure message of Islam. The Government Medical College should acknowledge the contribution of such men—those great men who contained men and their minds in what would have turned out to be a volcano that would have swept the college away and buried it underneath its molten lava. One such practising Muslim who was not shy to be a Muslim and practised his subject to perfection changed the fate of boys studying medicine in GMC. For all those who thought Islam made people extremists, this one represented a side of Islam which made us all proud. He went on to become its principal at a later date.

Incidentally, *Darul Ulooms* also started mushrooming all over the valley; people were keener to know about Islam, to seek refuge in it. Had turmoil not struck the valley, people would have never known Islam in depth. Was it a blessing in disguise? *Darul Ulooms* never interfered in politics; none of them taught jihad; in spite of such a neat image, media referred to them as preaching extremism. No one told them that preaching Islam is not preaching extremism.

And a Darbar Moves

Harsh winters, with their mishaps and mischief, leave Kashmir all alone. Even the Government offices migrate; they call it a *'Darbar move'*—a court which moves. It reminds a Kashmiri of an emperor and his court, a court that would close its doors in winters and would display its grandeur in summers, in Dal and Jhelum. With *Darbar* move, all that is official moves over—the civil secretariat, the ministers, the courts, and the officials. Trunks and truckloads of files, too, move, leaving the entire state in a vacuum of governance for more than a month involving shifting, packing, unpacking, adjusting, and restarting. Kashmir remains isolated, aloof, and calm during these months—politics-free, politician-free, and pollution-free.

Sometimes, winters are easy to tolerate, and sometimes they are harsh—the harshest portion coming in *'Chila-i-Kalan'* or the 'eldest winter'. The bite of cold winds is hard to tolerate. And the Kashmiris' struggle becomes a struggle for survival—no electricity, shortage of essential commodities, and an unbearable chill. Two human races are then pitted against each other—the ones in bunkers and the ones in warm but tense interiors. The rest enjoy the lovely sunshine in Jammu and Delhi . . .

When snow blocks the roads, we witness its preferential clearing. Roads are cleared for the convoys to move . . . nothing else is important. Civilian vehicles are not important; restoring essential services is not important . . . . Helpless Kashmiris watch heavy army vehicles race past them, splashing crushed dirty snow as they move towards their own destinations, leaving past gazing, waiting inferior beings called Kashmiris.

Off to the Boarding School

Our blue-eyed heart-throb was growing up, and we couldn't bear it any longer; we had to part away from him. A scratch on his forehead would kill us, we knew. And sometimes, we would not be around, or sometimes even being around would not help. What could we do then?

His growing height was a concern, not a relief! Very soon, he had to be part of a crowd that would parade in the lawns, raise hands, and stare before an unknown vehicle housing an informer.

His parents then sent him to a boarding school in Himachal. I remember his tearful departure as he cast his look towards us when he left; I remember how he collected his toys and put them aside for his siblings to play with. Our only joy was gone . . . . He had given us smile amidst tears; he had elevated our mood, given us a reason to live. But we all wanted him to live and to succeed. So, we sent him to survive and to succeed!

He was uneasy there in the boarding school, especially during first few months. Some kids would taunt him, 'You, militant'. Imagine the impact it had on a young boy's psyche. He would remember us and our agony. He would be worried about us and would write emotional pieces for us, expressing his love and his concern for us.

Here was a boy like many other Kashmiri boys, carrying an imprint of the beautiful place where he was born, carrying with him all the wounds that had torn apart his homeland, trying to build up a life of his own—in a place not really his own.

Chapter-3

Lulls

MD and All That

I was keen at specialisation—though not in medicine; it was hectic no doubt but a highly saturated branch. There was a huge pool of doctors waiting to be adjusted in medicine. Postgraduate entrance examination was not a regular feature. I had appeared in the entrance examination for post-graduation during my internship, and it was nearly 2 years and we were still waiting for the results. The hospital and college were suffering as postgraduates formed a very effective 'workforce' and their absence was felt in each postgraduate department. Five batches were waiting for the results which were long overdue. We would be surprised that not far away from our home, in Chandigarh and Delhi, entrance examinations for post-graduation were held 6 monthly and results were declared the very same afternoon. Here we all were losing time and no one was concerned.

Many bright students left Kashmir, tired of the inertia and extremely callous attitude of the authorities. They were justified in moving out to places where their talent was respected. So many doctors went away just to save their time and to hone their skills. But some were just waiting for MBBS to be over and were preparing to move out much earlier—those were the focused men and women, ready to fly!

Finally after waiting for nearly 2 years, our post-graduation entrance examination results were out. Many students who appeared in the list had already left Kashmir. I opted for pathology, a subject about which I had little knowledge, but I knew well that I would grow there and there would be no dearth of a job for me. To my distress, I was allotted a seat in Government Medical College, Jammu. I was quite close to my family, and the thought of going to Jammu disturbed me. I didn't know how it would be there and how I would be received there.

Love in Jammu

But anyhow, I couldn't miss the opportunity of going to Jammu. Jammu, the winter capital of Jammu and Kashmir State, had come into limelight after the eruption of militancy in Kashmir. Many Pandits sought asylum there and lived in one-room flats and ragged tents there. Dogras inhabited Jammu, which was a peaceful city and an entry point into Kashmir. The city was known for its hot summers and cold dry winters.

Not knowing how the journey would turn out to be, I left for Jammu to pursue post-graduation in pathology. My sister had talked to someone who would pick me up from the airport, accompany me to the college for admission formalities, and find a suitable accommodation for me till I could get hostel accommodation. The Jammu airport was smaller and less tense than the Srinagar airport, where the women in security would do a painful massage of your entire body and laugh out on finding all facts about you—the facts you would always conceal! And those men meant for searching your purses and wallets would carefully look at every chit and bit inside them. But in Jammu you could move, turn your eyes, gaze at anything, and you would see smiling faces here and there. And there was air there, which though hot and humid in the month of June tasted pleasant. I took a deep breath in the airport itself and gulped more and more of it. How soothing was the air of 'freedom'!

When I stepped out of the airport, I saw an old man waving at me. I smiled at him, and he called out my name. I was surprised; he had recognised me without having ever seen me. 'Adab,' he said, folding his hands.

'Adab, Mahra.' I returned his greeting with the words I had not used for years. The old man, who had fragile bones, a sunken face, and sticky white hair, took hold of my luggage. I resisted, but he pulled it away towards himself. There was a car waiting and we both got into it. The old man introduced himself as Koul Sahib.

I had not seen Jammu for ages; it had transformed so much. There were flyovers, new buildings, malls, and business establishments—visible everywhere in the city. The city looked happy and prosperous. At least there was a part of the state which was happy and thriving.

I loved looking at the kids sprinkling muddy water on each other, at young boys and girls skipping and hopping in their school uniforms, at men and women decorated and made up for a function, at snake charmers attracting huge crowds in the middle of roads—it was beautiful on the way. I had not seen those small yet subtle happenings of life in Kashmir for nearly a decade.

The car stopped suddenly, and Koul Sahib asked me to get down. He pointed towards a place where I had to stay for a few days till I could get the accommodation in the hostel. It was a huge house, and there were people who would look after me there—a maid, a cook, and a driver. The lonely house belonged to a friend of my sister who had gone 'out of station' for a month or so. My comfort and care was ensured, I was told. I suddenly felt scared in a new city and refused to get down. Koul Sahib sensed my apprehensions and smiled at me, and then we raced on. After a while, we reached a place called a 'rest house'. The place had many rooms, and there were many people from Srinagar there who had come for some work to Jammu. Food and accommodation was good and I should not be scared, I was told. But again I refused to get down . . .

The old man was a bit worried, but then I had my own worries. He asked me again as to where I wanted to go. I thought for a while and said, 'To your home, *Mahra*.'

'But . . . my home is too small,' he said. I convinced him that I would accommodate and that there would be no problem.

Away from the city along vast barren lands, we saw clustered tents and monotonous shabby buildings. This, the old man told me, was the place where migrants lived. Many more areas were inhabited by them. Muthi, he said, was the largest. As I stepped out of the car, women walking along those crude roads stopped to have a second look at me. They were amazed, I am sure, to see an *abaya*-clad girl walking with an old Pandit.

We stepped inside a two-room flat; the old man introduced me to his wife and his two daughters. The woman hugged me tight and kissed my forehead. Seeing her face brighten, I knew I was not an unwanted guest. I smiled at the young women—one I was told was married in Pune and had come for some time to her parents' home. The other young woman was dark and obese and had a depressive look, but she greeted me with warmth. A little doll peeped again and again from behind her grandmother's sari . . . . She was named Vidushi. I called her name, and she raced towards me—I kissed her lovely face. She was Koul Sahib's granddaughter.

It was a small place indeed. There was one small room which was used by the old man and his wife and another one by the daughters and granddaughter. The room used by the old couple was divided into two by an old sheet tied to a nylon rope and held tightly by a hook on the wall. On one side was a bed and on the other some plastic chairs and a small multipurpose table. There were a few *almirahs* there, which squeezed the already squeezing space.

The other room too was congested and crowded. There were two beds aligned together, many books, some *almirahs*, and a few toys. For the burden it bore, the room looked neat . . . . I complimented the family for the neat arrangement, and they showed me their rusted trunks and bags—all the treasures they had under those neat-looking beds.

I came to know that there would be a partition in the room when Koul Sahib's son and daughter-in-law would come on weekends from their job in Udhampur. As it was hot, they had removed the partition to put it back without fail on Saturdays—the day when the couple arrived. Monday mornings, they would again use the entire room.

I felt a little guilty for making the family uncomfortable, but I loved them all. They served me a strong cup of Lipton tea. I sat for a while, then asked for a rug to offer *Namaz*. They gave me a clean cloth for it and showed me the direction of Qibla.

While chatting with those lovely women about the day-to-day happenings in Jammu, Koul Sahib introduced me to a young boy; the boy was a domestic help for a Muslim family from Poonch who resided in a nearby flat. The boy was carrying a slaughtered chicken in his hand. 'This Halal chicken is for you,' Koul Sahib said. I was moved beyond words. How much care and concern the family had for me!

I had a lovely dinner—Koul Sahib's wife ensured that chicken was prepared without *yanga* (a spice added by Pandits and not Muslims), roasted well with onions and green chillies. I loved it—every bit of it.

And then as it was time to sleep, those lovely women and that little girl squeezed themselves to make a room for me. They slept on one bed and left one whole bed for me. A few horrifying mosquitoes danced into the concaves of my ears, but I wrapped myself in sheets, over my head, and closed my eyes to merge myself in the peaceful stillness of my first night at Jammu.

I woke up early the next morning to find a mosquito mesh spread over me and little Vidushi struggling to roll over on to my side of the bed. I got up, took the little one in my arms, and put her in the warmth of my own place. The two women were in deep sleep!

I went to the bathroom, made *wudu*, and offered my *Fajr* prayers. In the next room, the old man and his wife were already awake, chanting mantras in a small *puja* room created in a corner of their kitchen. While still on my prayer mat, I received a lovely cup of Kashmiri *kehwa* seasoned with saffron and almonds. After a while, a heavy breakfast was served, and off I went with Koul Sahib to Government Medical College, Jammu.

The Government Medical College in Jammu was a huge complex, and we went to the administration block to complete the admission formalities. Everyone in the administration block seemed to know Koul Sahib. He used to work as an officer with J&K Government and had retired long back. After the formalities were over, I applied for hostel accommodation but the college hostel was overcrowded. There was a lot of influx from Rajouri, Poonch, Doda, Ladakh, and many Kashmiri Pandit girls whose families had migrated to other cities had also opted for hostel accommodation. I was supposed to wait till a slot was free, I was told. That would mean another night or many more nights at Koul Sahib's house—another trouble for them . . .

I went back to Muthi. At Koul Sahib's house, his wife and daughters received me with great warmth, and I was happy to see them . . . again.

As it was suffocating inside, Koul Sahib's younger daughter asked me to come with her up on to the terrace. I happily went up with her, with Vidushi holding my little finger. The depressed, obese young woman talked about the area, her community, her simple parents, and herself. She was quite friendly with me. Her parents were worried for her, as she was not getting a proper match. She was not good looking and she was unemployed, she told me. With a scattered community, Pandit boys liked outgoing and smart girls, and for her, there was no hope. There was tough competition from girls of other communities too. I comforted her, reassuring her that all would go well for her.

I had to stay with the family for nearly a week. Koul Sahib's daughter would take me around every day after I would come from the hospital. People would notice and stare at me—but never say a word to me or to my companion. I would stare at all those faces—pale and gloomy—and try fitting them somewhere in the closets of my memory. Some faces would seem too familiar and some too plain and expressionless. The children playing in the vast space would not speak the language their fathers had spoken. The children were uncomfortable with the Kashmiri language, and parents too wouldn't care—my friend told.

For all the days in Koul Sahib's tiny home, I was treated like a VIP. I however avoided going into their kitchen. I knew Muslims had a restricted entry into the *wuza* of Pandits, but my lovely hosts never restricted me from going anywhere I wanted to.

I remembered all those teachers, those friends, and all those Pandits whom I had known since my childhood. I bothered Koul Sahib with names of almost everyone I remembered. Did he know where Handoo Sahib lived? Did he know where Sapru Sahib lived? Did he know where Dhar Sahib lived? He told me whatever little he knew about a few of them and about how he had lost track of a sizeable population—since their migration. Migration had made them selfish too, no one told the truth about himself and no one spoke to the other person about his plans, Koul Sahib said. He knew the whereabouts of a few close relatives and a few Pandits who lived close by in Muthi. When I asked him about Vishwa Bharti and its staff, I was told that Vishwa Bharti had a wing in Jammu too. I was keen to know where, but he kindly advised me not to think about going there.

The family weighed each word of their conversation. They never talked about anything that would displease me, never talked about their exodus from Kashmir, and never mentioned a word whether they were forced or not. But they talked about their past, their wholesome lives, and regrettably about their huge houses . . . their house—a house of thirteen rooms, an attic, and a lawn which was left behind when they came to Jammu and which was later sold to a Muslim neighbour. They talked about their maladjustment with the climate and people of Jammu. They felt like strangers in Jammu. There were many who hated the sight of them in Jammu. There were many who wanted them out of Jammu and so many who held them responsible for all the ills of their society and their economic woes; rising prices, unemployment, and social ills—all were attributed to their presence. But yes, they were clear they did not want to return to Kashmir to live there again; their kids were happily adjusting to the new life, I was told. Koul Sahib told me that he had enough to make him live a comfortable life and that he hated to line up for 'relief', but he continued to do so because he never wanted his men to think that he was different!

Koul Sahib introduced me to some of his relatives and friends in Jammu as a 'daughter from Kashmir'.

Well, a day more and Koul Sahib's son and daughter-in-law would come for a weekend holiday and there would be a greater discomfort for the family. I was on tenterhooks to leave, as my hosts I thought had enough of me. I asked Koul Sahib to accompany me to the hostel warden's office so that we could plead with him for my adjustment there. Surprisingly, the warden turned out to be an old friend of Koul Sahib. Without any further waiting, the warden asked me to shift to the college hostel.

I collected my luggage from the Koul Sahib's home and thanked the family, and as I was about to leave, I saw little Vidushi on the cloth I used as a prayer mat—in *Ruku* and *Sajood*. Without disturbing the little kid, I left. Huge tears formed in my eyes as I left with a promise to be back soon.

When I left, there were so many questions vibrating in my mind. How was it that I had entered the house of a Kashmir Pandit in the first instance, even when I had never seen or known him? Why did the family care so much for me, giving me all the comfort and putting themselves through all the trouble? Did they have no grudge against me, no complaint against me? Koul Sahib and his family had given me lovely memories to be cherished . . .

The hostel was a hub where we all came from mixed backgrounds: Pandits, locals, girls from Rajouri and Poonch, and all those 'non-locals' who held the state subject of Jammu and Kashmir. They were all lovely girls, full of life trying to do what we had done 10 years back—trying to learn, to know, and importantly to pass exams. There were some girls who did not mix up at all. They would just mind their own business; those were the ones who were VIPs—daughters of VIPs studying in Jammu for security reasons. Aloof and withdrawn, those girls would receive special attention—anywhere.

Meanwhile, I had to go to Chandigarh for an exam, and I met Koul Sahib there. He took me to a relative's house in Mohali. I had never heard of the place before. The family lived in a posh locality there .The woman there greeted me when Koul Sahib introduced me as 'a daughter from Kashmir'. The family seemed affluent; the woman was a widow whose son was working in a multinational company and had married a non-Kashmiri. Both the little kids of the couple did not speak Kashmiri. The Pandit family seemed warm and happy till we saw one unwanted family member who was sick, bloated, and anxious. Koul Sahib hugged him on his bed and wanted to know more about him. Never married, he was the brother-in-law of Koul Sahib's relative, who had migrated with them and now was a liability on them. When Koul Sahib told him that I was a doctor, he showed his entire prescription list to me. His liver had failed and he was counting his last days. He was missing Kashmir—his own Kashmir—and was waiting for the day when he would be there. The others in the family were not happy to have him, and he was feeling their discomfort. When I was about to leave, he requested me to take him along to Kashmir, where he would sit in his shop and chat with his Muslim friends. They would look after him, he told me. I knew I couldn't do it. He had to be where he was. I knew he could never make it there because he was very sick and weak. Also, he was dependent on a family which was busy, immersed in a metropolitan lifestyle. There was no room for a sick man's emotions in the practical world in which they were living. Our hosts treated us well. Before we left, Koul Sahib cried and so did the lady. I saw Koul Sahib covering his half open mouth to control the sound of his sobs. As the woman bade us goodbye, she asked Koul Sahib if they would ever meet again. 'Perhaps not,' Koul Sahib said. On the way back to Chandigarh, Koul Sahib didn't say a word. Sorry! I had no consolation to offer and I went my own way.

I felt sorry for this generation of Kashmiri Pandits. They were intimately wound around the nature, beauty, and charm of Kashmir, wound around its language, culture, prose, and poetry. Great works from Kashmir were translated by them. It must be painful for them to stay away from Kashmir. And circumstances had separated them from each other too.

The pathology department of Government Medical College, Jammu, was up many, many stairs, located on the fifth floor—a huge department with many consultants, demonstrators, and many postgraduate students. There were a few Kashmiri Pandits and a few Muslims from Rajouri and Poonch; the rest were locals.

They all looked at me with awe the first day, but we all became friendly as the days passed by. The department was well equipped and teaching was good. In the department, I would hear frequent arguments and witness 'word battles' between the people belonging to various communities. Arguments aside, they lived together in harmony, and thankfully, all were kind towards me.

I interacted with people of all communities in the hostel and college. Most were kind, but some Pandits were rude; they showed apparent hatred towards us. They held us responsible for all they had gone through. They called Kashmiri Muslims militants, called us anti-national, and wanted us out of Jammu, but who would argue with them in an alien land and why? But it was my wish that they would not celebrate our debacle or call our suffering as 'no suffering'. Was I secure when they moved out in search of their own security? Wasn't I too insecure? Wasn't my family also susceptible? When they were being chased, hadn't I already been mauled? If their moon had blood clots, was there any moon over our skies? Hadn't a sword instead replaced our moon, hanging over us, having chopped so many of us and ready to chop many more . . .

Jammu was too hot; the heat was unbearable for someone like me who had lived the entire lifetime in the cool valley. I wanted to go back. There was only one way, and that was applying for a slot in GMC Srinagar.

Many students had been adjusted in different corners of the world—long before the results of post-graduation entrance were out. The ones who left—created slots for readjustment of those who did not get the slot of their choice in the first counselling. And the vacancies thus created were to be filled by those who followed in the merit list. But the primary list was out after years, we did not expect the supplementary list to be out soon. I too applied for a 'change'. . All those students who desired to pursue post-graduation in a different subject from what was allotted to them would throng the office of the competent authority. I went many times to the office to plead for change but encountered indifferent officials. They never thought about us, never thought that we were losing time; instead, they would rebuke us sometimes and convince us at other times that the supplementary list would be out soon. We had thought Jammu would be different, but that indifference and laziness had gripped the entire state administration, and Jammu was no exception. No one had the time and patience to listen to us, leave alone to think about us. We lost a good 6 months or more till we were readjusted. I got a slot in Srinagar—for some time in Pharmacology and finally in Pathology.

Life as a Postgraduate

When I left Government Medical College, Srinagar, as a graduate, I thought it was sinking, but when I joined it as a postgraduate, it had already sunk. It was pathetically understaffed. One or two people in Anatomy, one man in Biochemistry, a lady in Forensic Medicine, and a couple of teachers in Pharmacology were running the entire show. The postgraduate turnover was poor because of the non-availability of guides; there was sadism on the part of the guides too, who kept the postgraduates hanging on for years together without signing their thesis or conducting their exams. I remember how a few gentlemen appeared in their MD exams after 7-10 years of admission. How depressive it was for us the newcomers!

Life was tough as a postgraduate. Our senior postgraduates seemed to be a terrified lot. They sat like KG students, moved with permission, and walked quietly in the corridors, preferably on the sides; a few females never wore sandals that made noise. It had been precedent there; we were told to be extra obedient and extra careful. Guides and heads should never be displeased.

Had I not been shuttled here and there for no fault of mine, I would have left the department. The fear and scare was intolerable. There was enough of it already outside. My heart which was already under pressure would not bear more of fear. But God was kind. My senior postgraduates were wise and kind. They gave me lessons on how I should behave in the department. They taught me the do's and don'ts of survival. And they taught me the basics of the subject. One senior postgraduate, Dr Nazir Ahmad Lone, a lovely human being, a practicing psychiatrist, a philosopher, a dramatist, and a writer protected me and another colleague of mine from all the noises and outbursts which would routinely fall on a postgraduate there.

Was being a postgraduate a crime? A postgraduate was a victim of frustration manifested by those small people who had seen a bigger and a happier world before and were terrified by the tightness of the shrunken space available to them now . . . . The targets for the frustrated mindset were still smaller people who didn't know what to do to please their 'bosses'. A colleague of ours before going into the room of his boss would always look at his dangling arms and hands and ask each one of us, 'Where do I keep my hands when I go inside—inside my pockets, at the back, in front, or on the sides'? He would tell us how he felt his hands were vestigial when a scrutinising boss would stare at him from top to bottom.

I was lucky. With the support of my other colleagues; and my excellent guide, Dr A.R. Khan, I survived as a postgraduate in the department of pathology Government Medical College. That was an achievement.

But events of concern were happening in Government Medical College—in general and in Pathology department in particular. The senior professors were retiring and no new recruitments were taking place. If at all someone was recruited, he was from Jammu. Those lucky ones citing security reasons would get themselves transferred within days—along with posts, depleting the already depleted department. Seventeen such cases happened when I was pursuing my post-graduation—Pathology lost five new consultants to the unfair arrangement!

The pathology department had a history about which we were unaware. But with time we came to know that post-graduation programme which was a decades' old programme in the department started by stalwarts and affiliated to the University of Kashmir was not recognised by MCI; there was no record even of permission from MCI for starting the course. No action had been initiated over the decades to get the programme recognised by the MCI. It bothered us, the new entrants, as we were not aware of this hard fact about our department when we had applied for post graduation there. Had it been made clear in the notification itself, we would probably not have applied for the course. But all those who were at the helm were interested just in running the college and never cared about the fate of the postgraduates it produced.

Pathology was interesting—it connected beautifully with all the clinical subjects. I enjoyed the challenge that each slide would throw before me, and it amazed me that everything which was seemingly abstract could be verified under a microscope. The department had competent pathologists.

But sadly, as the senior professors were getting superannuated, there were just two faculty members left in the department—one permanent and one adhoc. Those two shuttled between theory classes and practicals, between third year and fourth year, and between terminals and quizzes. Rest of the work was carried out by the demonstrators who were just MBBS graduates and by postgraduates like me. Those poor fellows were getting stretched beyond their capabilities when they were asked to teach MBBS students, who were brighter and smarter than them. We as postgraduates also had a lot to learn from them.

As I was doing my post-graduation in pathology, I like my other friends was assigned with something that would scare me—teaching medical students. As I had to teach a class of 100 or 200 (sometimes two classes combined), I would feel small. I knew a bigger authority was required to teach that crop of intelligent beings. Brilliant boys and diligent girls bursting with talent and bubbling with energy definitely deserved better teachers. But we were the ones they had to be content with. We would tremble when we would stand on the same spots where some great teachers of great times had stood.

Guiding students in practical classes was less fun. We would ourselves struggle with the eyepieces of microscopes to try and make them understand the complex architecture that would baffle ourselves too, but we were smart enough not to show our own discomfort with the slides and the microscope to the students.

As the post-graduation was getting done, I knew it would be hard to get adjusted without the degree being recognised by MCI. With courage, we were pursuing the degree in the hope that someday it would get recognised. A 50-year-old institution was in shambles. MBBS was all about postponements, taking 8 years to complete and post-graduation was recognised in just five departments . . . . The rest of the degrees that were awarded were unrecognised.

Meanwhile, for me marriage to a surgeon was on the cards, and perhaps it was a stress buster to overcome the depression of pathology. But leaving the warm environs of Downtown and bidding Kohimaran farewell was disturbing. The place where I went after marriage was different from the place where I was born. In my in-laws' place, people kept to themselves and neighbours were strangers. Huge houses were occupied by a few inhabitants. People met each other at weddings and mourning. Males sometimes would meet each other at crackdowns. The streets were usually empty. The tiny lanes and by-lanes were made tinier by the encroachments. No kids would be seen outside; there was more fear as bunkers could be seen at every intersection.

Back After a Decade

Being there next to the examiners and nodding our heads in affirmative or negative when the students would answer right or wrong made us feel all important in front of the students. We would try to help all those we could.

It was a 'send up examination', and I was entrusted with the viva of a batch of students who had to appear for a supplementary examination. I saw a boy, rather a man with a haggard look, an admixed black and white beard, and a swollen one side of face. I enquired from him if he also was to appear in the examination. 'Yes, madam,' he said in a soft tone. A fellow colleague of mine asked him as to which batch he belonged. He hesitated for a moment and said, 'I have done my first MBBS long back.'

I could trace him as a student somewhere near our batch . . . . He had done his MBBS first professional almost 10 years back.

Where was he all these years? That was a question we could not ask him.

When I went home and described the guy to my husband, he could identify the guy as his classmate; he told me the entire story of this man. An intelligent boy from a middle-class family, selected for MBBS on merit, he was doing well till one day he left his home and went for arms training. The boy was lost . . . and the other class fellows did not know where the boy was. Someone informed the class one day that he had received a bullet on his cheek. No one knew how the boy was and where he was; the college forgot about the boy, and he was not seen for years. Most students did not want to know more about the boy . . . . to avoid trouble.

What was his state now and what had happened to him all these years we don't know. How he had come to become a doctor yet again—we don't know. Had he left all that or was he still with the same engagements? Was he married or not? While accompanying the examiner for the final practical examination, I met that man again. Seeing his tense face, I comforted him. I mentioned my husband's name to him, asking him if he knew him. 'He knows me, madam,' the man said.

I felt sorry for the man who had lost a good decade of his life . . . . He visualised something that could not be accomplished. His career was marred; physically he was deformed and mentally I don't know what. His batch mates were done with their post-graduation and postdoctoral; they had married and had children. I pleaded with the examiner to be soft with the man. I don't know whether it was right or wrong on my part to do so . . . . I eventually came to know . . . that the guy had cleared second Professional MBBS. It would take him a few more years to clear MBBS. He had to join pre-final with a fresh batch—a batch 10 years junior to his original batch. And every time that 10-year gap would haunt him!

Shameful Fudging

In March 2000, armed men entered the village of Chattisinghpura, lined up local Sikh residents of the village, and opened fire. Thirty-six people were killed. The killings coincided with the visit of US President Bill Clinton to India. Five days later, on 25 March, the security forces killed five men in Pathribal village of Anantnag district, claiming that the militants were Pakistani and belonged to *Lashkar-e-Toiba*. Official reports claimed that the security forces had, after gunfight, blown up the hut where the men were hiding and retrieved five bodies that had been charred beyond recognition. The bodies were buried without any post-mortem examination. Two Pakistani citizens were arrested and paraded in front of the world media as the perpetrators of the massacre.

Surprisingly, in this so-called encounter, no security personnel were injured. The local villagers began to protest, claiming that ordinary civilians were killed in a fake encounter and not foreign militants. Five men in the neighbouring villages who had disappeared between 21 and 24 March 2000 were believed to have been abducted and killed by the security personnel and later on projected to the world as Pakistani militants who were responsible for the Chattisinghpura massacre. The protests and allegations were ignored, and the media as usual pointed fingers towards Pakistan; however, in these very protests eight men were killed. In order to establish the truth about the encounter and to pacify the people, an exhumation of the bodies was ordered. The exhumed bodies charred and deformed beyond recognition were identified by the relatives of the missing people as their own. DNA samples were collected from the bodies and from eight relatives and sent in April 2000 to the Centre for DNA Fingerprinting and Diagnostics, Hyderabad, an autonomous institute under the Department of Science and Technology. In its worst and most crude cover-up, DNA samples were fudged before they were sent to the forensic laboratory in Hyderabad; to ensure the tests would prove negative, officials apparently tampered with the relatives' samples. However, they did not realise that the DNA test would also be able to expose their attempts at a cover-up. While the report said the samples of the alleged terrorists did not match with the persons who claimed the deceased were their relatives, it also conclusively pointed towards a cover-up operation.

While DNA samples purported to have been collected from the relatives did not match with the DNA isolated from the exhumed bodies, in three cases, the samples of women relatives were found to have come from men, something that is said to have come as a shock to the forensic scientists. The cover-up strongly suggested the switching of DNA samples was a desperate attempt to disprove the claims of the relatives that the slain men were their relatives and had nothing to do with the Chattisinghpura massacre. The report made another interesting observation; one of the blood samples contained the DNA of two individuals, the blood that was supposed to be from the sister of one of the persons who was exhumed. The report gave rise to the doubts whether any of the samples of the relatives sent by the authorities for DNA testing to Hyderabad belonged to the relatives at all. [5, 6, 7, 8] It was probably the first time that an Indian reporter like Pankaj Mishra played a role in unearthing truth.

The Department of Forensic Medicine, GMC, Srinagar, came into limelight after this incident as all its faculty members including the Head of the department were suspended. The college already suffering from chaos and dearth of faculty crumbled further. No interim arrangement was made to address the issue of dearth of faculty. The doctors were blamed for fudging the DNA samples. Doctors in Kashmir always become soft targets when such investigations are under way. In a state where such episodes are so common, there should have been a well-equipped forensic department and well-trained faculty to tackle all medico-legal cases in an effective manner, but the department had dearth of faculty and a primitive infrastructure. I still don't understand how a single member was able to handle the department with all its hectic teaching. Suspension didn't last long, and finally there was a respite! It was interesting to note that before anyone could be booked for any crime, doctors were the first to be suspended. In other investigations involving allegations of rape or murder, doctors were the ones who were pressurised or punished. Doctors working in peripheries were the ones most vulnerable. They would face the wrath of the crowd, anger of the police, and punishment of authorities also. No one would think that doctors working in peripheries were no forensic experts who could divulge deeper truths about medico-legal cases presented to them.

Though Sikhs and people from other communities, i.e. Christians, did not leave Kashmir with the onset of turmoil, incidents like the Chattisinghpura massacre made them panic and put the cord of trust between Muslims and other communities under tension. However, 12 years after the massacre, the investigators told the Supreme Court of India that the army personnel who killed five people in Pathribal were cold-blooded murders and the accused officials deserved to be meted out exemplary punishment.

Pandit Doctors and De-recognition

Dr Sushil Razdan, a neurologist of high academic value, served at SKIMS as its pioneer. Known for his efficiency and his calm nature, he was the one who won the hearts of Kashmiris. A brilliant researcher, he conducted an epidemiological study on stroke in Kashmir. He resigned from SKIMS but continued to work in his private clinic at Srinagar. Once Pandits left Kashmir, he too left, but Kashmiri patients even in that uncertainty would go all the way to Jammu and continue to throng his clinic there. Son of a dedicated teacher who had taught science to thousands of Kashmiris, Dr Sushil lived true to his lineage.

Some prominent Pandit doctors did not leave Kashmir. There was a renowned chest physician Dr S.N. Dhar, who treated patients in his own clinic at Rajbagh. He too was abducted for weeks together and rolled from one village to another. He was let off eventually, but he continued to live in Kashmir and serve its patients. Another stalwart in surgery, Dr Brij Mohan Bhan, who headed the Department of Surgery at GMC, Srinagar, for a long time also continued to live in Kashmir even after his retirement. He too would see patients in his own clinic at Karan Nagar. Dr Kakroo a consultant in Microbiology at SKIMS, too dared to stay back. God knows what kept them glued to their motherland, while their brethren left. They must have felt insecure, I am sure, but they braved it all and stayed on. Some doctors from Jammu who had their clinics in Srinagar also did not leave Kashmir and continued to serve in Kashmir.

These doctors did exemplary work with a great mission, but there were no acknowledgements and no appreciations . . . for the doctors who lit the candle of hope amidst darkness. Elsewhere, these doctors would have become national heroes.

There was a Pandit consultant in our department at GMC Srinagar who stayed back when other Pandits in the department left for Jammu. Dr M.L. Bhat was unlike anyone—bold and enterprising. When his seniors retired, he took over the reins of the department. It bothered him that postgraduates from the department did not possess a recognised degree. He set out to correct the wrongs of the decades. In spite of a deficient staff and a poor infrastructure, he decided to gamble and go for an MCI (Medical council of India) inspection of the department— MCI inspection of a department with no teeth. All were surprised; de-recognition would be definite and a limping PG going on in the department would be stopped altogether. And that was what actually happened. The MCI inspector, going by the rules and norms, looked at the status of faculty and the available infrastructure and did not consider recognition of the department, stopping even the entry of postgraduates into the department till the prerequisites laid down by MCI were fulfilled. The unrecognised tag was humiliating; for all of us. All those who possessed a recognised degree made fun of us and our degrees. When the pathology department of Government Medical College, Srinagar, was not recognised by MCI, it was thought by some to be a game plan of a Pandit to stop the course altogether. But we trusted his sincerity. He tried again for the recognition in next 2 years with the same results, and MCI put it strongly in its report to stop further admissions. With such a directive from MCI, there was no hope left. Why would anyone in Delhi or Jammu and Kashmir bother whether a particular department of a medical college in Srinagar was recognised by MCI or not? Were there no other important issues to be addressed?

With all fresh recruits running away to Jammu for safety and security, no increase in faculty strength was expected. All doors we knew were knocked at. After all, it was a matter of justice. Someone had to do something. MCI could have given us a waiver, given us some relaxation, as the college was functioning in an area that was turmoil hit.

With a desire to help ourselves and the department in some way, we sought an appointment with a high-profile person on one sunny day. Four or five of us with our patron, the Head of the department, sat underneath the shade of a chinar and waited for the 'great man' to talk to us. There were people in groups of 10-20 waiting for their own turn to talk to the big man.

After a while, the big man arrived with his escorts and policemen. He went straight to a chair and sat on it, listening attentively to a 'delegation' from a village. He listened to all they said and responded to each query they raised. He read their leaflet, signed it, passed on the instructions, shook hands with each one of them, and hugged their chief. He went to another group; repeating the same process there, he went on to meet the third and the fourth group. We had been waiting for a long time for our turn to be heard.

He actually ignored us and started walking towards the exit till some officer reminded him that a delegation of doctors from Government Medical College, Srinagar, had come to see him. He looked at us with disgust, a frown on his entire face, and asked, 'What do you want?' He did not sit to listen to anything we had to say, leave aside giving the attention he gave to other groups. Somehow from what we could hurriedly pass on to him, he could gather that we wanted some concession at MCI for the recognition of our degrees. 'What concession?' he shouted. 'How will I ask concession for everyone, for every department of Jammu and Kashmir? Work for yourself to sort out your problem. Entire state cannot thrive on concessions,' he added. We were silenced. The high-profile man, who could have made a difference to the cause of Government Medical College, bluntly refused us. We wondered why those delegates from villages got so much attention and not us.

One of the secretaries working in his office remarked, 'Because they vote and you, the urban white-collared fellows, do not.' And we woke up to a new reality that sunny day!

Sad and huffing, I came back home. My mother, a wise woman with experience on her side, told me not to be worried. The people with power never treated ordinary people kindly, she consoled me. She remembered her own time; she told me the experience of her mother, when she went to a person of power in her time because her husband had died, leaving behind a large support less family. Her mother was chased away by a dog because the person in power wanted to scare her away, as the last word of her late husband's name, surname *Moulvi*, on the application form put before the man with 'power', irritated him. How that family struggled, pension less and head less for decades, on the earnings of that great lady (my grandmother) who would teach Koran to the children of neighbourhood—is another story.

The Shattered Dream of Dr Guru

There was a college in our state, whose conceiver was no more. The trust that created it was itself in distress—no staff, no facilities, and poor students suffering without a recognised MBBS degree. Known to most as Jhelum Valley College of Medical Sciences (JVC), it was the first private medical college of the state and Dr Guru was the brain behind the college. The college started its admission in first professional MBBS, the year we were admitted to GMC Srinagar. Many girls and boys whose parents could afford the capitation fees were admitted. The college was started in a barrack-like structure—with hardly any teachers. I remember how the teachers from our college used to be taken in special vehicles to teach the students of JVC. We would be sad and actually protested against this so-called 'injustice'. They should have recruited the faculty first before starting a college, we would always say.

Somehow, a few batches managed with difficulty to do MBBS—a degree unrecognised by the Medical Council of India. I remember the plight of those students when they would go pleading from one office to another. In a turmoil-ridden vale, who would look at their plight?

It was a great idea to start a private medical college in a state crazy about medical profession. But it should have been well conceived and well planned. Those poor students, it seemed, had committed a professional suicide. No career ahead and a loss of money! Many of my friends whom I had known in school and college left the profession and opted for other professions. A pass-out from this college went to America and after her degree from JVC was not recognised there; she left her profession to become a teacher in a school there. Loss of good 5 years of her lifetime! Another boy known to me, after doing MBBS from JVC, did his MBBS yet again from a private college in Bengaluru. The boy perhaps loved the profession; that is why he paid twice for a degree that he got after spending more than a decade pursuing it. Other students were made to beg from door to door for a fault that was not theirs-

Finally many years later, something good came about; the Government looking at the plight of so many students and unrecognised doctors and seeing the unwillingness of MCI to grant recognition to JVC conceived a merger with the Sher-i-Kashmir Institute of Medical Sciences, and JVC came up on the shore. It was a milestone for JVC and a relief for its pass outs.

Sinking and rising SKIMS

Sher-i-Kashmir Institute of Medical Sciences could not maintain its glory. The infamous 'take away group' squeezed life out of SKIMS; they sucked its jugulars and punished the performers. Some bright ones were compelled to leave. Machines became defunct and men behind the machines disappeared. Historical mistakes were committed by the administration at SKIMS to accommodate 'the blue-eyed boys'. Out-of-turn promotions and out-of-way favours became the norm at SKIMS. Where post-graduation was a requirement, MBBS was considered; where a postdoctoral degree was a requirement, MD was considered sufficient. The good lot was dropped. The rules and regulations were bent so much that no trace was left of them. So many good doctors left SKIMS at that point-manoeuvring and manipulations harmed SKIMS more than militancy did.

One of my dear friends admitted for MD on her own merit was threatened that she would be abducted if she did not resign from her slot so that the one next in the list could be accommodated. To save her life, the poor girl did as was asked—and the guy next in the list joined the MD course. No one listened to her plea; she too asked for migration and she too asked for security. But nothing was granted to her. She left her MD, and the oppressor at gunpoint took her PG slot. The hard-working girl tried yet again and got yet again into MD into a different discipline, which after 3 years of her hard work was labelled as invalid. She wasted three precious years of her academic life due to the politics and the dread that had enveloped SKIMS. Will she ever forgive those who massacred her ambitions?

There was some remarkable work done though by many doctors at SKIMS in spite of the odds. Commendable work was done by Dr M.S. Khuroo; the work he did in gastroenterology is possibly the best from India—till date. He worked tirelessly in epidemic-affected areas of Kashmir to find a cause of jaundice in pregnant women. His observations led to the discovery of Hepatitis E virus—the causative virus for jaundice that had escaped the attention and sight of many keen researchers in the East and West. His diagnosis and novel treatment of Hydatidosis liver led to the invention of a novel technique which could cure Hydatidosis liver. His work on Ascariasis and his novel observations about this parasite ubiquitously present in Kashmiris'surprised public health professionals, parasitologists, gasteroenterologists and radiologists of the world. This researcher became the Director of SKIMS eventually but could not take up the pressure and left for a foreign country, which was safer and where he was valued as a researcher. He left behind a great department. His junior colleagues too did a wonderful job.

A great clinician at SKIMS, namely, Dr Abdul Hamid Zargar, dived deep into an ocean of diseases to chase the base of a huge mass of preventable endocrinological diseases. With his clinical acumen, he looked differently at our so-called 'morons'. He analysed the swollen necks in our urban and rural population and suggested the cause. He studied 'stature' and 'bones' in our young ones. He applied his mind and studied 'depressed and weak women' treated wrongly for their depression which was unresponsive to treatment. He called it 'Sheehan's syndrome' and treated them to bring their life back to them. He found fire amidst a 'great fire'—a fire the flames of which could be doused. Kashmiris were obsessed with a 'salt' to which they were emotionally bonded. They were detached from it by this great man who advocated 'iodised salt' to a population suffering inherently from its deficiency. With his hard work and efforts, the iodine-deficient salt vanished from our markets and widespread consumption of iodised salt proved a panacea for the patients suffering from these diseases. His mind blowing publications in high impact journals do not have many contenders in the world.

There were others at SKIMS who too were doing their bit quietly and expeditiously; one such gentleman, Prof. Khurshid Iqbal, strived to provide cardiology services to patients who attended SKIMS at par with the best centres of the world. He remained a prototype of an 'ideal doctor' all through his career at SKIMS. He did not bend where others bent, did not compromise where others compromised and did not leave when others left. He remained a reliable cornerstone of SKIMS and still holds a great burden. His gentle manners and subtle temperament are so unusual with doctors nowadays. He was made mute so often and deprived of his due, but his uphill journey towards perfection never really stopped. A great doctor, who could have earned a better name and fame elsewhere. Is he our 'White man in dark'?

Work done in medicine and its allied faculties too was remarkable, surgical branches worked with dynamism and dedication to attend to trauma of all sorts, all organs . . . .

Was that peace?

All were waiting and watching with curiosity the happenings in Kashmir as it remained quieter in 2000 and onwards. There were subtle reminders of something lacking in the lives of Kashmiris, but all seemed quiet. New Delhi thought Kashmir had been won again. The lull was confused with peace. Indian media and magazines began flashing 'Sorry, Kashmir is happy'. Meanwhile the loot continued. Mansions and malls came up with what money, I am not sure. The gardens and parks were filled up; people started knowing Gulmarg and Pahalgam yet again. The last remnants of militancy were getting wiped out. But bunkers continued to be there and the military and paramilitary forces continued to guard us. Elections attracted some attention—in villages. Was it peace or the beginning of it? Were people tired of turmoil, rather sick of it? The popular mood was against guns; the organisations which had started guns were talking peace. But the opportunities remained the same—rather diminished. A state that was feeding lakhs of its employees without doing any work was feeling the pinch of it on the exchequer. Militancy-related expenditure too had dried up the state treasury. A slab on new recruitments with no private sector and thousands of youngsters without jobs created a crisis in the state. In villages, the people were fooled yet again—to vote for *Bijli, Sadak,* and *Pani,* and special whispers of *nokri* were also made into their ears. A Government job in Kashmir was very attractive. It meant lifelong security . . . for the most—without actually working. Business class too started asked for loan wavers and concessions. People at the helm thought that it was peace. We all understood it was no peace but a deception. But why were the people at the helm waiting for the tears to turn into storm, waiting for the anger to turn into rage? Why didn't they act when there was seemingly calmness all round?

Meanwhile, villages continued to suffer in spite of the enforced calm. I went to my sister-in-law's home in Handwara village and saw on my way the towns of Kashmir that had seen major trauma and borne maximum torture. I saw Sopore, a town ignored for long breathing heavily under siege. I was reminded of the massacres that Sopore had witnessed over the years. I saw Handwara with its occupied orchids and fields. There were unattended piled up apples. No children could be seen near them; because of fear, villagers would usually come in groups to collect them. We were advised by the locals to be back from Handwara before six o'clock because that was when the entry and exit into and from the village would be stopped by the troops. I heard about disappearances, encounters, and killings. I heard about midnight searches and a syndrome called 'midnight knock syndrome'. The villagers accustomed to late night searches by the security forces had developed this syndrome in which they were jumpy and could not sleep without pills.[9] On our way to Srinagar we were searched everywhere even when the words '*Jawan aur awam aman hai muqam*' (army and people—peace is the goal) were written everywhere near the army camps in bold.

There were areas which had mines and posed threat to the life of the villagers. There was a meek cry from the doctors in Kashmir to ban the landmines. 'We call on Asian countries to sign the Ottawa treaty in 1997 to ban the manufacture, use, stockpiling and transfer of anti-personal landmines. If such action is taken we can save lives of innocent people and prevent increasing number of orphans and widows in the subcontinent.'[10] This appeal from a reputed Kashmiri doctor appeared in Lancet. But who listened to him?

Data from Our Hospitals

Disturbing figures were accumulating in our hospitals. With regards to abdominal trauma, it was seen that gunshot wounds accounted for maximum cases of abdominal trauma in the Kashmiri population in the late 1990s (77.76%). Many patients of gunshot wounds in the abdomen (25%) required operative procedures which included removal of whole or part of an organ.[11] The data from the psychiatric hospital was more disturbing; the number of patients getting admitted in the psychiatric hospital had swollen from a few hundred annually in the 1980s to nearly a lakh in the late 1990s. Post-traumatic stress disorder (PTSD) hitherto unknown in Kashmir was observed frequently in patients who had experienced, witnessed, or confronted an event which involved threat to self or others or which involved witnessing death of someone close. The response of these patients was fear, helplessness, and horror. PTSD is a debilitating disorder in which as Dr Mushtaq Margoob well known psychiatrist from the valley who has extensively worked on it says, 'Patients see someone get killed in their presence, some friend, some relative and they get stuck in that moment.' Four hundred and sixty-nine consecutive patients of PTSD were evaluated at the Department of Psychiatry, Government Medical College, Srinagar, and 53% of these patients were females. Even children were also seen to be suffering from PTSD[12, 13]. There was extensive data on depression and other psychiatric ailments which had assumed epidemic proportions in Kashmir[9]

Kashmiri doctors dared to publish their observations in reputed journals, but there was silence from the medical fraternity of India. 'The medical associations of countries where torture is endemic often fail to speak out. In countries like Iraq and El Salvador doctors interested in justice have been prosecuted, whereas in countries like Israel medical associations are silent because they tacitly accept a definition of loyal citizenship which holds that human rights abuses may be necessary in the name of national security.'[14] Was the Indian medical fraternity keeping quiet in the interest of national security?

They Too Didn't Last

The fierce ones who had silenced thousands were rewarded by a nation claiming to be a propagator of peace. They got awards. They sat in legislature as honourable members and took an oath of loyalty 'towards protecting the integrity and sovereignty of a great nation'. They unfurled the flags in impressive ceremonies. They gave speeches too, on Gandhi and his philosophy, and a Gandhian recommended some important ones for 'Rashtriya Awards'.

But then who would tolerate those pampered brats for long? After their job was done, some of them were eliminated easily and some were blown to bits, but their pieces were packed together; they were wrapped in flags, they used to salute. Where were they were buried? I don't know. I know their burial site would be away from the population because their remains too would scare the human beings.

So much had changed in college also. That hefty girl who had spread terror in the college in our younger days, teasing and torturing the students, later married a notorious gunman, and they together spread the dread in the college. I remember how she had walked like a commander, talked like a dictator, and pounced at any easy prey. Her husband would enter any chamber at will, smash any table, or slap anybody. But, one day, we heard that her husband had been killed. When I came back from Jammu, I heard the self-styled commando woman . . . had become the wife of a powerful politician. I still remember how she victimised girls in the college and how she threatened them, asking them to wear a veil. She would wear the veil herself too for some time. But as politician's wife she gave up all. Which face should we trust? Should anyone remind her about her earlier days, seeking liberation of Kashmir? And when that woman proudly cheers in the stands while her husband salutes in a parade, I get confused!

The Arts and Crafts

The arts and crafts were dying their own death as were the artisans and craftsmen. The arts lost their markets; the admirers of Kashmiri crafts dared not to venture into Kashmir. Those who had passion for the art continued with it in spite of the odds, though raw material such as *Tila*—a special thread, and copper sheets were hard to fetch in 'disturbed Kashmir'. The upkeep and promotion of art was not on the Government's priority list. Elderly artisans continued with hiccups, but propagation of 'art' within the families stopped. Angry young boys did not get the environment to develop passion for the 'art' that their fathers and forefathers had. Living in the interiors of Srinagar, these young boys waited for their turn—to be arrested or lined up in queues for a Government job. The sad and sudden death of Kashmiri arts had no mourners!

That *Tila* design on my mother's *pheran* was beautiful. I was keen to have the same *Tila* design on my *pheran* too. I asked her if I could also have it. She recollected having got that design done from a *Tiladooz* at Barbar Shah. I and my mother went across the lanes in Barbar Shah to find him. Barbar Shah Area had a good population of Kashmiri Pandits, and once they left, some sold off their properties to Muslims around and the morphology of the entire area changed. Shops came up; new houses came up. My mother had known the old Barbar Shah—and it was difficult for her to make out where exactly was *Tiladooz's* shop. After repeated inquiries, we were told that the concerned *Tiladooz* had become quite weak and no longer accepted any assignment. However, his son had a shop somewhere near. With difficulty, we located his son's shop; the gentleman did not know my mother, but my mother described herself as a client of his father and a passionate lover of his father's art. The young *Tiladooz* was pleased. He wanted to know what we wanted from him. We showed him our two *pherans*—the one that belonged to my mother and the one that I wanted embroidered. He looked at my mother's *pheran* and said, 'Keep it well preserved. No one can make it now. It was my father's magic. I can never do it. Neither can any of my workers.'

When we asked him about his father, he said his eyesight had become weak and his hands had developed tremor—he could not hold a needle in his hand. I wanted to know more, so I asked him how many of his children were into this craft. 'Just me,' he replied. Before I could ask him the reason, he told me how difficult it was to earn two square meals out of the *Tila* work that he was doing. From getting raw material to retrieving money from customers, it was a long-lasting pain . . . . Turmoil had cut off the admirers of the craft. His brothers, he told, had studied and got adjusted as Government servants and he owned a shop nearby, but his father insisted that he should continue with the 'craft of his forefathers'. He didn't promise great to his son, but he promised that there was *barkat* in the work that he would do. For the sake of his father he was continuing, he told. He took both *pherans*, gave a receipt, and asked us to come after 3 months. Long wait, I thought, and risky too, as he had taken both *pherans*. When we left him, he sensed my apprehensions. 'Do not worry. I will give you the same design. *Toth* (Father) will guide me.'

Three months later, we went again. I saw my *pheran* . . . a piece of art, so much similar to my mother's *pheran*, yet so much different, so much distinct . . .

I cleared the bill, thanked him, and asked him if I could get another one done. 'No, please, not for some time,' he replied.

As I left, I came back from the door, and I don't know what provoked me to tell him, 'Propagate the art ahead. Teach the art to your children.'

'*Insha-Allah*,' he said.

Kashmiri art and craft has been an identity of Kashmir for ages. It has survived in tough times, survived in tumultuous moments, remoulded and recast itself, rejuvenated in form and feature, and lived on . . . not only in museums and galleries but also in the hearts and minds of its admirers . . . throughout the world. In spite of witnessing so much of trauma and pain, it is surprising that Kashmiris continue to look to nature for that inspiration. The almonds, the twigs, the tulips, and ever inspiring chinar leaves continue to be represented in our art works. Each form represents a unique art work, speaking on behalf of his creator who in spite of his own misery presents the onlooker with the richness that he finds around him.

But will our art be able to rise again from the death that seems inevitable? With carpet looms shut, craft centres closed, the nature around plundered, will a surviving sad artist again revert to his passion? What will be his inspiration? Who will be his resuscitators?

The papier mâchié workers licked 'lead' which 'rolled their hands and heads', but they still created those wild flowers and forests on the vases and lamps. The weavers got sores on their heels and thighs, their joints got locked, and their lungs shrunk, but they kept on weaving . . . weaving gold and gems for *Darbars* and 'walls' that never discussed them or their plight. The copper workers braved the deafening noises to inscribe on those Samovar bellies an art that would be inscribed on your heart. And those masters or '*Sozin* workers'—buried under the burden of loans—still created masterpieces with those needle-bitten hands . . . . How did they create that fine embroidery? Did that streak of light passing through those thick cataracts in their eyes have so much power? Unfortunately in the younger generation, sense was prevailing over emotion as they were moving away from a work that was fetching them nothing to more mechanised jobs that were giving them livelihood. Was Dacca being repeated here?

Off to Bengaluru

My husband got admitted to one of the finest institutions of neurosciences in Bengaluru, namely National Institute of Mental Health and Neurosciences (NIMHANS), for a degree called M.Ch. He was the first Kashmiri to be admitted to NIMHANS for a super-specialisation in neurosurgery. The bearded man was scared of being there. How would a Kashmiri be treated there? But when he worked there, he liked the place and in fact loved the work that was done there.

When my daughter was born, he came to see us in Srinagar, but one evening, my mother-in-law panicked as he had not come back from *Magrib* prayers. We went to search for him, but there was no clue. Ultimately someone who had seen him being pushed into a bunker at Ilahi Bagh, Soura, informed his cousin about the incident. My in-laws rushed with a few relatives to the bunker into which he had been pushed. They pleaded with the security forces to set him free. They told them that he was a doctor pursuing a degree in an institution at Bengaluru.

Imagine a doctor who was pursuing a super-specialty course in neurosurgery and had come to his home place to see his family was held up in a bunker and he had to prove his identity. The identity card that he had was not relevant, they said. His parents searched in their home for another identity card (voter's card), which convinced them that he was a local who had come home. Had the boy not been an eyewitness as my husband was pulled inside the bunker, what would have been the fate of a neurosurgeon? When my husband came home, uneasy and tense, his father said, 'Didn't I tell you not to wear a beard, but you never listen.'

My husband, a soft-spoken gentleman, was always at the receiving end because of his beard. He was frequently spotted and stopped while walking or driving in Kashmir. It was his choice to have a beard, and he had to bear its consequences so often. He was better off in Bengaluru than in Srinagar.

My daughter born after my post-graduation was a lovely little angel.
My husband was keen to have us in Bengaluru. After my daughter was
a little less than 2 months, I headed with her for Bengaluru. Travelling
with a tiny infant was not easy. On the way from home to the Srinagar
airport, where I had to report 2 hours before, they searched our car, the
pram of the baby, and me—too thoroughly. My little daughter was tossed
and rolled by those security personnel who seemed so emotionless and so
shrewd; the sight of a small lovely child could not make them smile, alas!

As I got into the airport having braved one security party after the
other, I finally got the boarding pass. After I got my boarding pass,
negotiating the innermost shell of security was another headache. Those
rough women looked in every pocket of my purse and every part of my
baby's pram. They took hold of the 'baby bag' and questioned about
each item therein. As I had left home early, my child needed milk and
I pleaded with the security to allow the milk that I was carrying to be
taken on board. With difficulty, they allowed it, throwing off the rest
of the things, i.e. cream, etc. I was carrying. They asked me to taste
the milk. They put all their probes into the milk even after I had tasted
it—never considering the fact that the milk was to be taken by an infant
and it would get contaminated. My baby was massaged, beneath her
diapers too, for a trace of ammunition. They pinched her knowingly or
unknowingly, and she screamed . . . . A sad day for me indeed! I felt like
a criminal in my own land. I hugged my daughter tight and marched
towards the plane. And I pitied myself as I saw how all non-locals were
treated with kindness and etiquette by the same security fellows who had
harassed us so much.

The flight to Delhi was a 1-hour flight. After reaching Delhi, I had
to take a connecting flight to Bengaluru. There too the crime of being a
Kashmiri haunted me. I was treated no different from how I was treated
at Srinagar. In Delhi, I was getting more conscious as I was checked at
every step, cross-checked, shouted at, and my little daughter manhandled.
My little one tasted her first pinch of being a Kashmiri in India. But on
the flight from Delhi to Bengaluru, the fellow passengers were kind and
treated me and my daughter with kindness and love.

I got an opportunity to work and study in Karnataka after I reached
there. The climate of Bengaluru just suited us. I saw the remarkable work
that was being done at NIMHANS. Labs remained open till late hours,
people worked hard, and there was never a break, never a hartal, never
a curfew. NIMHANS was an excellent institution for neurosciences.

Psychiatry was state of art—possibly the best in Asia. Lush lawns, green trees, and cool breezes were enough to revitalise a tired mind, not to speak of the impact it would have on an ailing patient. Neurosurgery, neurology, and neuro-radiology were too advanced. There was neuro-rehabilitation too, where all those with neurological disabilities were trained to earn their livelihood. Neuropathology, the department I worked in, was a temple of learning. Those great people were avid learners besides being excellent teachers themselves. My daughter was looked after by a young Kannadiga girl when I was away during the daytime. Since we lived in the hostel, my chirping little daughter became the darling of the entire hostel. Fellow doctors and their families would run after the little Kashmiri princess. In the afternoon, she would come to my department and excite the over busy faculty of our department. Dr Shankar, the Head of the department, was especially fond of her. A shrewd administrator, a thorough academician, and a researcher par excellence, he would rotate and revolve around my daughter. I had not known Indians like him before. The ones from the military and paramilitary forces had presented a different image to me. Who was the real Indian? I wanted to know.

A Deprived Lot!

IT revolution had swept through Karnataka. Major IT players had established their companies in Bengaluru and nearby areas. NIMHANS had a computer everywhere. All records were preserved in electronic files. When I would look back and think about my own land, I would remember the disorder, the chaos, the poor planning, and that thick layer of inertia enveloping all of us. When would this all reach us? When would we become tech-savvy? India was not, after all, all that backward. When would we all do what NIMHANS was doing? I would think. There was something more that should have happened to our land. A computer, a mobile phone, and something called Internet should reach us too. That all didn't come for a long time to us . . . . The said facilities, it was believed, could prove to be dangerous and could pose security concerns. There was Kiran Bedi fighting with all her might for such facilities to be provided to the inmates of Tihar Jail and there was an entire nation using mobiles and Internet. And there was a deprived land . . . which deserved to be deprived of it all—mobiles, Internet, and computers. Incredible . . . India! We got a reliance mobile phone in Bengaluru, and I loved to use it. Back home, I gave it to my 2-year-old daughter to play with as no mobile services existed in the state.

But then that was not all. On return to my land, there were new problems at hand. There were people still dying; young boys who had witnessed the tragedies in the 1990s had become teenagers—angry teenagers on the roadside, protesting for small things and bigger things. There were huge bunkers still there, reminding us of our history; there were those who were disappearing, and there was pain—the pain of not having something important in our lives . . . that freedom we cherished for ages! Massacres were rare, but isolated deaths were a regular occurrence. Why didn't all that stop?

The politicians who had forgotten Kashmir had arrived on the scene and displayed their power and arrogance. So petty they were before the police and military. Sometimes those self-proclaimed bosses were humiliated, but who would care?

They Too Didn't Help

Government Medical College Srinagar produced greats in medical and surgical specialties. Innovators and directors, specialists and consultants of various reputed institutions of the world were graduates of this seemingly insignificant college. Turmoil drove more of the capable doctors to every corner of the world. It was a drain of the sane!

But this mass exodus bothered none. All those doctors got settled in 'dream institutions', but our dear brothers never looked back—not a second look at the sorry state of health in 'their own land', not a patch of adhesive for a college that nourished them, not a small concern for the patients on whose bodies they were trained. They dreamt only for themselves, not for their mother institution or their motherland. That is what turmoil had made us-insensitive and selfish. They would come someday and deliver a talk on gene therapy, liver transplantation, or new receptors or an unknown molecule, showing little concern for the diseased health care institutions of the valley which they could have attempted to revive. An odd computer on a lucky day was all that the college would receive from a generous one! Did the 'sons of the soil' need reminders to perform some service for their own people? A free OPD, a free medical camp, an awareness talk, or a casual visit to the wards-they did nothing. They should have initiated collaborative research initiatives with the local institutions or a support to establish a trauma centre; surprisingly, there was none in a place where trauma was an epidemic. They could have provided life support system equipment or essential drugs to the people or the hospitals. Who would have stopped them from doing all that? They did not do the least. They gave explanations . . . sometimes huge ones for not doing what they ought to have done in a place where healthcare was in shambles and incidentally that was their home too!

I met a 70-plus non-resident Kashmiri doctor who had served in USA for 40 years. The doctor was in Kashmir looking for some land where he would construct a house. He intended to spend the rest of his life in Kashmir. This to me looked like a selfish proposal—spending your most productive years in a land and amongst people who at the fag end of your life feel are not your own. Better do that productive work at a place where you are valued . . . . Many more non-resident Kashmiris, he told me, had purchased land in Kashmir to spend their old age in Kashmir. And if this was the situation, our non-resident Kashmiris should have tried to improve the health care in Kashmir, as in their old age, they would have to be content with what meagre we had.

But whether they liked Kashmir or not whether they were concerned about its plight or not-Kashmiris always were proud when a son of soil achieved the unthinkable. If not anything else, the world was acknowledging the intelligence and hard work of a Kashmiri.

And away in the Far East and West, some sons of the soil wrote; they spoke about our world and their pain. Their audience appreciated the beauty of their words but not our anguish; for that matter, no one, it seemed, understood our pain. Those little souls cried in futility; the world was unmoved and our lives remained unchanged. Quite a few publishers published a few touching accounts, little poetry, and a few stories—some true, some impressive, some dull, but God knows whether their rhymes were resonant with our lives or whether they were enjoying the climaxes of their own stories while we suffered . . .

Odds and the Hope

Well, coming back to our unrecognised degrees—as I joined Govt. Medical college after coming back from NIMHANS we were still feeling the pinch of unrecognised degrees. We were worried when our forms were not accepted for a faculty position at SKIMS also, which was an institution within the state. That place too was seeking a 'recognised lot' to give a boost to its own ongoing postgraduate programme. With difficulty and a lot of negotiations with the administration, our forms were accepted, and the non-availability of 'recognised candidates' contributed to our selection as faculty members in Pathology at SKIMS.

Pathology at SKIMS was another enigma. There was a shivering and stammering flock of consultants who were so because their degree was not recognised by MCI. Quite senior people who had given a good part of their lives to the development and upkeep of the department were mocked at because of their degrees. Me and my other colleague selected as faculty members were shrunk into the corners, as we could foresee our fate looking at the state our seniors were in. Those meek ones were called the 'unrecognised lot' by all those who would pass by the department— casually or formally!

It was a sorry state of affairs yet here—and no respite at hand! The Department of Pathology at SKIMS was tagged unfortunately with the Department of Pathology, Government Medical College, Srinagar. There were we seeking recognition, and there were 60-year-old pass-outs from the department who could not become guides and had retired as the 'unrecognised lot'. Looking at how things were going on, we could not think of recognition till we were buried deep into the soil, but we were thinking of requesting our younger colleagues to whisper on to our graves—when the great happening of our degrees being recognised would take place. Would that mean a change in epitaphs?

And then, help arrived from Delhi. An angel, I should call him, who was appointed as an MCI Inspector came to Srinagar for what would be the last chance for Government Medical College Srinagar to seek recognition for its 'unrecognised lot'. He felt the pain for Government Medical College, felt the pain for SKIMS. He felt we should have been treated better. He argued on our behalf in 'Higher offices' to grant us recognition. After three inspections had failed to grant recognition to Government Medical College Srinagar, he along with Dr Bhat, worked again with the help of the principal of GMC Srinagar, then Health Secretary Mr Jandial, and approached the Ministry of Health and Medical Education, Government of India, to grant recognition to the post-graduation course in pathology at Government Medical College, Srinagar. The Ministry of Health and Medical Education was pressed to see some sense in what we were asking for. The efforts of the group worked, and finally the Medical Council of India posted Government Medical College, Srinagar, on its website as an institution that granted a recognised postgraduate degree in pathology. What a relief it was!

How great of the man who did it! All thanks to Dr M.L. Bhat for the work he did to get pathology department of Government Medical College Srinagar recognised. We benefited from his presence. The courage and commitment of this Pandit made a difference to our fate. Had Dr Bhat left Kashmir when all Pandits left—what would have happened to our unrecognised degrees?

My Koshur Hero

That winter night, I lay on my bed, half conscious, half unconscious, my ears trying to catch the sound of my newborn. The sound seemed to come from a distance, but the murmur between my husband and my mother was clear. My heart was shaken; a bullet was tearing through my gut as I heard the unfortunate news. I had given birth to a second daughter, and this one was born with a congenital anomaly. It is termed as bilateral cleft lip with a cleft palate. I heard the unfortunate news before anyone could hide it from me. No one was eager to show me the split face, which was helplessly looking for the first sip from her mother. Tears rolled down from my eyes as I spent the longest night of my life. Finally, morning arrived, and I caught a glimpse of the snow-white hand, blackened perhaps because of the intravenous line meant for feeding the little one.

The real tragedy arrived with every new visitor. Some sighing, some crying, some stunned—each one had his own theory about the unfortunate happening. This one should die—soon, I heard my dear ones making this unanswered prayer!

My husband kept his cool; he reassured me and called for someone who is my hero. He arrived, saw my baby, looked at me, and said, 'Don't worry, this deformity is hundred per cent curable.' He added, 'You will not be able to recognise this child after we do her repair.' He gave feeding instructions and asked us to get the child to him when she would be 6 kgs for the first sitting. I had no option but to believe what Dr Sahib was saying. I took up the challenge of increasing the weight of my baby and confined myself to a room, which was exclusively meant for my baby.

No one believed that my child would ever be all right; no one believed she could ever suck. Every now and then, people greeted me with fresh apprehensions. Those disturbing stories of failed repairs and those sad anecdotes about our poor health care facilities gave me jittery nights and unpleasant mornings. Me and my husband, both of us doctors earning a humble salary, contacted all those people who could possibly help us. Corporate hospitals of Delhi promised a five star treatment for 8 lakh. PGI Chandigarh promised an early repair at 1 year. G.B. Panth set a date for us for the next year. I looked here and there for reassurance, for consolidation, for some help at least—but nothing great came up. A reassuring programme on Reality TV *about an infant who was repaired for a cleft lip and palate gave me hope that something good was in store for my daughter too.*

I believed this man—Dr Shabir Iqbal, Additional professor, Plastic Surgery at SKIMS, Srinagar. Somewhere deep within my heart there was a feeling that what the doctor was telling was true. I cannot describe my plight. How hard I struggled for those 3 months. My daughter knew only one thing properly, i.e. to vomit. The feed I used to give would regurgitate through her nose, and that uncomfortable infant used to struggle, making my heart burst with heaviness and helplessness. I didn't know much about Dr Iqbal's academic achievements, didn't know much about his family background, but I knew for sure his conviction to stand by his promise. At 3 months when my daughter was 6 kg, he planned surgery for her. He operated my little heart, repaired her lip, a part of palate in a major surgical procedure, which lasted for 6 hours. After the operation, I saw my little one was calm and quiet. The next day she had a face—a beautiful one, a lip which could suck, and a sutured palate. Ten days later, all my fears vanished. I had a daughter whose face was cuter than anybody else's, who could suck, and above all who could smile. Nobody wished for her death now . . . . My daughter's repair was better than the 'small miracle' episode shown on Reality TV. *Oh my God! Our doctor in our set-up had done better than a doctor in the USA. Did anybody know that?*

I wanted to thank Dr Sahib, call him for a dinner—he politely refused. 'I do it routinely', he said. Dr Iqbal made a difference to my life, to the life of my family especially the life of my daughter. But his contribution was much more than this. He and his team have been doing on average two clefts per week, which means more than 1, 500 in 15 years; 1, 500 families, 1, 500 mothers, and 1, 500 infants who would otherwise lead a socially stigmatised life owe their smiles to this great man. Kashmir has a high incidence of cleft lips and palates, and the treatment available here was not at par with the best centres but better than them. I had a short conversation with Dr Iqbal before I wrote this one. He talked to me about other work that he, a humble diligent gentleman, was doing towards the betterment of the neglected and ailing Kashmiris while at SKIMS.

1. ***Burn reconstructions:*** *Patients especially ladies falling prey to burns require reconstructive surgeries which were provided on a 'compassionate basis by Dr Iqbal's team. Faces distorted by traumatic burns were made to glow again. Thousands have been helped.*

2. ***Other congenital anomalies:*** *Besides cleft lip and palate, other congenital anomalies, e.g. hypospadias, accessory digits, etc., were taken care of. New and simplified techniques were devised to help infants with these anomalies.*

3. ***Tumors:*** *Mutilating tumors especially of the head and neck regions leave behind horrifying defects when removed. Free-flowing muscle grafts were done to bridge those defects. More than 100 grafts had been done, of which more than 80% are successful. This was possible by the use of microsurgery in which Dr Iqbal and his team had gained expertise. Bilateral trapezius graft was successfully accomplished in a patient afflicted by electrical injury. This grafting was the 'state-of-art' technique performed for the first time in India; AIIMS, PGI, and other institutions had to follow!*

4. ***Re-implantation:*** *Sounds like a fairy tale—a patient has his arm trapped in a machine and comes to the hospital with blood gushing out from the amputated site with attendants carrying his dissociated arm in a bag. Dr Iqbal was not the one to disrespect this arm, and he and his team successfully re-implanted amputated arms and hands on the patients (with almost full recovery of function in the affected arm).*

5. ***Bear mauls*** *The distortion is pathetic but Dr Iqbal and his team were ready to face the challenge. The reconstructions were simply unbelievable.*

6. ***Accidents/injuries:*** *Our valley afflicted by ongoing trauma had seen accidents of every sort. Besides the common road traffic accidents, injuries due to grenades, bomb blasts, gunshots were common, and Dr Iqbal and his team did all to help these patients (whether skin grafts, muscle grafts, or treatment of ugly scars was concerned).*

7. ***Calling us back to home:*** *My husband, a neurosurgeon, had wonderful opportunities outside—me and he would have preferred to serve there. But our daughter's surgery was an eye-opener. My*

husband said once, 'What if Dr Iqbal would have preferred to go out?' Surely there was a whole world waiting for him! I agree—what would have happened to our daughter then? When Dr Iqbal could stay back, help people, and excel in the field, why not we? We may not contribute as much as Dr Iqbal is doing, but for us, he was an inspiration.

Dr Iqbal did not take any credit for himself. He looked towards his seniors for help, guidance, and encouragement. He had tremendous faith in his junior consultants and residents from whom he received fresh ideas and a constant feedback.

My hero deserves recognition, an encouragement the magnitude of which would belittle a Nobel Prize. I have tried in my humble way to put him in a place he deserves, for in spite of the suffocating atmosphere and too many limitations, the hero is ready to do more and has no hangovers about what he has done!

This write-up of mine was meant to be sent to a Kashmiri group in USA, who invited essays from Kashmiris on *'Kosher hero'*. A hero in their lives who had made a difference to their lives. In their advertisement, the group claimed that they would give awards in Dollars to the three best essays and compile the best ones in the form of a book. I could not think of a better hero than Dr.Shabir Iqbal. I wrote my essay and sent it to them, but there was no response from them ever. No awards were ever given to anyone and no books were ever published. This unpublished acknowledgement to Dr Shabir should form a part of my book, I thought. When I wrote this piece about my hero, he was still at SKIMS, but then he left the place—willingly. He was not getting his due, he thought, and he worked in private in Srinagar hospitals and did the same wonders as he was doing at SKIMS—'a shining white man in dark.'

Chapter-4

Replay

Now, coming to the last part of the book; this is where I lose my continuity, my coherence, and my rhythm. So much has happened during the past over two decades—and yet so little has changed on the ground.

I don't know if all that has happened or is happening is relevant . . . to be written here considering the fact that I am trying to write an account of Kashmiri doctors in turmoil, but then I just cannot dissociate myself from all that was happening around us. Some events might not have affected my working as a doctor . . . but yes, all that which kept happening affected me as a Kashmiri, affected me as a sufferer. I have reached the part where my narrations are no more narrations but quotations from the hearts of all those who suffered.

We lived and lived amidst insecurities and perils, and we are lucky we survived when so many died. The official death count stands at more than 60, 000 and the unofficial at more than one lakh. We lost the count of orphans, disabled, and half widows. Amidst the moments of pain and tension, there were moments when violence was a little less. Though our backgrounds remained unchanged, during those moments we forgot about everything and just were busy living our own lives—in the best possible way to keep ourselves sane. The great nation mistook the lull for peace and aimed not at soothing our pain, but at total integration. Kashmiris were exploited in the name of 'Kashmiryat', a loose term which was being thrust on them to dilute their identity. Kashmiris were no doubt for the most part of their history in a state of togetherness and in perfect harmony with people of all faiths. As of now also, there were no issues about coexistence with other faiths, but there was a denial about a basic historical fact—denial of a basic human right called 'freedom', and Kashmiris were in no mood to barter it for something less. Their masters forgot their vows, pledges, and promises and imposed 'rulers' over them. Some of those rulers were too funny and some too shrewd.

The lulls didn't last long, and there came three horrible summers when our youngsters were yet again showered with bullets. It started in 2008. In 2008, 20 years after the gun was introduced in Kashmiri streets, there were no gun-toting youth, just stones in the hands of our youngsters. Poor boys—they sought to achieve what could not be achieved with guns or with resolutions. So they died—8-year-olds, 10-year-olds, and so many 18-year-olds. We wept again. Again we took to streets. This time some sane voices started erupting from Indian intelligentsia. They cried for us too—Gautam Navlakha, Arundati Roy, and a few more. Massacre of children on the streets terrified the nationals but not the nation.

Those three summers had three different inciting factors: Amarnath land transfer, murder and rape of two Shopian girls, and death of a young boy Tufail Mattoo, following the infamous Machil encounter. In 'stone', our boys found a respite. It was an unrest of humiliated souls and hundreds died . . . in those demonstrations. The repulsive emotions were crushed and tapped under the feet, and they called it *Ragda. Ragda, Ragda, Ragda*—there were 3 years of *Ragda* in a row . . . These were the summers of curfews, hartals, uncertainties, and deaths . . . and Kashmir was in turmoil . . . again.

Bullets and Grenades

Tufail's death provoked the 2010 uprising in Kashmir—one of the worst in the history of Kashmir. Tufail, a young class 12th student, was hit on his way to tuition by a tear smoke shell. Tufail, police said, had died after being hit by a stone, but the post-mortem report of the body revealed that he was hit by a tear smoke shell in the head. It was alleged by the witnesses that Tufail was chased by police, who fired a tear gas shell at him from close range. The shell hit in his head, killing him instantly.

His father had advised him to use lanes and by-lanes. And that day he had done everything perfectly, everything right, but still he was killed. His father narrated the painful tale of his son's death to the press many days later—he narrated how the entire *mohalla* was submerged in silence when the news of his son's death spread, how no one could gather the courage to tell him the bad news, and how his neighbours struggled to say those words of consolation after the news of his son's death was broken to him by a policeman in casual wear.

With Tufail, 113 more boys lost their lives . . . . 2010 gave us more pain—our kids demonstrated their disgust towards all that was happening to them collectively. Our children used to relative calm of the early 2000's now saw a cycle of death and destruction. They saw what we had seen in our youth—burning tyres, huge processions, massacres, loots, tortures, and torments. They were terrified, like we had been when we were young, like my nephews and nieces were then, so the cycle was repeated. No Kashmiri was spared. We never talked to the 7-year-olds and 10-year-olds about our trauma, but seeing the odd events happen yet again, they learnt the wrongs of being born as Kashmiris. We tried to shield them; we tried to avoid answering their queries. But how long could we do that? They learnt their history early, learnt about their misfortunes too early. We could not stop the knowledge explosion around us. Were we raising another generation which was ready to die?

This time my destination had changed from Downtown to Buchpora, my in-laws' place, so had my workplace. Those weren't now the same outskirts, which had been quiet and secluded not so long ago. But there was a battleground here too. Soura, Aanchar, 90 feet Road, Ganderbal, and Nowshehra were witnessing huge demonstrations. Stone pelting became infective and was not restricted to Downtown.

Downtown was exploding each day with anger. Bullets changed lulls into storms, pellets changed peaceful demonstrators into angry mobs, and torture yet again was a brutal reminder of an acrid history. Our hospitals were swollen with dead and injured. The blood of our youngsters stained our scarred souls yet again. We again moved about in those rattling vehicles called ambulances, carrying on their bodies' dents and holes of a two-decade violence. We were stopped yet again by another generation of military and paramilitary forces; we were stared at yet again, shouted at yet again, humiliated yet again, and killed yet again. Who says our fate had changed?

SKIMS, Soura, again worked non-stop; SMHS Hospital and Bone and Joint Hospital too were flooded. The work done by our doctors surprised the world. New York Times featured an article on how SKIMS tackled victims of 2010 violence. Voluntary blood donors queued up for blood. *Langar*s for stranded ones again came up, and people stayed awake to hear good news about the critical ones they had never known. Soura and the adjoining Aanchar harboured those emotional ones whose blood would boil at every killing. Their men were dragged, boys tortured, and houses vandalised. That Downtown of the 1990's seemed so close by. A study conducted on 35 ambulance drivers of four major hospitals of valley during 2010 found that on an average the ambulance drivers worked for 60 hours/week and drove an average of 160Km/day .Twenty nine (83%) of drivers experienced more than one threat of physical harm, 18(54%) experienced physical assaults and 31(89%) reported evidence of psychological morbidity associated with their jobs. The study concluded, '*The atmosphere of conflict on streets of Kashmir had an adverse effect on ambulance drivers, both physically and mentally. The stress faced by them should be recognized and corrective measures taken*' [15]

After bullet showers on our innocents raised a hue and a cry, rubber bullets and tear gas cartridges were used indiscriminately on our protesting mobs, but the studies published from Kashmir in international journals reported that neither rubber bullets nor tear gas cartridges were safe tools to control mobs. Some outstanding literature in medicine came from turmoil-hit hospitals of Kashmir. The recommendations of the experts in the field were never thought about; leave aside talk of implementing them. A study was carried out on 100 patients admitted to Bone and Joint Hospital, Srinagar, from May 2008 to July 2010, who had sustained injuries due to rubber bullets. The rubber bullets used had a tiny pointed tip with a muzzle velocity of 73 m/s. Of the 100 patients studied, 95 were males and 5 females. The age range of the patients was 12-60 years; 59% of the patients were in the age range 12-20 years. In 80% patients, injury was seen in lower limbs and 10% patients had injuries involving head, neck, and face. Sixty-five per cent patients had blunt injuries and 35% had penetration. The study concluded that '*improper ranging with inaccuracy of rubber bullets with improper aiming can result in severe injuries and sometimes in death. This type of ammunition should never be considered for mob control*' [16]

Another study from SKIMS on five teenage patients of head injury caused by tear gas cartridge also concluded that '*tear gas cartridges considered as one of the benign modalities of controlling agitated crowds is not really benign. It can cause serious injuries and mortality.*' Out of the five patients admitted with tear gas cartridge induced head injuries to

SKIMS, one died, one went into a persistent vegetative state, while three recovered.[17]

Pellets, stones, rubber bullets, slingshots, and tear gas shells caused severe injury to the eyes of our youngsters. In an analysis on the pattern of ocular injuries assessed in the Department of Ophthalmology, Government Medical College, Srinagar, from June to September 2010, sixty cases of ocular injuries were received by the Department of Ophthalmology, GMC, Srinagar. Seventy-five per cent of patients were school-going boys in the age range 16-26 years. Injuries due to stones occurred in 48%; pellets accounted for injuries in 30% patients, slingshots in 10% cases, rubber bullets in 8%, and tear gas shells in 3% cases. Injuries due to pellets were mostly perforating, and associated IOFB (intraocular foreign body) which had a very poor prognosis. Most of the ocular injuries suffered by the people during the unrest were visually disabling .The study concluded that '*given the seriousness of the damages caused by the methods used to control public demonstrations, use of less lethal weapons becomes imperative.*'[18]

Sometimes our youngsters and adults involved in their routine, fell prey to the stray bullets fired in the air, shot miles away to terrify the mobs. A 7-year-old boy was playing in a field; he suddenly fell down unconscious. The patient was evaluated for loss of consciousness; a CAT (computerized axial tomography) of his head revealed that a bullet was lodged in the cerebellum. Nobody in the family knew wherefrom the boy had received the bullet. The patient was managed conservatively at SKIMS but died on the third day of injury. Another boy walking in his village suddenly fell down with weakness on the left side of his body and became unconscious. On investigations, a bullet was seen lodged in his right parieto-occipital region. He was operated—a bullet was removed with evacuation of hematoma. The patient survived, but he needs support for his daily activities. Another young male while playing cricket suddenly fell down, due to complete paraplegia. Investigations revealed a bullet in the spinal canal at L3-4 level. Though the bullet was retrieved, the patient's condition has not improved after 2 years of follow-up. The young male has become a paraplegic and a burden for his parents and his own self. A young woman was working in her kitchen garden when she suddenly felt pain in her back and became paraplegic. Her family members noted a wound in her back, which was bleeding. When the patient was brought to the hospital, she was in shock. An X-ray showed a bullet in the pelvis. Her abdomen was opened in emergency surgery with evacuation of hematoma, and the bullet was retrieved. MRI (magnetic resonance imaging) of the dorsal spine showed a bullet tract at C7-D2 level. The patient in follow-up continued to be paraplegic.

In all these four cases, the patients were not aware of the bullet injury, and it was after enquiry that it became clear that at the time of injury, the security forces had resorted to aerial firing for crowd dispersal some 1-3 km from the site of injury. These cases formed a case series published from SKIMS on the so-called unintentional bullet injuries due to stray bullets, describing the pattern of injury due to stray bullets in our patients. Unintentional firearm injuries occur usually due to celebratory gunfire, handling of weapons, i.e. cleaning, playing, accidental discharge, or due to game shooting. Law enforcement agencies resorted to aerial firing to scare away the mobs and added another cause of unintentional firearm injuries. Never before in world literature has 'injury caused by stray bullets in riot control been reported'. The study concluded that *aerial firing considered innocuous should be banned because of the harm it causes to innocent bystanders.* The modern police rifle bullets travel a long distance from the site of firing with a high velocity up to 2, 000 m/s in a parabolic trajectory and hit the unintended targets.[19]

So, for Kashmiri teenagers, death and disability were coming together. Bullets, pellets, or tear gas shells were spreading death and causing severe disabilities. Nobody paid attention to the literature that was published on the callous handling of mobs in Kashmir. The nation was silent and so was United Nations and its allied agencies.

Somehow, the internal and external pressures worked, and they all came here to condemn the loss of young lives in Kashmir—all the worthy politicians and leaders. We heard them on television say how sorry they felt for the youth of Kashmir! I always knew what the writing on the wall in Kashmir meant, but in 2010, those writings on walls, those graffiti's became more visible. When they came here, they must have looked at the real writings on the wall . . . . Didn't they ponder over those writings? They came here to justify oppression, not to pacify us. When our rustics talked and asked simple questions, their debaters, lawyers, and parliamentarians were silenced . . .

Some interlocutors too were appointed. An academician, a journalist, and a bureaucrat were asked to solve an 'ages old issue', and a special investigation team (SIT) was constituted under the court directions to investigate the circumstances which led to the death of Tufail Matoo. Time-pass!

The Story of a High-headed Tailor

He was a poor tailor who worked hard for his living. A father of five daughters, his gentle manners and subtle temperament would move you. He did his job well and stitched the clothes to perfection in a small rented shop in the backyard of my father's home. He started from nothing, and we were overjoyed to see his growth from scratch to a modestly settled tailor. I went to him in the month of Ramadan that year (2010) as he had opened his shop on an odd day when 'all was normal'. He looked weak and seemed a bit worried as I handed over to him a bag of clothes which needed to be stitched. He promised to stitch them before Eid, and I left, handing him over the stitching charges. I knew what was troubling him; perhaps the ongoing turmoil had affected his work and he was not earning enough. He had a large family to feed, but the trouble in the valley had forced people to care for the basics; getting clothes stitched in the trouble-torn valley seemed a luxury which people did not like to avail. True to his promise, he stitched my clothes before Eid, but when I saw him pre-Eid again, his anxious looks and pale face troubled me. I wanted to help, but I knew he would hesitate; I liked it when he held his head upright, at times too high to be bent by our request for any help. 'May God help you to keep your head high-always!' I would pray.

Post-Eid, the valley turned upside down. Government imposed strict curfew and people were paralysed in their homes. Even stray dogs feared to trespass through the streets. In this killing silence, I received a phone call; my sobbing mother said, 'The tailor is dead.' I couldn't believe what I heard. What had happened to him suddenly? I thought. After a few days when the curfew was lifted, I went to the tailor's house; the sight of his young wife and five daughters was touching. How would they live? I thought. There was no male member in the family, and none of the girls was employed or in the know of any skill. They were just studying—their father had great plans for them.

Now why is it that I am narrating this tale of a tailor? There are thousands of people who succumb to a disease, leaving behind families in a more deplorable condition. Why is it that I am talking about this tailor?

The death of this tailor is a murder. I'll let you all decide who killed him. He complained of pain, I am told, in the right side of his lower abdomen. He rushed to a nearby hospital, where he received some preliminary treatment and was asked to go home. The next day, he again developed pain but did not get any vehicle that would take him to the hospital. He could not walk down to the hospital because of the intense pain that he had. He took the painkillers, preferring to be at home because curfew was very strict; even ambulances and hospital vehicles were stopped. His disease intensified; he had an inflamed appendix that burst, spreading the poison (toxins) to his entire gut. The poison did the damage—he became listless and was taken by neighbours to a referral hospital where he was operated upon. He died—his five daughters shouldered his coffin.

No bullet pierced this tailor, no pellet hit him, and no torture cane tortured him. Even then he died—helpless—because of a disease which was otherwise curable. He will not get the label of a 'martyr', nor will any Government agency give his family 'compensation'. This death did not contribute to the toll of 113 deaths that the valley had that summer. Which agency will take the credit or discredit of 'murdering' this breadwinner? Where will the tailor fit? Where will his family fit? What will be the fate of his five daughters and his young widow? Will somebody own the blame? The high-headed tailor is underground, so I won't ask for compensation on his behalf. All I do is to ask for justice— will I get it in the world's largest democracy?

The tailor was not the only one who suffered; there were countless patients with treatable medical and surgical conditions who could not reach the hospitals. Some died in their homes, relying on the remote prescription of a doctor, some died on the way to the hospital, and some in the hospital because of complications from an ailment for which help could not be sought in time.

'Yeti kyah karan'—What will they do here?

In search of a safe place, a secure surrounding, the youth kept going out of Kashmir, out of the state, and out of the country. No sector actually was thriving in Kashmir. Frequent curfews, hartals, and bandhs affected education. Employment was a dream come true in a bankrupt Government sector with too many employees to feed, and the private sector was non-existent. Who would invest in a trouble-torn state with a difficult terrain and a hostile climate?

Over the years, the conditions deteriorated; unemployment was at its worst, and parents saw no hope in holding back their children here. Though many parents sent their wards off to distant lands for want of employment, many more who could easily be employed here were sent off for a better quality of life—uprooting them from their land permanently and themselves living as miserable 'alones' in those bungalows which were built for large prosperous families. Even when parents wanted their children with them in Kashmir, having tasted the joy of being independent, who would come to live in a prison? The children never really returned.

The popular phrase with Kashmiri parents, when they would send their children outside, was: *Yeti Kyah Karan*. What will they do here?

Old men and women were alone—shrunk into a corner of those beautiful bungalows, made from money their sons and daughters struggled to earn abroad. Charming villas with lonely inhabitants . . . waiting for a day when they could be together. When elderly parents also go to their sons and daughters who live in distant lands during winter months-*chowkidars* are made the custodians of those huge bungalows.

Some parents opted to keep one child back home and send the rest out—creating divisions and discord between the families. The one who stayed back always felt overburdened whereas the one went overseas felt he was helpless and that living in Kashmir would shatter his and his family's dreams. What would you say in such a situation?

I read a headline in a local daily about an old couple—ailing and alone, living in a bungalow in a posh locality of Srinagar. One of them had fractured his limb and the other one was bedridden. There was no one to take care of them. Money they had in plenty . . . stacked in *almirahs*. They had three wall clocks in three rooms with different timings matching the time of the countries where their sons lived. Once the old man went up on a stool to change the battery of one of the clocks; his shaky legs could not maintain balance on the stool and he fell down and fractured his leg. As the old man and old woman were both bedridden now, there was no one to take them to a doctor; they requested a pharmacist neighbour to administer an injection to the old man. He saw their plight, their helplessness. The woman had incontinence; her bedding and all her clothes were soiled. The old man who was previously looking after his ailing wife was himself incapacitated now. The pharmacist was moved by their condition. After he helped them, they showed him the money they had in their *almirahs*, which their sons had sent them. The pharmacist narrated their tale to the press so that society would be more caring towards its elders. I don't know what happened to them, now that a year has passed by since this episode became the headline in Greater Kashmir.

Yeti kyan karan? The question posed by these very couples when they sent their children out . . . is answered by their own shattered selves.

There are my friends and colleagues in the West who call us occasionally for a dear one here who is sick—their father, mother, brother, or a sister. They want some attention from us; in all humility, they beg us at times. I don't know if our attention satisfies them or not.

But how many will keep on going outside Kashmir? From education and employment to business—how many Kashmiris will leave their motherland? Isn't it the same Kashmir which was a dream for visitors, a heaven for tourists and life for those who lived here? Now this haunted piece of land has become a place where one does not want to reside . . .

When Pandits left the valley, it was called 'mass exodus', and now when youth have left Kashmir to seek better opportunities and better life, what should we call it? Moving out of Kashmir may be a survival instinct-but what is being done to provide education and employment for Kashmiris in Kashmir?

They Learnt to Live and Tell Their Tale

As Kashmiris moved into the plains and plateaus of India for education and career, there were difficulties, especially for the youth. How does it feel to be in India, the major cities and the minor cities, facing the taunts and the ebullition, braving communal forces, talking to nationalists, and tackling them? There was harassment and humiliation. A single act of violence anywhere—in any part of any city of India— would have an impact on a Kashmiri studying or doing business in any corner of that city. There would be raids, there would be questioning, and there would be a harsh time in lock-ups and jails. The torture and torment would not leave a Kashmiri, no matter where he was in India.

But the new generation had learnt to live, learnt to survive with dignity amidst hostilities. They sought asylum, won hearts, competed, and excelled in whatever field they tried. They learnt to 'cheer for India' to keep their friends happy and to keep the hostile ones at a distance. But, they never felt shy to ask for a right so long denied to their fathers and forefathers. They managed to have at their back the entire carefree cosmopolitan Indian youth who thought with a difference but who made no difference to Indian policies and its politics. They asked for justice; they asked for an end to hostilities—right there in the capital city of Delhi, braving the uncertainty and unpredictability of their moves. They stared into the face of Indian democracy—reminding it about the hollow 'dummy' that had been in place in the so-called crown of India. They spoke it out straight, argued about their viewpoint, and confronted the 'defenders' of democracy, making them speechless on the television shows being aired during the days of visible disturbance. They feel bad about a ravaged place called Kashmir which is their home place—they care for it.

They desire a lot. They desire peace and prosperity for this land. My dear green-eyed nephew-our companion during the days of turmoil went ahead to do his law in a top Indian university, and the topic he worked on was Public Safety Act in Kashmir.

He wrote when he saw us in pain, he wrote when he saw our suffering. He won't forget his childhood—those traumatic and painful moments. And he wants to do something about our today and tomorrow. Here is a little bit from what he wrote in a local daily when in the summer of 2010 he came here and witnessed death and devastation. This is an excerpt from what he wrote:

> 'Violence is an inseparable part of our existence. There are no two ways about it. My home, which I cherished with love, has become a volatile paradise, the waters of which are being tested by the tormentors of humanity.
>
> I have been hearing gun shots, cries for help from the last two decades, I don't know how louder we have to scream for the world to hear our cries and bail us out of it. It's been always fake promises and neglect which has made the present situation in Kashmir so volatile. Everyone is out on the streets, in the hope that someone would hear their cry for help, a cry for freedom and liberate them from suppression.
>
> The people in New Delhi do not understand the basic fact that it's easy to kill a person's right to freedom, it's easy to deny the people the right to live, but no force can break the thirst of a wounded soul, to rise from the ashes and liberate itself. This is the same power which against all odds is making the people come on streets and protest against the brutal force with which the people are being treated. The voices of Kashmiris

have been choked due to which the cries of mothers and the
pain of our brethrens have been lost . . .'

My niece, who has lived her entire childhood in the trouble-torn valley, is doing Economic Honours in a top Indian university. She wants to pursue her dreams further and wants to do her master's from a foreign university. She showed me the 'statement of purpose' that she wrote for admission in a University in the West. It pained me when I read it, but it gave me hope too—these guys and girls are sincere. I quote:

'Apart from my interest in Economics, one needs
motivation to pursue a particular subject, and my motivation
is derived from the homeland, where I have been born and
brought up. I am from Srinagar, the capital of the State of
Jammu and Kashmir, which is situated in the northern most
part of India. Since 1989, militancy engulfed the beautiful
vale of Kashmir. Hence, the childhood I stem from is a period
which terrifies any Kashmiri even today. The pain of the
valley, seen through the ordinary eye, only made us thank
Lord for sparing us our lives, as being alive and physically
unscathed seemed the only asset in those times. But, every
child in the valley was emotionally scarred seeing atrocity
at its peak, when our playgrounds were turned into burial
grounds, right before our eyes.

With twenty years gone by, I realized how a valley which
was so abundant in resources got whirled up in a web of
turmoil. The growth it could manifest seemed lost, as the
natives started perishing gradually. The valley could have
highly contributed to the growth of the country. Recovering
from the scars, while still a student of economics and walking
towards a new outset, I tried to learn about the economy
of my native state. The present scenario was not a treat to
the eyes. Difficult terrain, militancy related loss of human
capital, low productivity, unemployment, malfunctioning of
public sector with an almost nonexistent private sector have
caused low economic growth. As a native of the State and a
student of Economics, I believe, it is my duty to care for the
ailing economy of the State in some way, so that development
could proceed again . . .'

They are keen to do something for their people and their land. From applying minor balms to pressing the major players to address major political issues concerning their state, they are determined logically speaking to do something!

I read something more—a sensitive and a small booklet on Kashmir and its tragedy by Sajid Iqbal. This collection of few pages has a whole ocean of sense, hope and tragedy narrated beautifully in it. The youngster who wrote it did not live to see its release. 'My road to freedom' is a melody written for the boys who were lost one by one in that jolting summer of 2010 and all this is connected to the 'sins' of our history.

There are questions they ask: Why shouldn't they be living freely in India without coercion and suppression? Why should they be subject to suspicion and harassment anywhere they go? And a major question is why should they love India when so much of pain and trauma is being inflicted on them? These youngsters brought up in difficult times, these survivors who were chased and tortured because they were Kashmiris, they fought it, survived it all, and came out victorious. And they seek answers for their questions from the sane and civilised. Can anyone in India answer them convincingly . . . ?

A young son of soil, mad for cricket, was out in an Indian city for playing a match when he was arrested and falsely blamed for carrying ammunition. The young Kashmiri's hope was crushed before he could rise. Our cricketing hero—Parvez Rasool—rose after a hard hit on his honour. He a Kashmiri boy had learnt well how to cope with fall, learnt to prove his mettle after each debacle, and learnt to startle the world with his performance! He wishes to play for a country which treated him like an animal or a criminal. He has made it to team India—when he eventually plays will the nation enjoy his heroics or will Parvez carry with him the taint of being a Kashmiri? A suspect. A traitor.

Decaying Downtown

Downtown or *Shehr-i-Khas* is seeing its worst days. All those who could, migrated to other unknown areas of the city. Those who could not are still living there . . . facing the wrath every time, any season. The business houses of the area also have migrated to Uptown or to the outskirts. Plenty of godowns have replaced lines of glittering shops. The wholesale dealers dump their extra material in old shops or buildings there. The huge houses in Downtown which housed traders have heavy locks on them or have been sold off. Some lovers of Downtown who like to be in those very lanes—like to touch that ground, to taste that air, and to cling to that warmth and love which is so much an indigenous part of it—still come here with their hand-driven carts and sell their goods there.

Standing still, here and there, are the houses of Pandits. A witness to the sufferings of Downtown, these structures made of mud, brick, and beautiful woodwork are decaying with the decaying Downtown. Some structures are burnt, some half burnt, and some sold off to Muslims who have put in patches of concrete in them, reflecting a changeover for which these structures were just not ready! Some more houses tell a tale of devastation, with huge pillars and elegant verandas, but broken windows, stolen doors, and shattered interiors. These are the ugly reminders of all that should not have happened. But I am sure if I leave my house and go away, its fate will be the same.

Some houses of Pandits are occupied by the forces, changing those beautiful ones in Karan Nagar and Habba Kadal into ugly monsters. Waves of panic and anxiety grips the onlookers of these houses. These dandified structures were meant to be treated better. How that affluent Pandit must have built his house . . . thinking it would last generations and would bring good luck and joy to his family, never knowing that unknown men would come there, occupy them, and spread the dread . . .

Years of turmoil replaced the prosperity of Downtown with poverty. Young girls lost their breadwinners—and some were exploited by a group or groups that had learnt to make merry while Kashmir burnt. Those tender girls were pushed into the webs of filth from which they could not escape. The exploiters were big men and powerful women. Though the valley reacted to expose those involved in the infamous 'sex scandal', a few middlemen were apprehended but the main culprits who had strong political connections were never caught. And perhaps they continue to make merry! Those victims were never rehabilitated. They continue to suffer . . . . as victims of an inexpressible pain. Has any NGO in India heard about them? Are merrymakers using more girls from other areas of Kashmir for satisfying their lust?

The city of Srinagar was occupied by all who could; footpaths were consumed, roads were encroached upon, and entire lanes were merged with private lawns. The paddy fields were sold off at high prices and converted into unplanned, disorganised colonies. The land the tiller had owned under a landmark decision of the State Government was no more cultivated—the tiller had sold it off for a high price. Surprising, would the tiller remember Sheikh Muhammad Abdullah for changing his fate?

Our governments gave Srinagar roads that were dug mercilessly. All roads in Downtown and Uptown were dug without purpose. The Downtown suffered more because it was seen as a seat of unrest. Digging and further digging made it more deplorable. They planned for drainage, but ended up creating havoc. The pits took years to fill, the pipes took decades to be laid, and macadamisation of roads became a distant dream. Initially, it was toy guns that our children wanted to play with, but with the changing morphology of their environment now it is a JCB machine—the yellow machine used in digging our kids want. The kids find it too fascinating.

Those youngsters from Downtown, those street-smart and good-looking boys—nothing has changed for them. Sometimes they are caught and killed and sometimes beaten in lock-ups. Each house here has lost an inmate, each house has witnessed a tragedy, and each shopkeeper here is an eyewitness to a bloodbath. How will they forget? Why will they forgive?

No politician cares and dares to go there, while villages rumble at times with politicians or queuing voters—these men and women never come out to vote. Their message and clear: 'No more cheating . . . . We have had enough.'

All along they smothered it with oppression, and now they want to bring tourists to Downtown to show them its remains:

Come along, dear tourist, I will take you to the Downtown . . .
Come along, I will show you uneasy remains of a fallen town.
A town caught in history,
A town shrouded in mystery,
A town wrapped in resolutions,
A town moved by revolutions.
Come along, I will show you uneasy remains of a fallen town
A town that couldn't weep,
A town that couldn't sleep,
A town that couldn't even peep,
Come along, I will show you how it turned into this heap.
A curious gaze was chased here,
A civilisation was razed here,
The world stood amazed—but away from here,

Come along now, when those asphyxiated residents have left the town.
Come along now, when its lanes have turned from red to brown.
Come along today, I will show you where those artisans taught,
Come along today, I will show you what those poets thought,
Come along into the lanes where those innocents were caught,
Come along, I will show you uneasy remains of a fallen town.
A town where the mosques remain locked,
A town where the dwellings were rocked,
Come along on to the banks where once cried Vitasta.
Come along to watch a (mass) grave along the banks of a dried Vitasta.

Who should accompany the tourist and show him all this? Would the tourist be happy meeting Syeda Begum, a 66-year-old widow, who lives in a shack-like two-room home in Darish Kadal—Downtown of the Srinagar city? The woman is frail, poor, and has only one working eye. She lives there with her 9-year-old adopted son[20].

Syeda, who was a blessed mother of four young sons, lost each one of them to the turmoil. Her eldest son was killed by the forces in 1998. Her second son, an 18-year-old chap, drowned after he was chased by troops after a firing incident. Her third son was shot in head and killed . . . . Her fourth son lost his mental balance—he would roam about and then disappeared. He has not come to her for the last 7 years now.

She reconciled with the fate, but she wanted to live with a hope, with a support, with a purpose. Her wish to live and to be called a mother again was fulfilled when a poor woman at a maternity hospital gave her own baby boy to look after. The woman had delivered twins. She accepted the challenge of looking after yet another boy—and the boy is now ten. She lives on what her kind neighbours give her and a meagre pension of Rs. 500. She calls her adopted son her world . . . but who will ensure the safety of her 10-year-old adopted son when four of her sons were swallowed by turmoil? Who will plead for this poor woman? Who will seek justice for her sons? Who will secure the future of her adopted child?

Many more widows—young and old, thousands of orphans, and many girls of marriageable age in Downtown are looking through the cracked glasses of their past into their insignificant present. Their future terrifies them and me too!

Lakes and Flakes of Money

They talked about Dal and invested crores in men and machines to get it cleaned. But its fate was never really altered. They talked about Dal as if it was the only lake polluted, the only lake encroached. Possibly it was the only lake visible to them as they would race their cars past Boulevard Road or would look at its deceptive calm through their posh bungalows in the down slopes of Zabarwan. They forgot about Aanchar—a lake near Soura which had been converted into a marsh. No one asked about its glory; no one talked about its revival. They were forgetting their own history; their own leader living nearby must have swum in its waters. Not only this, one of Asia's largest fresh water lakes was becoming unrecognisable below its weeds. An odd boat moving through its bushes carrying *Nadroo* or *Singhara* would give you an indication that life was going on inside it. So much security around Wular—gives it look of a spiny garland around . . . it. They say Wular has swallowed many a generation; were the weeds now covering its angry face? So many have drowned into it and were lost in its historical depths during turmoil. There have been many instances of capsized boats, many deaths which were never traced—so many boys on so many unfortunate days. Will Wular dry up with all its secrets or roar again to swallow this civilisation?

Natural Resources—the Plunder

The Hindu carried an interesting news item about a clash between the army and the J&K Police when a convoy of Territorial Army (TA) was intercepted at Heeri, 6 km from Kupwara in North Kashmir. Two feeder trucks were seized carrying smuggled timber after jawans of TA 160th Battalion had illegally felled green conifer trees and sawn it into logs in a dense forest cover. Three hundred cubic feet of timber was to be smuggled from Zirhama to the battalion headquarters at Heeri.[21]

Wajahat Habibullah admits in his book on Kashmir that Kashmir's forests have been among the principal casualties of violence. He writes, "only fitfully challenged by forest officials, people in the security forces set about felling trees to build their homes in villages across Punjab and Haryana.[22] You talk about green revolution elsewhere, and here in Kashmir does felling of trees happen in national interest or in global interest?

The water resources of the state too have been exploited and power projects have come up which supply electricity to the northern states of India. Though water resources of the state are being utilised for power generation, Kashmir continues to be dark in summers and winters— powerless before the powerful. The politicians talk about handing over of power projects back to the state, but one generation hands over the projects and the progeny cries over them!

The symbolic Amarnath Yatra where a limited number of *yatris* would go yearly to have a *Darshan* of the Holy Lingam is being converted into a mass annual pilgrimage. Chopper rides and plastic have damaged the sensitive environment near the cave. The rush and display of might is being portrayed as Hindu revivalism in Muslim Kashmir.

Health Care for Which No One Cared

In disturbed Jammu and Kashmir, health care was not a priority but security was. Those who were health conscious went to Delhi and other metros to care for themselves. Some were treated and some came home . . . cheated! The private sector floated touts, utilised agents, and organised OPDs in the valley to hunt for patients, hook them to Delhi and other metros, and operate them there . . . . No attempt was made to engage big players in private sector for setting up state-of-art hospitals in Kashmir, where people could pay and get treated.

A doctor known to me who worked in a private Delhi-based hospital told me about a Kashmiri patient who came to Delhi for surgery of a brain tumor. The patient had a huge tumor in close proximity to the vital structures. The neurosurgeons in Kashmir told him that only a part of the tumor would be removed; the rest of the tumor would need radiotherapy. But aspiring to be treated by better doctors in Delhi, the patient went to a private hospital in Delhi, where he was told that his tumor would be removed in toto without causing any damage to the vital structures lying nearby. When the patient was operated, the Kashmiri doctor, who was working as a resident there, was surprised to see in the post-operative scan that the doctors had just nibbled at the tumor, taken a biopsy, and closed the case. The patient was asked to be on the follow-up of radiation oncology. That Kashmiri patient went home boasting that his tumor was removed in Delhi without giving him a deficit. He cursed the Kashmiri doctors for being incompetent and shying away from accepting the challenges. The resident doctor, also a Kashmiri, did not divulge the details of the surgery . . . . Poor doctor could not act against the interest of his own hospital.

Doctors from Delhi and other metros were air-dashing to Srinagar, charging a heavy fee and promising an A class treatment. There was no vigil on what they were prescribing and where they were referring Kashmiri patients for costly investigations and surgeries.

Back home, major Srinagar-based hospitals were getting overburdened, treating everything from common cold to valve replacement. Overload and overcrowding ensured that doctors were busy, but many patients were ignored. The hospitals would proudly put the graphs for the load they received and the tests they conducted on their annual reports. The Government would proudly quote the figures—counting it as an achievement and bag awards for the 'best health service provider'. However, many figures were not encouraging; a large number of deaths unrelated to turmoil were being recorded in Government-run hospitals.

There was a strong syndrome engulfing Government hospitals. The patients who knew some hospital employee or a high ranking official would be treated kindly and early. Their tests would get done for free, and they would be seen by the best doctors available. There would be special attention given to VIP patients too. These patients would never line up in a queue and never wait for their turn. But they would suffer—suffer themselves—the God's wrath. They are the ones who would never get well and land up in complications. The syndrome called as 'VIP syndrome' was perhaps God's way of doing justice . . .

An early date for surgery in a Government hospital was a dream for a common man . . . a 2 months' wait, 3 months' wait, 6 months' wait, and a wait for years. Many patients were left with no option but to go to private nursing homes or fly over to Delhi and other metros for the desired surgeries. Most of the private hospitals in Kashmir were ill equipped and primitive. None of the hospitals had a licensed blood bank or a working intensive care unit.

The stress in the valley has not deceased; besides government hospitals and an international NGO called Doctors Sans Frontiers, there are no notable organisations working in Kashmir to help a huge population of patients with psychiatric ailments, hardly any NGO's. The stress of conflict and the fear of loss of life, property, or honour are reflected in various physical manifestations of psychiatric disorders. There are patients who have witnessed the events of violence in 1989 and 90's and patients who have witnessed events in years 2008, 2009, and 2010. And there are people who have suffered in both uprisings; the fresh pain and old pain have coalesced to give rise to various psychiatric disorders.

A cluster two-stage household survey conducted in 2005 by Medeins Sans Frontiers found high levels of ongoing violence across the region with civilians caught in the middle. The majority of people surveyed stated having been exposed to crossfire (86%) and round-up raids (83%). High numbers of people reported being subjected to maltreatment (44%), forced labour (33%), kidnapping (17%), torture (13%), and sexual violence (12%). One-third of respondents reported psychological distress, whereas using the same methods in a non-conflict area in India, a study done on low-income urban women found a prevalence of 18% for psychological distress. Suicidal thoughts were more common in one-third of respondents. The study concluded that *mental health problems in context of chronic violence should receive full attention through the provision of appropriate community-based services that would improve access to care and reduce the burden on the health system*[23]In another study conducted by SKIMS medical college, the prevalence of depression was seen to be 55% in Kashmiri population. The study concluded, '*To live in a community of total 6 million people having more than one million depressed and more than 10, 000 thinking in terms of ending their lives is a matter of great concern and a big challenge for medical professionals working in Kashmir.*'[24]

Although the look of the psychiatric hospital is changed lately, Kashmir with its burden of psychiatric diseases needs bigger and better psychiatric hospitals. There is no help available in villages from where the bulk of psychiatric disorders are reported. Except for a few NGOs working in villages, there is little initiative on the part of the Government to take care of people afflicted with psychiatric disorders in villages. An analysis done by State Human Rights Commission (SHRC) highlighted the malfunctioning at Psychiatric Diseases Hospital in Srinagar, indicating to the government that the facilities and care available there was inferior to that available in Jammu. In Jammu, the diet and other facilities were as per the PGI norms, whereas in Kashmir, patients were given a cup of tea and one *roti* for breakfast, *dal, chawal,* and vegetables for lunch. Patients were not given regular haircut, their toilets were not cleaned, and other inhuman conditions prevailed there, noted the SHRC.[25]

Cancer too came as a demon which seemed to swallow Kashmiri population. However, no policies were framed to detect cancer at an early stage, no awareness programmes were conducted, and no epidemiological studies were made. Whatever little work done was insignificant. A few beds for cancer patients at SKIMS were not sufficient to tackle cancer. Jammu and Kashmir was lagging behind in procuring advanced instruments for diagnosis and prevention of cancer. For certain investigations which could have been done well here, material and patients were referred to outside the state.

Cancer statistics were alarming. A 5-year retrospective analysis of malignancies diagnosed in the Department of Pathology, Government Medical College, Srinagar, from 1994 to 1998 showed that 1, 680 malignancies were diagnosed in the said time period with gastrointestinal malignancies constituting 42% of total malignancies (720 in total).[26] If this is the statistics from one hospital, then if the statistics from all hospitals of the valley is pooled, the figures will be more alarming. Gastrointestinal cancers in Kashmir are present in the form of an epidemic, but there is no strategy to look into its causation, pattern, early diagnosis, and treatment. Other cancers like lung cancer, breast cancer, and hemato-lymphoid malignancies are also on the rise. Women usually report very late for breast cancer and genital tract cancer because they are not aware of the warning signs of cancer as awareness programmes are lacking and they also feel shy to narrate their symptoms to over-busy health care professionals.

Immunisation programmes for infants and pregnant women also suffered as the health care professionals could not move about during hartals, curfews, and crackdowns.

While some attempt was made to recruit faculty into Government Medical College, Srinagar, to prevent its final fall 'adhocism' still prevailed. Again about nine super-specialists trained from the best institutions of the country were put on contractual assignment as 'adhoc consultants' at GMC, Srinagar. These doctors managed super-specialty clinics and helped to set up super-specialty services in various wards of SMHS hospital. Dialysis and ERCP was started by these dynamic ones who were really keen to give back something to their mother institution. But no one bothered to regularise their services; no one bothered to give them their due. These doctors could have been absorbed in any other institution of the world, and for their services, they could fetch hefty sums, but how was our state treating them? I see two PGI Chandigarh trained super-specialists—one an endocrinologist and another a gastroenterologist—still serving as adhoc employees in SMHS Hospital. They were my seniors in college and have been slogging for years. They endured humiliation for years . . . without confirmation. Why won't they leave Kashmir?

Our administrators did not have an understanding about the needs of our health institutions. Our teachers would tell us how in the past Government not only sponsored the advanced training of doctors but also on completion gave them responsible and respectable posts which would suit their merit and qualification. Each doctor trained was supposed to deliver . . . . That was the mindset. In these times, there are thousands of them but they are not being utilised.

2012 began with sadness for the health care of the valley. We lost more than 400 neonates in a span of 2 months at the valley's sole pediatric referral hospital named G.B. Panth, located on the busy national highway. G.B. Panth Hospital—meant to take care of neonates and children—witnessed its worst year in 2012. The deaths raised a hue and cry, and various theories came up about the loss of lives at G.B. Panth. Poor sanitation, lack of ventilators, and the callous attitude of the authorities were cited as the possible reasons. The hospital was ill equipped, overburdened, and understaffed. An inquiry was conducted to probe the cause of death of those neonats; the inquiry revealed that the grossly negligent hospital staff was spending more time in their clinics than in the hospital. The hospital facilities had not been upgraded for years and the deficiencies were coming to the surface now. The hospital was marred by something called 'dual control'; the Cantonment board and Jammu and Kashmir Government were controlling it jointly, adding to the confusion already existing in the hospital. Though there were warning signs about the mismanagement in G.B. Panth, those were never heeded to and the authorities did not care to set right the mess into which G.B. Panth had plunged.

People in villages and outskirts dying to see a pediatrician carried their sick children to G.B. Panth, which increased the load to the hospital. While trained pediatricians remained jobless, children continued to die in the outskirts too . . . . The 'doctors at the helm' were put under suspension for some time, other remedial measures were also looked into.

The issue of infant deaths was a serious matter—the public outcry forced the authorities to go for certain short-term measures . . . . We heard about a new pediatric hospital that would come up at Bemina, new ventilators which were being procured, a microbiology laboratory that was being set up, and the faculty that would be recruited. Did the lack of all this cause the infants to die? Perhaps 'Yes', or perhaps 'No'.

When I recollect the time I had spent in the pediatric hospital that used to exist close to the maternity hospital, it seems like a bad dream. Nothing was OK with the hospital then, but still not many infants would die. We knew it then that we were working in suboptimal conditions, but still patients would survive. We would attribute all to the Divine Hand—then.

With the shifting of the pediatric hospital to a bigger place, we thought things would change for good. But increase in space did not mean a better output. As an attendant of a neonate, I saw the horrifying state of the intensive care unit—how adults and neonates were packed together into it with their blankets and sheets, how infants in intensive settings were cared for by their attendants and not the nursing staff, and how nursing mothers who had recently delivered would fall helplessly on the floor—as no beds were available for them. Nobody took a note of anything that kept on happening at G.B. Panth in the name of patient care . . .

But 2013 solved the riddle, solved the issue of infant deaths. Infant deaths that occurred in G.B. Panth were attributed to the supply of 'Spurious drugs' to the hospital. The primary antibiotic used in the hospital was tested to be 0% pure: 'It contained no antibiotic at all.' Almost all sick infants who had been treated at G.B. Panth in 2012 were given spurious drugs, and naturally they died. The fake drug was recommended by the drug committee and was interestingly supplied to the hospitals in Kashmir only—it had a selective target population, it seems. Four hundred kids lost their lives and many more adults too must have lost theirs—because we don't know how many drugs that were supplied were fake and how many fake drugs were supplied to how many hospitals and medical stores. They promised an enquiry, but will the influential guilty be ever punished?

Health care is still not free from the cage. The military camps are still flourishing outside and inside our hospitals. The prime land of SKIMS with a huge building meant for mortuary is occupied by the security forces. This land would have been utilised by the authorities for extension of emergency, for making a passenger shed, or for making an auditorium.

Night-time, the doctors, staff, and attendants fear for their lives. If a cracker is burst or a juice pack bursts under a tyre, an alarm is sounded. Green heavy vehicles, barbed wires, sandbags, and angry soldiers on their toes carrying 'ready to fire guns'—are guarding SKIMS. Similarly in SMHS Hospital, there are huge areas occupied by the forces. What could have been used for patient-related activities is used by the forces for their own purpose. Soldiers occupying the bunkers in hospitals live in unclean surroundings. Lavatories and eating places are all clubbed together in one place, adding to the dirt already existing in our hospitals.

Dog's Days

Who would imagine that Srinagar, the pride of Vitasta, would soon become a 'city of dogs' where thousands would roam free, thriving on the garbage which was omnipresent? Dogs too did not spare our children and youngsters. They mutilated young kids, at times scaring them away in nearby lakes and rivers where they drowned. Name a place in Srinagar which is not a dog's hub. Poor Kashmiris projected as militants the world over were helpless before these creatures whose abundance in the city had terrified them. Meanwhile, Srinagar earned the distinction of being one of the dirtiest cities of India.

Animal rights groups all over India were united to protect the rights of dogs to live in Srinagar city. They came over in groups to see if the dogs were looked after well, but they never showed a concern for all those who were bitten . . . or the ones who died.

A sterilisation programme was launched to interrupt the breeding of dogs; kennels and dog ponds were established and crores spent on dog welfare. Young boys of the valley were employed to 'take care of dogs'. In a valley of dogs, humans were insecure, and the security of dogs was becoming an important issue . . . . In a shocking revelation on dog menace in Kashmir, at least 20 persons died of rabies in 5 years (2008-2012) while 80, 000 cases of dog bites were reported in the valley during this period. In 2012, 18, 228 cases of dog bites were recorded in district hospitals. ARC, the anti-rabies clinic at SMHS Hospital, recorded 5, 406 cases of dog bites in 2012. Nearly half of the cases of dog bites were class-III bites (where the victim has one or further bites, scratches, licks on broken skin, or extra contact that breaks the skin).[27]

There seems to be confusion regarding the number of dogs in the valley. As per the Minister of Housing, the actual number of dogs in Srinagar is 91, 110, whereas SMC (Srinagar Municipal Corporation) puts it as 48, 949. For every 13 persons in the valley, there is one stray dog, and the dog-human ratio is 1:13. If the present rate of dog reproduction continues in the valley, the dog population is expected to cross 20 lakh by 2015 in comparison to the expected 14 lakh human population.[28] The dog sterilisation programme, operational in the valley by which 10 dogs are sterilised every day, is a time-consuming project, requiring a lot of infrastructure—and a sterilised dog does not stop to bite, does not stop to defecate, and is not immune from rabies. In a conflict zone, should the dogs exceed humans and keep them in check?

Other Man-Animal Conflicts

Passing through the corridors of SKIMS, I stopped when I saw something frightful; waiting outside a doctor's room was a woman—less clearly delineated as human. She had a sunken face that looked like a badly broken pot; her jaw was gone, her face had stitch marks, and she had scars everywhere. Her mouth was drooping, with saliva drooling. I asked someone what was wrong with the woman. Some kind of accident, I thought. A bear maul, I was told. Two women were walking in an orchard in South Kashmir when a bear attacked them . . . . One died and the survivor was in front of my eyes. The patient was on treatment for the last 2 years. If this was the state now, how bad must have been her state earlier? I could not guess her age and didn't know if she was married or not. There was a young man accompanying her . . . . I didn't know whether it was her husband or her brother. If married, her family had a lot of burden to bear, and if not, I was sure she would never find a match.

Had this been an isolated incident, perhaps I would ignore it, but every year hundreds of Kashmiris are mauled by bears. In villages, other wild animals too are after human life. Bears, wolves, and lions, feeling insecure in the jungles made thin by jungle smugglers, venture often into nearby villages and pick up a kid, a woman, or a man. Sometimes, they eat poor villagers and tear them to bits, and sometimes their mauls turn beautiful faces into ugly ones. The attacks have considerably increased over the past few years because of extensive deforestation. A study done at Government Dental College by A.A. Shah has analysed the data of 200 bear maul injuries, who reported to Oral and Maxillofacial Surgery Department of Government Dental College from January 2005 to October 2009.[29] Most patients were males in their fourth decade. Breadwinners were made defunct. Studies from Sher-i-Kashmir Institute of Medical Sciences (SKIMS) on incidence and pattern of bear maul injuries based on a study of 417 cases has been published in reputed international Journals.[30]

In November 2010, more than two dozen people were injured by bears in South Kashmir, but after an attempt by a group of people to allegedly burn a bear, the Minister of Environment asked the Honourable Chief Minister of the state to take action against those involved in the attack on the bear. This news was highlighted by news channels all over India.[31] But what about all those injured in bear attacks, all those who died in such attacks? According to Wild Life Protection data from 2006 to 2011, 118 human deaths have occurred in Kashmir because of bear attacks, and there have been 1, 147 attacks over the said time period. Leopards also are known to attack humans in Kashmir, and a comparative study on 35 cases of Leopard attacks and 120 cases of bear attacks has found leopard attacks to be more severe than bear attacks.[32]

Jammu and Kashmir is a region where bear-human conflicts are rife with one in every ten hospital beds occupied by a victim of bear attacks.[33] A fund for the rehabilitation of the victims was promised—I don't know where it halted.

If these mauls would occur elsewhere, how would the governments and the press respond? The plastic surgeons of SKIMS spend nights operating upon such severely injured patients, which involves flaps, grafts, re-grafts, re-implants, and cosmetic surgeries. There are just six faculty members in the Department of Plastic Surgery at SKIMS, who have to bear almost the entire brunt of bear maul injuries. There are many plastic surgeons whose services are not being utilised; some of them are on contractual arrangement at SMHS. There should have been a separate unit to tackle all the mauls in a place where such happenings are common. Incidentally, an NGO from Germany recently set up a medical camp in which many patients with facial deformity were taken up for surgery at Rainawari hospital. I saw so many desperate women hiding their mauled faces behind veils and so many men with masked faces trying to hide their facial deformities-one of them did not have a nose. They all had come for specialist consultation. How many specialists were brought by the Government to look into the mutilating and disfiguring injuries of our brethren? Is bear conservation a national priority and not the treatment and rehabilitation of bear maul victims? What has the government done about these victims?

A Teenager's 'Lost' and 'Found' Story

Sarmad, a teenager, was sold for Rs. 10, 000 by a nurse in Srinagar's biggest maternity hospital to a childless couple on 2 August 1994, soon after he was born. Separated from his twin brother, at that time Sarmad made a tortuous and heart-rending journey back to his biological parents . . . . 17 years later, his story was published in a local newspaper.

A woman admitted to a major maternity hospital of Srinagar delivered twins on 2 August 1994. Though she did not know what she delivered, the attending nurse told her that she had given birth to a single baby boy who was in the cradle alongside her bed. But the woman insisted that she had given birth to twins as an ultrasound done prior to her admission in the hospital had shown that she was carrying a twin pregnancy. No one believed her and her ultrasound report.

The boy she delivered was sold for Rs. 10, 000 by the attending nurse to a childless couple. But after the boy was taken, his foster father and mother who were not getting along well with each other fought with each other bitterly. When the fight reached its zenith, his foster mother left her husband and came to live along with the boy with her father. The boy's foster grandfather brought him up with love. When the boy's foster grandfather died in 2004, his foster mother took him back to her husband's home where he was no longer welcome.

Sarmad's foster parents, especially his father, hated him, and spitting out his internal froth, he said to him one day, 'Go find your parents. You are not our blood.' The boy was shattered. He left his home, not knowing where to go. He spent three nights in a local mosque without food till he met one of the relatives of his foster parents and insisted him to tell him the truth about his birth. The relative was moved by the condition of the boy and told him the names of his biological father and mother and also gave him the address of the place where they lived.

He was curious to go to the place which was his lost home, hoping to see his parents, but the poor boy did not know about their state and whether they would recognise him, believe him or actually accept him. With these very thoughts in his mind, he located the house which was supposed to be his home. As he entered it, his mother recognised him the moment she saw him. Sarmad narrated his tale to his biological parents who were too happy to have him and accepted him as their own son. He met his twin brother there and was shocked to see how similar they looked. His parents wanted to do DNA analysis on him so that he carried a proof of his lineage—just in case the question of property inheritance demanded so.

Sarmad was stolen from Srinagar's biggest maternity hospital but returned just by sheer luck to his biological parents as a teenager. The boy was too overwhelmed to find his parents and did not want to fight a legal battle against the hospital authorities. His parents were too happy to have their son back and were not interested in punishment of anyone involved in the crime.

'I want my story told so that no greedy nurse or doctor dare sell someone's baby in future' Sarmad said without any anger in his voice to the news reporters.[34]

Sarmad was lost in 1994 and found in 2011. How many more Sarmads' were lost in those terrible 1990s and never returned to their parents, when those who sold precious lives were left free to steal? Is this what happens to the babies born in a zone of conflict?

An error done 17 years back will never be owned and yes, will never be probed. Like all mysterious happenings in our Dark Valley, all errors will be forgotten and manipulated to be forgiven. I recollect my days in maternity posting, my days during internship at LD Hospital. Those women who counted money in evenings, were they the ones who stole Sarmad from his mother or was it some other woman in some other hospital?

Those Doctors by Default!

Thanks to Facebook, I saw bald man. The terror man, the postponement man of our college days. The bald man was no more—bald . . . . He wore a wig, looked younger, and posed handsomely with his wife and kids. He was serving as a doctor in a rural area, perhaps in Kashmir, earning a good sum. And his friend in USA is doing well too. And another one in England is well settled there, posting huge articles for a popular newspaper in Kashmir—sermonising, teaching, and criticising us . . . . Those three doctors by default, should I hate them or not? They

used the turmoil and the gun to clear MBBS. They terrorised us. They
asked us to cover, and as I see their wives on Facebook—the modern
wives of modern gentlemen, I am not surprised. God forgive them! They
have got nothing to do with a pain called Kashmir or the painful called
Kashmiris. That was emotion; this is maturity. That was eruption; this is
sense . . . .

Many more mature and sensible guys and girls from Kashmir used
turmoil for their petty needs; when the need was satisfied they left for
greener pastures and are in different corners of the world .As of now, they
are relishing tinned Kashmiri *wazwan* and when on vacation enjoying
the scenic beauty of Kashmir. Occupation or no occupation, Kashmir is
not their headache now. These opportunists were never punished, neither
by the system nor by the Government. Separatists never loathed them;
the army never punished them. They were opportunists here; they used
Kashmir and its suffering for their own gains, and they multiplied their
opportunities wherever they went.

Turco

The faithful citizens of India, meanwhile, enjoyed their engagement
as 'interlocutors' and faithfully submitted the desired report. The report
was fluid . . . which could fit into any space—yet another *Turco* signed
by two men and a woman of conscience. We learnt how effectively the
reputed citizens could be used. Tufail's case too was closed in 2012—the
culprits were untraced. No justice to the victim, no justice for his parents.

Would those leaders and politicians visit Kashmir again and tell its
population how the case of Tufail Matoo was closed? The other 113 boys
and their families are not asking for justice as yet. Will it take 113 years
for the authorities to label the culprits as untraced and eventually close
the cases?

I thought I was done with Chattisinghpora in my book till some
dear one reminded me that it was the biggest joke, biggest mockery that
one of the biggest nations was playing in the name of justice. Massacre
of 36 Sikhs in Kashmir, subsequent killing of five innocent civilians who
were projected as militants behind the massacre, the frantic attempts
to tamper with the proof of their innocence, identification of guilty in
uniform who were proved to be guilty by court of law-what more do
you need to punish the culprits? Guilt was getting covered under thick

shield of AFSPA and guilty were roaming free. Chattisinghpora cannot be separated from Pathribal. Mind you, we are talking about secular India and justice to Sikhs of Chattisinghpora is important for the secular image of India. The victims of other grisly crimes in Kashmir who have been denied justice are not expecting justice, but justice should come to victims of Pathribal as Pathribal is linked to Chattisinghpora .Aren't there just orders from the Courts and no follow up? How far will the *Turco* go?

Recollections

On 31 July 2012, 24 years after the armed struggle began in Kashmir, I read a memoriam in Greater Kashmir, which recycled my pain, all through my body, my soul, and my senses. I don't add a word or subtract a word from what I read:

Memoriam

In the memory of our two beloved sons Taj-ud-Din Ahmad (20 years) and Imtiyaz-ud-Din (13 years), who were put to eternal sleep by the irate Jawans of BSF 30th Bn on this fateful day (31 July 1992), their separation has left us in a state of perennial agony and shock. We continue to mourn their separation even after 19 years. We are unable to reconcile with the idea of their separation from the family more so when the killers are at large and justice eludes the 'Shaheeds'. We know that when the Prophet Muhammad's (SAW) own son died, he said, 'The eyes shed tears and the heart is grieved, but we will not say anything except which pleases our Lord.'

We know that one should strive to be patient and remember that Allah is the one who gives life and takes it away, at a time appointed by Him. It is not for us to question Allah's wisdom.

We too are mortals and till we survive on this earth, we cannot forget the horrifying scene enacted by criminals in uniform. On that fateful day, our darling Imtiyaz-ud-Din, on hearing a knock at the door and presuming it to be his father rushed in excitement to open the door, was shot in the head at point blank range and on hearing the gunshots, his elder brother Taj-ud-Din came down only to find his brother lying with his head blown. He too was not spared the bullets by the killers. They pumped in a hail of bullets into his abdomen leaving him in a pool of blood with his mother crying for help and any help that could come by was prevented from reaching them by the marauding Jawans.

Rest is history! The sad plight of the bereaved aged parents in absence of their male children can only be imagined!

To our beloved sons, we in our old age could not do much to get justice but we believed in the Divine justice and on the day of justice, we will definitely challenge the perpetrators of crime and seek justice for you. May Allah bless you with Magfirah and help us to bear your separation . . . Ameen.

Mehmood-ul-Hassan Farooqi and Family, Lal Bazar, Srinagar.

Show me an eye which will not drown in tears on reading this pathetic story. Show me a heart which will not explode with gloom after going through this painful happening.

Will all those who have borne this tragedy and many more tragedies of this sort ever reconcile to the fact that 'all is well with/in Kashmir'?

Mother of Tragedies

What has been India's worst massacre? Was it the massacre at Jallianwala Bagh, the one at Jammu, at Surat, at Delhi, or was it here in Kashmir—the massacre at Hawal, the massacre at Khanyar, the massacre at Sopore, or the mother of tragedies, the massacre at Gawkadal? Over the last few years, my memory is getting unwound; my tears are rebuilding as I read those obituaries—the obituaries of three young girls: Saltanat, Uzma, and Neelam, who lost their father on that fateful day at Gawkadal on 20 January 1990. Their father worked with Cable Car Corporation and had promised them a ride along the snow-covered peaks of Gulmarg in the Gondola. That day never came as they lost their father at Gawkadal. Their father had received 32 bullets. The educated daughters of a Gawkadal martyr tell their tale of loss and pain every year.

They were so tiny when their father fell to bullets. They survived the calamity but they remember him, and they recall what it means to lose father at a young age. They recall how it feels like not getting justice.

There was an engineer, an eyewitness of the tragedy who was dumped with the dead and later on found to be alive; many bullets had pierced him. At bone and joint hospital Dr Ashai had helped him relive his life; he had died in Gawkadal and was reborn in the hospital. Every Kashmiri who had not been to Gawkadal or who was born after Gawkadal happened knows the story of the engineer-it is a story that is too real to be believed.

On the day of a massacre, the hospitals would be drenched in blood and drowned in cries. All would volunteer for help, strangers would line up for blood donation, and heads of the departments would clean the operation theatres, wards and wash off the blood.

Massacres are not worth forgiving; they are never forgotten. Every time there will be a person recapitulating as to what happened to him, to his dear one, or to his distant one . . . on the day of the massacre. If justice doesn't come by, it becomes an agonising oozing sore.

I cannot narrate anything about that massacre in Gawkadal on 20 January 1990. For the last 23 years, I have been hearing different stories about what happened to us on that day. But I read in Wikipedia recently about all that happened to us on that sad winter day, just to refresh my memory. Wiki knows it, so does the world; they know it all, and they say all that happened to us was inhuman, but that is it. Didn't we deserve anything more . . . not an atom of justice? Let me recall the concluding words of the greatest tragedy of my life as reported by Wikipedia.

> 'No known action was ever taken against the CRPF forces officials responsible for the massacre, or against the officers present at Gawkadal that night. No government investigation was ever ordered into the incident. Fifteen years later, the police case was closed and those involved in the massacre were declared untraceable. No challan has been produced against any person in court'.[35]

The British Prime Minister arrived in India this year to seek support from Indians living in England for the forthcoming elections. Indian media and Government was not interested in what Mr Prime Minister was asking for; they only wanted an apology for a crime committed by British soldiers more than a century ago at Jallianwala Bagh where innocent Indians were killed. The British Prime Minister called the massacre unfortunate, but India is waiting for a formal apology. Ask the nation who should apologise to Kashmiris for their massacres? What do Kashmiris do with the memories of their tragedies? Who will give them justice? Why are their killers untraced and their innocents easily traced?

Is rape here different from rape there?

I read about the gang rape of a medical student in a Delhi bus. I felt sick and sad—the incident is a shameful one for the entire humanity. The nation was all in unison against this crime, out on the streets, pelting stones and demanding protection for women. Women in India deserve to be secure—we understand that!

But, somewhere in the northern mountains, thirty women of two villages, Kunan and Poshpora of Kashmir's Kupwara District, were allegedly gang-raped by army personnel of 4-Rajputana Rifles on the intervening night of 23 and 24 February in 1991.[36]

Interesting, the Press Council of India (PCI) team led by Mr B. Verghese visited Kashmir in June that year and claimed that charges against army were a 'well concocted bundle of fabricated lies'. The committee commenting on the medical reports of the victims called the abrasions and torn hymens seen in some of the victims as 'common among village folk of Kashmir' and attributed those to 'natural factors, injury or premarital sex'.[1] The allegation of mass rape was seen as a conspiracy to malign the image of the armed forces.

The J&K Government closed the investigations as 'untraced', and many years later, the State Human Rights Commission was approached by the petitioners in 2004. The commission gave recommendations to reinvestigate the 1991 Kunan-Poshpora 'mass rape' case. Justice (Retd) Javed Kawoosa observed, 'Right from February 1991, all successive governments and district administrators have been guilty of callous, negligent, insensitive and indifferent attitude towards the victims as if nothing has happened in these two villages on the intervening night of 23 and 24 February and 1991.'[37]

I watched the video on YouTube. The women who suffered on that dark night were narrating their tale, hesitantly, with hiccups and interruptions. They were shy, humble, and modest—narrating ugly stories about themselves. That sadness, sorrow, and humiliation they experienced had made them restless forever.

Why didn't we hear about a probe? Why didn't a single soul cry for these women? The governments I know are run by politicians who sideline issues like this. I wonder at the silence of civil society groups, women's groups, national and international human rights groups . . . . Why the silence on these particular incidents? So much time has passed by, yet justice to the victims has not come by.

There is a ray of hope for the victims lately; the case has been reopened. After 22 years, politicians are apologising. The women met the press a week after the case was reopened in a press conference organised by the group namely Jammu Kashmir Coalition of Civil Society where they renewed their resolve to fight the mass injustice. They narrated their tale yet again, how they were assaulted physically and mentally, how they kept quiet about their young unmarried co-sufferers' sufferings, who they believed would not get a match if people came to know about the assaults on them, how a woman who was in her post-partum period was also raped, how a pregnant woman (who later gave birth to a deformed baby) too was raped, how so many of them became so sick that hysterectomies had to be performed in 18 of them, how they have been telling the reporters about their sufferings, how have been clicked over and over again, making them repeat their sad tales, and how justice has been denied to all of them. Even the people of Kashmir, the victims felt, were not proud of them though they suffered at the same hands as other victims of conflict, i.e. martyrs suffered but no Kashmiri was proud of them.

After decades of silence the civil society groups in Delhi are also crying for help for the victims of Kunan-Poshpora. The Centre for Policy Analysis, New Delhi, a think tank of civil society activists and experts under the Directorship of Seema Mustafa has since 2009 been involved with the people of Kashmir in the search of a peaceful and just solution. Over the years, several groups of civil society activists and experts have visited Kashmir; this year they visited Kunan-Poshpora to find the facts about the alleged mass rape. They wrote a letter to the Prime Minister who was on a recent visit to Kashmir to ensure the delivery of justice to the victims of Kunan-Poshpora, the women who were allegedly assaulted and raped.

Interestingly, the officers who showed solidarity with the Delhi rape victim whitewashed the sins of the culprits in Kashmir. Don't call them shameless, O defenders of a mass crime. They are powerless, we agree!

Though probes don't reveal what the authorities conceal, the results of probes into murders and rapes stunned us. Aasia and Neelofer died as a result of drowning in the shallow waters of a stream which was just ankle deep—reported the CBI, the premier investigating agency of this country. The alleged rape and murder of these young Shopian women became a mystery. The storm seen on the streets of Kashmir didn't bring out the truth. We lost two women and many more young men—but still truth was packed layers deep . . .

The young child of one of the ladies murdered in Shopian has yet to grow, has yet to look for his mother, and has yet to crave for the truth about her. His motherless childhood will trouble him, and the knowledge about her mysterious death will twinge him. How will he respond to his mother's call for justice? Won't he look for the spot where she breathed her last? Won't he scan the bushes where she walked last? Won't he stare at the stream that she last negotiated? Rape is rape—a horrifying crime. With or without justification, it is still rape. You cannot remain silent over one rape and stage protests for another. What is rape for a Delhi girl is rape for a Kashmiri girl. If you demand capital punishment for a rapist in Delhi, I demand the same for a rapist in Kashmir. No cloak should cover a rapist; no uniform should shield him. I hope they understand it well.

Why don't they all understand this, when I tell it?

When we protest, why do they want a sense in our protests? But when Delhi erupts, why do the senses get blocked, the roads witness roars, and policemen are pushed to the walls? You should hear those TV anchors and watch their rage on their TV shows when such incidents happen in their communities, and when such incidents occur in Kashmir, they always support the official version, defend it, or else ignore the incident. Thousands of rapes have gone unaccounted for in Kashmir . . . . How do we bring the culprits to justice?

Vanishing juveniles and expanding mass graves

That boy was just 14 when troops of 163 Battalion of Paramilitary Border Security Force arrested him on 13 March 1995 from his home in

Wagoora, Varmul. The family kept on searching for the boy, and after a prolonged struggle to know the whereabouts of their son, a four-member committee constituted by the Government established that two members of 163 Battalion were involved in the disappearance of the boy. And the committee reached a conclusion that 'Muhammad Iqbal Shah, son of Muhammad Yousuf Shah, a student of class 10th is presumed to be killed and his dead body disposed off somewhere'. Iqbal holds an unenviable distinction—being the youngest amongst thousands of Kashmiris who disappeared in custody.[37] Why don't the saviours of the nation light a candle for him? At 14, he was not a criminal. We hesitate to punish the juvenile killer rapist of Delhi, but here we can kill a boy and conceal the body somewhere.

Justice for juveniles in the conflict zone is a far-fetched dream. A report by Asia Centre for Human Rights (ACHR) established that juveniles in the conflict area of Kashmir were denied access to juvenile justice unlike their counterparts in the rest of the country.[38] No wonder Kashmiri boys were detained, tortured, and sexually assaulted; add to this list the ones who were getting killed and ones who were made to disappear somewhere.

What and where is that somewhere?

This somewhere has haunted Kashmiris over the last two decades. Those known and unknown faces who left behind waiting families and could not come home were buried in these graves. International People's Tribunal on Human Rights and Justice in Kashmir published a document called 'Buried Evidence' in 2009 in which they documented the presence of 2, 700 unmarked graves in Kashmir.[39] Activists from the valley, including the most prominent one, Parvez Imroz, a lawyer, struggled to find facts about these graves. The fake encounter at Machil in 2010, in which three boys were killed and projected to the world as militants, caused a stir in the entire valley. But Parvez Imroz and his men found about the entire drama as to how three men were lured, trapped and killed by the army on 28 May 2010. Three bodies were exhumed and were identified by their family members. From this painful episode to thousands of unmarked graves, Imroz and his field workers identified more than 8, 000 unmarked and mass graves in Kashmir spread across all the districts of Kashmir.[40]

'Mass graves' existed in Kashmir, we knew it long back . . . but this question has never bothered anyone in the country. For the relatives of disappeared persons, mass graves matter. They would like to perform

the last rites of their dear ones. They would like to get rid of a painful
wait . . . . They would like to pray for the peace of the departed souls. A
son would see his father's grave, a mother would choose her burial site—
next to her son's grave, and a 'half widow' would plan ahead with her life.

UN says that Kashmiri families have a right to know the truth and
that when a disappeared person is found to be dead—the right to have
the remains of their loved one returned to them and to dispose of those
remains according to their own tradition, religion, or culture; however
the DNA profiling of the graves and identification of the people in those
graves has not been undertaken as DNA tests are believed to create a law
and order problem.[41] So, if a major step in the journey towards truth is
missing, how will truth come to the surface?

In Lal Chowk, the hub of the city, there is a park called Partap Park,
where a few women, old men, and children arrange a sit-in. They wear
badges and bands and sometimes hold placards of 'APDP'. They are the
members of an association of disappeared persons, the members of a
group started by a woman whose teenage son disappeared 23 years ago.
The unlettered woman, Parveena Ahangar, better known as the 'iron lady
of Kashmir' who lost her 'apple of the eye' is tired but not losing hope.
She believes she can find the truth about her son and about others who
disappeared. In the sit-ins that are organised by APDP, some members are
seen regularly while some know that nothing comes out of such sit-ins.
Some women love to be there . . . to share their grief with each other.
They hope against hope, waiting for a miracle to happen. No politician
talks to them ever or hears them ever. Some parents have died in wait
and some orphans have lost their mental balance waiting for a parent they
never saw.

Initially, there was a denial about the existence of mass graves; later
on those buried in unmarked graves were labelled as militants, but as
more and more facts came up on to the surface, there was discussion on
the unmarked graves in the assembly with legislators for the first time
in 2011 talking about the 'need for identification of unidentified men
buried in thousands of unmarked graves in the state'. Though legislators
called those buried in unmarked graves as their own 'Lakhte-Jigar' and
quoted examples of a few men of their own district who disappeared . . .
nothing more happened in this regard.[42]

Adrian Levy and Cathy Scott-Clark in their revealing book 'The
Meadow: terrorism, kidnapping and conspiracy in paradise' talk in depth
about the mass graves and enforced disappearances in context to the

abduction of six foreigners in Kashmir. 'Get them by balls, minds and hearts will follow' was the torture slogan used by renegades who caught and killed the innocent. The authors claim that far from being utterly clueless the Indian security forces identified the hostages' exact location early on, but chose not to act simply to prolong the adverse international publicity for Pakistan. One foreigner was killed, one ran away, and the other four were sold to surrendered militants and shot in cold blood on 24 December 1995. And if authors are to be believed, are the abducted foreigners too buried in unknown graves? [43]

When 'The Meadow' came out with revealing facts about the abduction of foreigners, SHRC wanted the case reopened, but the state police informed the SHRC that the master file of the case of the kidnapping of six foreigners was gutted in a fire incident. [44] The truth about the foreigners' kidnapping would have thrown many skeletons out of the cupboard . . .

Truth Sprouting

There was a time when except for the BBC Urdu Service no channel spoke about us. But then over the last few years, cry for justice is erupting from conscious citizens of the world. Many documentaries and movies are being made, attempting to tell the truth about Kashmir. Jezza Neumann, a BAFTA award winner, made a documentary on Kashmir—'Kashmir's Torture Trail' aired on Channel 4 in United Kingdom. The documentary highlighted systematic human rights abuses in Kashmir. It exposed a network of Government-run torture centres in Kashmir. The film had the highest number of viewer comments after its transmission; Amnesty International also featured the film.

Jezza Neumann in an interview to Daily Greater Kashmir (1 August 2012) told that he is not surprised at the silence of USA and Britain on all that is happening within the valley as 'the lure of Indian markets' has silenced everyone. He asks certain thoughtful questions about India's moral and human obligations. Talking about Kashmir, Neuman says, 'Here is a place where there is no comeback, no oversight, no monitoring or accountability. It is a morality vacuum where any crime can be committed without the intervention of the criminal justice system—if you are a security force trooper or a policeman. But if you are a citizen, you can be preventatively arrested for 2 years. It is difficult to think of anywhere else in the world where such an imbalance has occurred. Once it was claimed that these measures were necessary to fight terror. But what now? No justice, no peace. That is the old rubric. In Kashmir it is undoubtedly true.'[45]

Thanks to Neuman for recognising what was left unrecognised for ages.

As kids we always heard in our dining rooms and around gossip centres (i.e *Tare boonie*) about *Centre ki chal* but Gen. V.K Singh has removed the tight lid from the secretive missions of Army and other agencies operating in Kashmir. Much more needs to come to forefront.

Dr Guru and the Truth about Him

Wajahat Habibullah—a bureaucrat of high rank who practiced all his wisdom in Kashmir—opened up in his book about many things that had happened in Kashmir when he was posted here. He maintained a criminal silence over many cover-ups for decades together. He pretended to be sympathetic but recommended our killers for national awards. In his book, he talks about the killing of the most respected person in our fraternity, Dr A.A. Guru. He writes:

> *In April 1993, the Chief ideologue of the JKLF, Dr Abdul Ahad Guru, was kidnapped and brutally murdered by the Hizb-ul-Mujahideen militant Zulqarnain. Guru, a leading Srinagar physician who had founded a medical college, had commanded wide respect; he presented a reasonable face of separation. He was therefore an inconvenience to the police. The police made an arrangement with the terrorist Zulqarnain, then in custody, who agreed to kill Guru in exchange for his release. But to ensure that this collusion remained secret, Zulqarnain was killed shortly thereafter, and the Director General of Police, B.S. Bedi, trumpeted his death as a triumph for the security forces, who had killed a dangerous terrorist in an armed encounter. But the truth was somewhat different. Instead of killing Zulqarnain in a armed encounter, the police stormed the home where under the mistaken presumption that he was safe after having fulfilled his end of the bargain, he was consorting with a girl friend.[21]*

Years have gone by since that son of the soil was silenced. His family must have never heard from medical fraternity about how they were doing. No one talked about him. No one possibly thought about him. No lecture was ever conducted in his honour. No talk was ever delivered in his memory. The college he conceived and erected with hope did not have a single stone bearing his name. Was it all a consequence of fear and suppression? Or was it a blunted conscience of the entire medical fraternity or a collective thought block?

We all came out on streets, remember? We all waved for *azadi*—then what was it that Dr Guru did? Didn't he do all in open what we did behind our veils? I heard his son—a successful urologist in USA—speaking at a urology conference in Kashmir. He was on a mission to help earthquake victims and other downtrodden in Kashmir. Selfless service for Kashmiris was his goal too. He spoke in the same hall where his father had spoken; he spoke about robotics, urological advances, and his will to help SKIMS and other hospitals of Kashmir. But I heard others too, who called him 'like father, like son' . . . . Strange that never before did they utter a word, never before did they demand a probe into his killing, never before did they demand a help (not that they needed it) for his family. His son must have his story, which no one shared with him; he must have felt lonely, depressed, victimised at times, but we left him all alone—to fight his own battle. Now that when he was back, without a grudge, a grievance, or a hope from us, we dare call him a 'son of the soil', knowing how we forgot his father. He must be obsessed with his father and his memories. Will he forgive us?

I write these lines with great humility, an apology to the family of a great man. Strange that Kashmiris realise most things much later after the events have gone by. They identify the traitors later; they identify the martyrs later. Is it innocence or an unpardonable ignorance?

Another Guru and the Collective Conscience

The Honourable President of India turned down the mercy petition of Mr Afzal Guru—a surrendered Kashmiri militant who was blamed for an attack on the Parliament House based on circumstantial evidence. Guru was to be hanged 'to satisfy the collective conscience' of the nation. The verdict was a gut feeling, a feeling in the subconscious that sending a Kashmiri to the gallows would satisfy the nation of India.

It was done as planned without any information to the family of Afzal Guru. The information to the family that their dear one was to be hanged reached them 3 days after he was hanged. For 2 weeks curfew was clamped in Kashmir. No protests were allowed and Kashmiris sobbed and grieved yet again in February 2013—inside their homes. Military and paramilitary forces showed their might again on the roads, highways, and meadows of Kashmir.

Afzal Guru had been a medical student at Jhelum Valley College of Medical Sciences, the same college that produced Shah Faisal, the IAS topper of 2010 batch. Afzal left his studies midway and went across the border for arms training. He returned dissatisfied and gave up the gun in an official surrender ceremony and vowed to live a normal life. He was never allowed to lead a normal life. Playing hide and seek with the people who were chasing him, he was somehow caught in the Parliament House mess. Whether he was guilty or not, he was not allowed a last appeal. So a doctor who couldn't become one, a Kashmiri was silenced forever. Incidentally, he was a close relative of Dr Guru—the famous surgeon. With Ashiq Hussain and Dr Guru, Afzal was the third member of the Guru family to be killed. Had he become a doctor, he would have been my contemporary, but Allah had a different plan for him—he was hanged to let the world know how much Kashmir is cared for . . . . That is why he superseded all others waiting in line to be hung.

Another Kashmiri down . . . how do I gulp it down my throat?

Besides their necks getting twisted, bullets are tearing the atria and ventricles of Kashmiris making huge holes there, disrupting the continuity of major vessels-the doctors present the data of ill fated and yet there is stubbornness . . . . on all sides[46]. Our eyes have enough tears, was there a need really to torrent them with teargas and blind them with pepper gas? And will these measures stop Kashmiris from asking for their due?

Musical Concerts and the cry of art

One of the noted singers of Kashmir, Mr Ghulam Nabi Sheikh was killed on his way to Delhi in a train. No one probed his death. His daughter who accompanied him on the train has bitter memories about the entire incident and she keeps on recollecting them in obituaries which are published every year in newspapers. She is not tired of asking for justice . . . . No Indian music lover asked for justice for Ghulam

Nabi Sheikh or his family. No Indian music lover asked for justice for a young handicapped musician who was shot dead by the security forces at Khayam. 'His time of death had come' is all they said. In a nation where music is worshipped-two Kashmiri artists-died mercilessly. It bothers our youngsters that reaction to 'Pragash' ban was so different and that there was no reaction at all to these cold-blooded murders!

Drama after drama is being enacted in Kashmir. One such drama was calling Zubin Mehta to perform in Kashmir. In a company of India's elite and Kashmir's insensitive he played *'Ehsas-e-Kashmir'*. No stones were pelted on his cavalcade but Kashmir bounced back with *Haqeeqat-e-Kashmir*. There was a dramatisation of our tragedies by our artists and yes, there was real tragedy too that day-a bunch Kashmiri youth were killed that day—a *Haqeeqat* the world witnessed. And Zubin Mehta had come to command us to keep mum. We want to question Zubin Mehta;

> *When our musicians could not perform in a sieged vale,*
> *How dare you Zubin Mehta? . . .*
> *. . . Can you construct tunes for the lost voices of Kashmir?*
> *We will provide the background on the screen of our sorrows . . .*

Leaderless or Pathless

The most unfortunate thing about Kashmir has been its inability to breed a leader—a leader who could earmark a path for people to follow. There are just too many of them—each one with a different agenda. The leaders do not converge but resonate at varying wavelengths. Whom to trust is a big question?

The plight of Kashmir and its leaders is described aptly in this line by someone who has known our leaders.

Kharabi kismatas ya cha khami rehbaran hinz . . . . (Was it our bad luck or a deficiency on part of our leaders?)

The blood that has stained the soul of Kashmir is restless to question its long lineage of leaders:

> Why did you speak something here and something else in
> New Delhi?

Why did you enter into accords and agreements without
telling us the truth?
Why did you use us?
Why did you fool us?
Why did you loot us?
And why do you rule us?
Oh you, standing meekly and apologetically before a
powerful country
Do you remember whom you represent?

They have questions for separatists too:

Why did you belittle us?
Why did you hurt us?
Why did you crack us?

Our sufferings gave you a name and fame . . . . Introspect. Unite.
Unite for the sake of truth. Unite for the sake of our today and tomorrow.
Don't divide the people but devise strategies to help them. Learn from
the history; it will not forgive you if you don't unite for a common
purpose . . . . It is merciless. It made dragons out of heroes. Fear it . . . for
God's sake.

Shreds of Kohimaran

I do go to see my parents twice or thrice a week. So many people
moved out of Makhdoom Sahib to the so-called posh areas of the city.
Some of our uncles too moved. But my parents are happy to be there.
Much has changed in Makhdoom Sahib over the last 20 years. Huge
concrete houses have come up everywhere, and they are now obstructing
the view of the shrine. *Tare-Booni* has been occupied. When the *Booni*
was occupied, a structure called a house was raised around it overnight.
No one objected. And now it is shrivelled and shrunk. Its trunk tapers
into a branch and escapes through the roof of the house that has encircled
it. The trunk adorns the drawing room of the occupier. How long will
Tare-Booni be able to stand this strangulation—I don't know. And how
long will the people around be able to tolerate the chinar? God alone
knows.

The stairs of the shrine are shabby; those makeshift shops with thick plastic sheltering them have blocked those rocks where we would play and shout. The graveyard up therein has been walled with glass, and many people dear to me are buried there. They died without their wish of a peaceful Kashmir being fulfilled. I can spot the graves of all those boys who died during the turmoil. The massive lawns where pigeons would perch have a beautiful though dingy mosque in the middle named Masjid-i-Aisha.

As you go further, the vandalisation is apparent. Kohimaran will soon have a Gondola. The pillars are already up and the digging is on. The long stretch of land which had blossoming almond trees looks desert-like as each tree was cut to make space for something that has not come up over the last 15 years. And there lies a mosque—the battered and lonely Malshah Mosque, with some reconstruction going on there. It was destroyed periodically by different rulers who ruled Kashmir—by Dogras and Sikhs, each group leaving its scar on the mosque, each different scar reminding us about our new ruler. The painted rocks which were sacred for Pandits and where they used to bow have faded. After sometime, they may not be visible.

On the fort too, some reconstruction is going on, but no one is allowed up. The fort reminds us about another set of rulers. It is still occupied. Occupiers may leave it, but they too will leave behind their scars. The Gondola—which was neither wanted nor needed . . . was brought here to eventually destroy the peace and tranquillity of the area . . . . Its existence will be a reminder of another rule . . .

Down there is Nowhatta—the chowk of unrest—guarded by those huge vehicles with big words 'RIOT CONTROL' written on them. It is an effective method of population control.

My heart is here . . . . When I die, I would love to be buried here with all those and all that I loved. But I belong elsewhere. I will have to be buried elsewhere. Will my father give me a strip of land here . . . or will my brother?

Epilogue

I feel sorry for my father—he saw 1947, 1948, 1953, 1965, 1971, 1989, 1990s, 2008, 2009, 2010, and 2013. How unlucky has been his generation! He has heard his father recount to him the tragedy of 'Quit Kashmir'. His brother died in the 1990s without his wish of a peaceful Kashmir being fulfilled. His cousins too died . . . without a major wish of theirs being fulfilled. At this stage, he reads four newspapers daily and keeps his television constantly on; the news channels flash news every second. He reads the captions with care . . . hoping every moment that something positive about Kashmir will come out. He pins hope on every meeting, every foreign secretary level talk, every minister level talk and continues to hope against hope. An optimist, he believed in peace and in peaceful resolution of Kashmir conflict. He and the survivors of his generation are all like him. I feel sorry for my mother too, who has so many of her relatives in Pakistan. She has seen her widow mother and siblings suffer, when they had no assistance from any quarter. She sings Kashmiri *wanvun* (songs) for all those who died and for all those who migrated . . . to the other side.

My parents and their generation are peace-loving, meek, brotherly, and progressive. They never thought of guns and never talked about rebellion but had the desire for a solution to the Kashmir problem deep inside their heart. They wished for 'freedom'. But they were keener to fight the illiteracy and poverty that was imposed on their fathers and grandfathers by the oppressive regimes. They voted in elections which were rigged and cheered for leaders who backtracked from their promises. They begged for their sons and daughters sponsorships, scholarships, seats for them in professional colleges, and jobs for them in the Government sector. They succeeded in all that . . . but could not hide that sentiment deep inside their hearts . . . the sentiment of 'freedom', the sentiment of *azadi*. A serious promise was broken and all were silent.

But their kids had a stronger desire. Their disgust grew stronger with every rigged election, with every selection, with every dismissed Government, and with every imprisoned leader. They revolted with guns . . . died and were devastated. Their children, another generation of Kashmiris, rose again and demanded the same with a stone in their hands. Now they have nothing in hand, just a tongue to shout *azadi*. Who will contain them and for how long?

Our parents do tell us sometimes, '*Aes aus theek*' (we were OK). Gun spoiled us.' But we know that is not true. They were never happy with how they had been treated. It was they who would grow hopeful of the Kashmir resolution with each war; it was they who boycotted Independence Day and Republic Day celebrations; it was they who kept on hoping . . . When our generation took to the streets, they were the greatest supporters; when they took to guns, they welcomed both gunmen and guns. The two generations had a different modus operandi but the same motive . . . . Our generation called their previous generation *buz dil* (weak-hearted), and they in turn called our generation *baykel* (foolish). In the pursuit of its goal, I hope Generation Next has overcome both. But sadly for a Kashmiri, two innocent unarmed youngsters were killed the same fortnight Parvez Rasool was inducted into Team India. What do I conclude?

I as a doctor have seen suffering closely; this loss of life, this destruction taking place periodically or continuously has shattered generations of us. We have been living in *phreth* (exteme fear) amidst *chrati chrath* (physically manifest struggle) of our fellow beings. As I enter my workplace, I see some photographs on the walls; these are the photos of the employees who died in conflict, and as I ascend upstairs, I see an employee on a wheelchair waiting outside the lift for his turn to move up. He was shot long time ago in his back, which bound him to a wheelchair. He smiles still . . .

This pain won't leave us. Is there no remedy? Is there no cure? Whom should we approach for a solution to our pain? Or will the ooze continue to feed the hungry hawks?

References

1. Gossman P. The human rights crisis in Kashmir: a pattern of impunity. New York: Human Rights Watch and Physicians for Human Rights; 1993. p. 8, 50, 93, 112-125.
2. Jaleel M. Army takes away groom on day 1 of wedding, sends his body back. Indian Express. 2003 Sep 17.
3. Reshi AR, Najar MS, Ahmad A, Masood T. Acute renal failure following further physical torture. Nephrol Dial Transplant. 1995; 10(2):198-202.
4. Malik GH, Sirwal IA, Reshi AR, Najar MS, TanvirM, Altaf M.Acute renal failure following physical torture.Nephron 1993;63:434-437
5. Sharma J, Varadarajan S. Panchalthan case an embarrassment for Farooq. Times of India. 2002 Mar 6. 11.50 a.m.
6. DNA fudge: forensic lab stands by report. Times of India. 2002 Mar 6.
7. Kounsar H. J&K fudges DNA samples to cover up killings. Times of India. 2002 Mar 6.
8. Evidently wrong. So, the lie has finally been nailed. Editorial. Times of India. 2002 Mar 9.
9. Nessman R. Amid conflict Kashmir man tries suicide 13 times. NBC news.com. 2010 Aug 14.
10. Malik GM, Basu J. Landmines: time for ban. Lancet. 1997;350(9081):891
11. Lone GN. Experience with abdominal trauma in Kashmir. JK-Practitioner. 2001;8(4):225-230
12. Margoob MA, Firdousi MM, Ali Z, Hussain A, Mushtaq H, Khan AY, et al. Treatment seeking posttraumatic stress disorder patient population: experiences from Kashmir. JK-Practitioner. 2006; 13 Suppl 1:57-60.

13. Margoob MA, Firdosi MM, Ali Zafar. Defeat depression program. JK-Practitioner. 2006; 13 Suppl 1:123-124.
14. Summerfield D. Medical ethics: the Israeli Medical Association. Lancet. 1997; 350(9070):63-64.
15. Dhar SA, Dar TA, Wani SA, Hussain S, Dar RA, Wani ZA et al.In the line of duty:a study of Ambulance drivers during the 2010 conflict in Kashmir .Prehosp.Disaster Med 2012;27(4):381-4
16. Wani MI, Sultan A, Wani MM, Malik M, Baba MA, Masrat N. Pattern of injuries due to rubber bullets in a conflict zone. Internet J Orthop Surg. 2010; 17(2):1. DOI: 10.5580/Ic92.
17. Wani AA, Zargar J, Ramzan AU, Malik NK, Qayoom A, Kirmani AR, et al. Head injury caused by tear gas cartridge in teenage population. Pediatr Neurosurg. 2010; 46(1):25-28.
18. Khan S, Maqbool A, Abdullah N, Keng AQ. Pattern of ocular injuries in stone pelters in Kashmir Valley. Saudi J Ophthalmol. 2012; 26(3):327-330.
19. Wani AA, Ramzan AU, Shoaib Y, Malik NK, Nizami FA, Dhar A, et al. Stray bullet: an accidental killer during riot control. Surg Neurol Int. 2011; 2:122.
20. Maqbool M. Being Syeda Begum: a mother's tragedy-II. Greater Kashmir. 2012 Dec 9.
21. Fayyaz AA. Army police face off over timber in J&K. The Hindu. 2013 Jun 12.
22. Habibullah W. My Kashmir: conflict and the prospects of enduring peace. Washington, DC: United States Institute of Peace; 2008. P 82, 135.
23. de Jong K, Kam S, Ford N, Lokuge K, Fromm S, van Galen R et al. Conflict in Indian Kashmir valley II: psychosocial impact. Conflict and Health. 2008; 2:11 Available from: http//www.conflictandhealth.com/content/2/1/11.
24. Amin S, Khan AW. Life in conflict: characteristics of depression in Kashmir. Int J Health Sci (Qassim). 2009; 3(2):213-223.
25. Facilities and care in Srinagar mental hospital alarmingly inferior to those available in Jammu hospital. Fresh Initiative. 2012 May 18.
26. Rumana M, Khan AR, Besina S, Seema A, Shah BA, Nayi K, et al. Cancer profile in Kashmir valley: an institutional experience JK-Practitioner. 2011; 16(1-2):50-54.
27. Hasssan M. Kashmir: 20 rabies deaths, 80,000 dogs bite cases in 5 years. Greater Kashmir. 2013 Mar 25.

28. GK News. Dog census figures go chaotic. Greater Kashmir. 2013 Mar 26.
29. Shah AA. Pattern of maxillofacial injuries in Kashmir. Natl J Maxillofac Surg. 2010;1(2):96-101
30. Rasool A, Wani AH, Darzi MA, Zaroo MI, Iqbal S, Bashir SA, et al. Incidence and pattern of bear maul injuries in Kashmir. Injury. 2010; 41(1):116-119.
31. Iqbal SZ. Mob tries to set helpless bear ablaze in Kashmir, probe ordered. NDTV. 2012 Nov 24, 14:34 IST.
32. Nabi GN, Tak SR, Kangoo KA, Halwai MA. Comparison of injury pattern in victims of bear and leopard attacks: a study from a tertiary care centre in Kashmir. Eur J Trauma Emerg Surg. 2009; 35:2153-2158.
33. Rossi V. Reinventing the public image of bears. The Hindu. 2012 Nov 26.
34. 'Stolen' as infant, back as teen: Kashmiri twin's tale (IANS). Greater Kashmir. 2011 Sep 26.
35. en.wikipedia.org/wiki/Gawakadal_massacre (accessed 20 July 2013).
36. Ali M. Govt forgets Kunan-Poshpora 'gang-rape' re-investigation. Greater Kashmir. 2012 Dec 21.
37. Wani AS. Valley's youngest missing in custody still untraceable. Govt says he was killed; family demands body. Greater Kashmir. 2007 Mar 7.
38. Gohain MP. Nobody's children: juveniles of conflict affected districts of India. New Delhi: Asian Centre for Human Rights. 2013 Mar 22.
39. Peer B. What lies beneath? Foreign Policy. 2011 Sep 29.
40. Unrest outcome of Machil fake killings: Govt. PBI. Greater Kashmir. 2010 Oct 2.
41. Those buried in unmarked graves are militants: Government. Greater Kashmir. 2012 Sep 5.
42. Jaleel M. 'A thousand ft deep gorge where crows are eating human corpses' and other tales from Kashmir. Indian Express. 2011 Sep 29.
43. Levy A, Scott-Clark C. The meadow: terrorism, kidnapping and conspiracy in paradise. New Delhi: Penguin Books; 2012.
44. Bhat A. The way to the meadow: a review. Available from: http://www.amazon.com/review/RP5U60ZA.
45. Jezza Neumann interview with Majid Maqbool. Kashmir: the story of control. Greater Kashmir. 2012 Aug 1.
46. Wani ML, Ahangar AG, Lone GN, Hakeem ZA, Dar AM, Lone RA et.al. Profile of missile induced cardiovascular injuries in Kashmir, India. J Emerg Trauma Shock. 2011; 4(2):173-177.